LABOR MARKET INSTITUTIONS AND
THE FUTURE ROLE OF UNIONS

𝕁𝔹

Labor Market Institutions and the Future Role of Unions

Edited by

Mario F. Bognanno
and
Morris M. Kleiner

BLACKWELL
Oxford UK & Cambridge USA

Copyright © Regents of the University of California 1992

First published 1992

First published in USA

Blackwell Publishers
Three Cambridge Center
Cambridge, Massachusetts 02142
USA

108 Cowley Road
Oxford   OX4 1JF,
UK

Library of Congress Cataloging in Publication Data
Labor market institutions and the future role of unions / edited by
Mario F. Bognanno and Morris M. Kleiner.
p.   cm.
Includes bibliographical references.
1. Trade-unions—United States.   2. Industrial relations—United
States.   3. Labor market—Government policy—United States.
I. Bognanno, Mario Frank.   II. Kleiner, Morris M.
HD6508.L228   1992
331.88′0973—dc20   92–17206
ISBN 1–55786–342–3

British Library Cataloguing in Publication Data
A CIP catalogue record for this book is available from the British Library.

Typeset in 11 on 13pt Times
by Huron Valley Graphics Inc., Ann Arbor, MI, USA
Printed in Great Britain by T. J. Press Ltd., Padstow, Cornwall

This book is printed on acid-free paper

Contents

Contents

Contributors

Mario F. Bognanno – University of Minnesota, Minneapolis, MN

Morris M. Kleiner – University of Minnesota, Minneapolis, MN

Charles McDonald – AFL–CIO, Washington, DC

Ray Marshall – University of Texas, Austin, TX

John T. Dunlop – Harvard University, Cambridge, MA

David G. Blanchflower – Dartmouth College, Hanover, NH

Richard B. Freeman – Harvard University, Cambridge, MA

Jonathan S. Leonard – University of California, Berkeley, CA

Barry T. Hirsch – Florida State University, Tallahassee, FL

Joseph D. Reid, Jr. – George Mason University, Fairfax, VA

Sanford M. Jacoby – University of California, Los Angeles, CA

Anil Verma – University of Toronto, Toronto, Ontario

John T. Addison – University of South Carolina, Columbia, SC

Pedro Portugal – Institut für Industriewirtschafliche Fortschung, Westfälische Wilhelms Universität Münster and Universidade do Porto

James E. Pesando – University of Toronto, Toronto, Ontario

Morley Gunderson – University of Toronto, Toronto, Ontario

Pauline Shum – University of Toronto, Toronto, Ontario

Peter F. Orazem – Iowa State University, Ames, IA

J. Peter Mattila – Iowa State University, Ames, IA

Sherry K. Weikum – Iowa State University, Ames, IA

Introduction: Labor Market Institutions and the Future Role of Unions

MARIO F. BOGNANNO and MORRIS M. KLEINER*

THE POLITICAL, ECONOMIC, AND SOCIAL roles of unions, government, and industry have changed dramatically over the past four decades. Following World War II, there was increased concern over the dominant role played by unions in the industrial relations system, specifically their considerable economic power. Thus, in 1947 the Taft-Hartley amendments to the Wagner Act were passed, and, thereafter, in the fifties, the relative standing of unions began to fall. The question for the nineties is, "Have the economic, political, and social roles of unions—relative to management and government—now become too weak for the good of the industrial relations system and democratic societies?"

During the late 1950s about 35 percent of wage and salary earners in the private sector were union members, and thousands more nonunion workers were covered by collective bargaining agreements. Comparable 1988 estimates put union membership density at 16.5 percent, with 18.8 percent of wage and salary earners covered by union contracts (Curme,

*The authors' affiliations are, respectively, Industrial Relations Center and Hubert H. Humphrey Institute of Public Affairs, University of Minnesota; and the Hubert H. Humphrey Institute of Public Affairs and the Industrial Relations Center, University of Minnesota.

1

Hirsch, and Macpherson, 1990). In 1990, as a result of more intense organizing activity, the AFL-CIO organized 250,000 workers in the private sector, yet overall membership fell by 25,000—from 14,525,000 to 14,500,000.[1] Clearly, the relative role of private-sector unions has slipped sharply.

Throughout the decades of the sixties, seventies, and eighties, a series of federal laws covering employee relations was passed, increasing the government's role in industrial relations and potentially acting to the detriment of unions. Similarly, private-sector businesses were increasingly able to effect new employment policies such as health and child care, pension, and other compensation policies without going through the collective bargaining process. In fact, as the union-free environment has expanded, the labor relations policies of businesses have become more constrained by government regulations than by collective bargaining.

The unfolding of these trends prompted many questions, among them being, "What does the future hold for the institutional actors in industrial relations?" and "What impact will these relations have on the employment relationship?" Because these and related questions are not adequately addressed in the literature on industrial relations, an effort was launched to attract leading academics to probe these trends in order to acquire deeper insight into their causes and consequences and, perhaps, to mount public policy initiatives designed to affect the trends.

As a result, a symposium was organized to solicit analytical and policy-oriented papers dealing with the future role of unions, government, and industry in industrial relations.[2] Ultimately, eight prize-winning papers were accepted for the symposium presentation and publication in *Industrial Relations*.

The symposium convened on April 28–29, 1990, at the University of Minnesota. Academic discussants presented the issue, method, conclusions, and policy recommendations of each paper. Then, two discussants, drawn from unions and public and corporate policy institutions, offered "advocate" critiques of each paper. Finally, the authors of the papers reacted to the comments and clarified issues. Thus, the following papers reflect the final results of this interaction.[3]

---

[1]*Wall Street Journal*, January 26, 1991.

[2]The symposium's editorial board included Mario Bognanno, Morris Kleiner, Richard Freeman, David Lewin, and Paula Voos. Other referees were Ross Azevedo, Brian Bemmels, Frederic Champlin, John Delaney, Avner Ben-Ner, Jack Fiorito, Michael Keane, Brian McCall, and James Scoville.

[3]Discussants included Ross Azevedo, Donald Bauer, Betty Bednarczyk, Charles Davis, Karl Egge, Terry Erskine, Jack Fiorito, Richard B. Freeman, Paul Goldberg, Robert Hobbins, David Lewin, David Lipsky, Daniel Mitchell, Barbara Nelson, Russ Norha, Craig Olson, Kenneth Peterson, Adam Pilarski, Robert Pleasure, Roy Richardson, Markley Roberts, James Vaupel, Paula Voos, and Norman Weintraub. Session moderators included Francine Blau, Mario Bognanno, Morris Kleiner, George Neumann, Fun Koo Park, and Myron Roomkin.

In addition to the eight prize winners, three invitees, distinguished by their expertise and extensive practical involvement in industrial relations, delivered papers at the symposium. Assistant to the Secretary-Treasurer of the AFL-CIO Charles McDonald explored the future role of unions, Professor and former Secretary of Labor F. Ray Marshall examined the future role of government, and Professor Emeritus and former Secretary of Labor John T. Dunlop assessed matters from his renowned "actors" perspective.

An international audience of approximately 150 academics, business leaders, labor leaders, government officials, and graduate students attended the symposium. Its threefold goals were: (1) to encourage innovative, policy-relevant, "gap"-filling research in industrial relations, (2) to share academic and practitioner reactions to such research, and (3) to identify issues that will shape a future research agenda in industrial relations.

Funding and logistical support for this project were provided by the U.S. Department of Labor, the Bureau of Labor Management Relations and Cooperative Programs, the Twin City Area Labor-Management Council, and the University of Minnesota's Center for Labor Policy, Hubert H. Humphrey Institute of Public Affairs, and Industrial Relations Center, Carlson School of Management. Academic and professional guidance was provided by members of the symposium's editorial board and the Industrial Relations Center's graduate faculty.

The prize-winning papers can be divided into two groups. The first deals with the institutional state of unions, explaining why union representation is in decline and what can be done to slow this trend. The papers in this group also account for the expanding role of business human resource management in a union-free industrial relations environment. The second group of papers shift attention away from labor and management to the role of government in the labor market. Specifically examined are the issues of employment effects of public policies regarding plant closing prenotification, pension program design, and comparable worth.

What follows is a summary of the papers presented in this volume, with the invited papers first, followed by the union-focused papers, the government policy papers, and, finally, a future research agenda and a brief conclusion.

Policy Perspectives on the Future Role of Industrial Relations Institutions

Charles McDonald, Assistant to the Secretary-Treasurer of the AFL-CIO, argues that the economics of the 1990s will not produce the private-sector, union-density declines characteristic of the decade of the 1980s, and he shows why this is the case, detailing a host of social, political, and

AFL-CIO policy innovations impinging on future union organizing and suggesting that academics have failed to consider the positive affects of these changes on future union density when conducting their analyses. McDonald is not compelled by the economic argument that deunionization stems from the fact that unions have done *too good* a job of achieving members' goals. Nor does he ascribe to the notion that enlightened employers obviate workers' demand for unions.

McDonald presents an important, pro-union critique of contemporary academic thinking about industrial relations. He wonders, for example, whether workers would want to belong to unions that are so "voice"-oriented that employers would find them too good to refuse. Under such a new model, would the interests of workers be adequately protected? He acknowledges that academics can be friendly toward labor, but he criticizes them for being unrealistic in their suggestions for labor movement reform. But for a few strategically placed amendments to the NLRA, McDonald envisions a private-sector labor movement that would be flourishing as it does in the public sector.

Former Secretary of Labor Ray Marshall argues that the United States is losing its status as a high-performing country because its economic and industrial relations policies have been slow to adjust to the new world order. The core of Marshall's thesis is that increasing global competition and accelerating technological change demand quality, productivity, and flexibility. He contends that U.S. post-Keynesian policies are not responsive to these demands, systematically develops the policy innovations needed to return the economy to its high-performance status, and draws some dramatic conclusions. They include an explicit government declaration that "high income" become a national economic goal. Moreover, he shows this goal to be consistent with: (1) low unemployment-high wage policies, (2) stronger protective labor standard policies, (3) major policy innovations to enhance educational and human resource development systems, (4) significant reforms in workers' right to organize and bargain collectively, and (5) new European-like policies in worker participation and cooperation.

Former Secretary of Labor John Dunlop reexamines the thesis presented in his famous book, *Industrial Relations Systems*, in the context of recent developments, concluding that the major issue for the future is the development of greater human resource productivity. He criticizes the state of human resource development in the United States and its consequent impact on productivity, economic growth, and international competitiveness. The solution to increased human resource development lies in increased cooperation among the major institutional actors—labor, government, and business. He argues that a transformation to problem-solving techniques among these actors is needed at the local and national level in order to accomplish requisite human resource development.

Declining Unionism: A Uniquely American Problem

David Blanchflower and Richard Freeman introduce a global perspective to the issue of declining unionism by analyzing intertemporal data and industrial relations developments in Organization for Economic Cooperation and Development (OECD) countries. Two general conclusions follow from their analysis. First, they do not find support for the theory that market-based industrialization will cause disparate countries to converge toward a common industrial relations type. Second, they estimate that the United States' union wage premium is much larger than the premiums paid in the other OECD countries. This fact explains to a great extent declining union density in the United States, which is not manifest elsewhere among developed countries. In these countries, there is also less resistance to unions than there is among American businesses.

During the seventies and eighties inter-OECD country comparisons reveal that in Japan, the Netherlands, and Great Britain, union density declined but at a slower rate than in the United States, and union density increased or maintained high levels in Canada, Australia, and most of Continental Europe. Thus, while the importance of national boundaries has decreased with economic globalization, there has been significant union density divergence, not convergence. Moreover, this divergence correlates with varying union effects on wages and profits. Generally, unions in the United States produce larger union wage effects and greater adverse effects on firm profitability, ceteris paribus.[4]

Relatively speaking, successful rent seeking among U.S. unions accounts for a large share of the dramatic decline in membership density during the 1970s and 1980s. The theory behind this conclusion is that large union wage effects produce large worker incentives to join unions, but they produce even larger profit-based incentives among employers to resist unions. According to Blanchflower and Freeman, during the past 20 years, increasing market competitiveness has shifted the union wage premium

---

[4]Discussant Jack Fiorito asked, "Should application of these limited criteria, i.e., union density and union wage effect, serve as grounds for disproving the convergence thesis?" In his judgment, Blanchflower and Freeman go too far in drawing this conclusion. In the area of nonwage employee benefits, the OECD countries and the United States seem to be on converging paths. This fact and the fact that U.S. unions seem to be uniquely "out-of-step" with the others, suggest support of the convergence thesis.

threshold downward to a point where the incentive to resist unions dominates the incentive to unionize.

The authors intimate that if American unions continue to emphasize "rent" over "voice" maximization, industrial relations in the United States may become a management-only activity. They also dismiss centralized or corporatist collective bargaining arrangements in North America as unworkable. However, they believe that a reversal of the trend might be possible if the link between union membership and bargaining unit membership were loosened; if the public, service, and white-collar sectors were organized aggressively around nonwage issues; and if there were legislation to establish "works councils," which, in the absence of collective bargaining, would provide workers with a "voice." These prescriptions would, however, dramatically change America's industrial relations system.

Jonathan Leonard's thesis complements Blanchflower and Freeman's. Under conditions of heightened competition, he argues, rent-maximizing unions negotiating with profit-maximizing firms tend to destroy union members' jobs—not create them. However, Leonard acknowledges that the alternative hypothesis—that firms destroy union jobs out of anti-union animus—is still viable.

Leonard suggests two challenges facing labor organizing: to build up union density by organizing workers faster than the labor force is growing and to make up for lost union jobs at previously unionized firms. Using a sample of California manufacturing plants, Leonard estimates that between 1974 and 1980 the employment growth rate in union plants lagged behind the growth rate in nonunion plants by 9 to 18 percent. Consequently, just to maintain union density, previously won certification elections must eventually be matched by an equivalent certification victory somewhere else inasmuch as jobs in union plants have shorter life spans than those in nonunion plants. Leonard also found that the slower growth of employment within union plants accounts for 61 percent of the decline in the proportion of the California workforce that was organized during this period.

This growth of employment differential seems to have less applicability in the public sector, a strategic signal to unions about the industrial sector in which organizing could be stressed. Moreover, Leonard concludes, the NLRB and the courts have excluded capital-spending decisions from the set of "mandatory" subjects of bargaining, and researchers have not been able to isolate the anti-union animus versus profit-maximization (cost-minimization) causes for laying off union workers and for closing or partially closing union plants. Leonard's empirical findings support the idea that when unions join management in the search for efficiency gains, it helps to alleviate the job loss incidence implied by a negatively sloped labor demand curve.

Barry Hirsch recasts the negative union/nonunion employment growth difference—brought on by the positive union/nonunion wage difference—as a long-run investment problem. Contrasting the investment behavior of union versus nonunion firms, Hirsch demonstrates that relative to their nonunion counterparts, union firms should theoretically invest less in physical capital, R&D, and other modes of firm innovation because unions can appropriate a part of the quasi rents accruing to long-lived capital, a result that attaches more strongly to noncooperative bargaining outcomes. However, it also applies to cooperative bargaining outcomes because a union's marginal rate of time preference is controlled by myopic, short-tenured, or senior union members and because workers' future returns from firm investments are nontransferable (property rights) assets.

Hirsch tests his idea about the deleterious effects of union representation on investment behavior using investment and union coverage data on 706 publicly traded U.S. companies over the 1972–80 period. He finds that unionized companies invested roughly 20 percent less in physical capital than nonunion companies—two-thirds owing to the union's ability to tax future earnings, and one-third owing to fewer available firm-specific investment resources because of union effects on firm earnings. Similar results were found in relation to firm investments in R&D.

In the extreme, union firms stop investing and ultimately cease operations, and thus union jobs are lost. Hirsch's results indicate that the loss of union jobs due to relative disinvestment by union firms portend continued union density decline. Unions can help their cause, Hirsch argues, by moderating their rent-seeking objective, and he contends that adverse firm investment effects on union membership can be ameliorated by creating mechanisms tying wages to the firm's stock market price rather than current or past (profit-sharing) profits. This strategy may have the effect of motivating workers to moderate current wage demands for future stability in an appreciating stock market.

Joseph Reid takes a historical view of the labor movement's decline within the context of public choice theory. His exploration focuses on whether unions' demise should have been expected and what, if anything, should be done about it. Reid's analytical model leads to specific forecasts about the "future" of industrial relations.

Generally, Reid forecasts that private-sector unions will survive and public-sector unions will thrive. In the private sector, unions will have less presence in large old-style assembly-line factory settings, where the demand for union representations was traditionally strong; they will have a moder-

ate presence in "modified" factories where labor-management "cooperation" is a survival imperative; and they will have an increasing presence in
service operations, particularly the deskilled ones. Moreover, future
private-sector unions will forego monopoly returns in favor of efficiency-
enhancing returns (via emphasis on agency "voice"), and they will work to
deliver to their members off-the-job consumables, such as discounts offered
through group purchases. Second, Reid sees the continuing rise of monopoly unions in the nonfederal public sector, with greater efforts toward
rent-seeking activity.

In the case of private business, Reid believes that low-wage industries
will view unions as a cost-minimizing vehicle for communicating with their
culturally mixed and largely uneducated workforce. Other "voice" arguments apply to high-wage industries, particularly among those that interact
with "cooperative" unions.

Reid concludes that the overriding future role of the government sector
will be to promote efficiency. However, within the industrial relations
arena, he forecasts more or less a partnership in the private sector and
more militant public-sector unionism.

Sanford Jacoby and Anil Verma continue the theme of "cooperative"
unions, specifically focusing on a study of independent labor unions
(ILUs) as an alternative—autonomous and collective—institutional model
of employee participation in industrial relations. ILU organizations are
not well understood, but they are generally believed to give meaningful
emphasis to cooperative, as well as to combative, approaches to industrial
relations.

The authors observe that over the past 20 years employee involvement
programs (EIP) have made important inroads in the country's growing
number of nonunion (NU) workplaces. Even the nonunion model of industrial relations recognizes the need for an employee "voice" in the workplace, and similarly, these cooperative initiatives are on the rise in union
plants. Thus, whereas business opposition to traditional unions, that is,
those affiliated with national unions (AU) and the AFL-CIO, has been on
the rise, businesses may find ILUs to be a more inviting organizational
form with which to interact.

Using the wage and benefits data of the 84 domestic plants of the aerospace firm TRW during the period 1979 to 1983, Jacoby and Verma show
that, in general, compensation in the firm's nine ILU plants was higher in
both years than in either their 19 AU plants or their 56 NU plants. After
controlling for other effects, the authors found that ILU members were
paid as well as or slightly better than workers in the AU facilities and
significantly better than those in the NU plants.

Jacoby and Verma interpret these results as support for the idea that TRW paid ILU members as well as they did in order to keep them from affiliating with a national union and, perhaps, because ILUs, as with AUs, do have bargaining power. Thus, their case study lends support to the idea that firms would rather have their workers represented by ILUs—if at all—and that ILUs can provide workers a genuinely independent "voice." The authors offer ideas for reforming labor law that follow from these conclusions. Specifically, they see a potential for coupling the NLRB's company union revisions—section 8(a)(2)—with those parts of the law governing organizing campaigns and elections.

Public Policy and Employment

John Addison and Pedro Portugal extend an earlier model of the role of prior notification of plant closure on the search behavior and employment outcomes of employees. They examine both the potential costs and benefits of advance notice. On the cost side, firms' operations can be adversely affected by prenotifications just prior to plant closings or layoffs through a premature loss of highly productive employees. On the benefit side, displaced workers' transitions to new jobs can be eased by the search-time increment afforded by prenotification. Ultimately, policy resolution should be based on balancing employers' costs against workers' benefits. A central aspect of the authors' model focuses on the potential for contracting failure and, consequently, the room such failure affords to policy regulation in this area.

Using data from the Current Population Survey's displaced worker file from 1984 through 1988, Addison and Portugal estimate a hazard model and find that advance notice resulted in pronounced reductions in median weeks of postdisplacement joblessness due to heightened search intensity on the part of those notified. They conclude that the 1988 Worker Adjustment and Retraining Notification Act (WARN) can reduce durations of unemployment, and they speculate on the reasons for union support for this legislation. They argue—in a manner consistent with the Blanchflower and Freeman analysis—that unions may be trying to increase nonunion labor costs through this type of legislation to reduce the adverse union member employment effect caused by the union/nonunion wage differential.

James Pesando, Morley Gunderson, and Pauline Shum examine the impact of "flat benefit plans" on mandatory retirement and pension policy using data from Canada. They define a "flat pension plan" as one in which the pension benefit is equal to a fixed dollar amount for each year of service. The major issue is to identify the work incentives created by flat benefit plans, with particular attention to the role played by periodic enrichments and early retirement incentives.

The authors first document the evolution of flat benefit formulas over the period 1974 to 1984. Next, they build a database consisting of all flat benefit plans under the jurisdiction of the province of Ontario, having 200 or more members as of January 1, 1984. This sample contains the majority of plans in Canada. Using these data, they develop a simulation of benefits and accruals under alternative formulas, giving particular attention to the effects of early retirement provisions.

Their simulation shows that the periodic enrichment of the flat benefit formulas has served to redistribute wealth across different age and service cohorts. These results are consistent with Freeman's finding (1985) that older workers exert a disproportionate impact on collectively bargained outcomes, which is consistent with median voter models of union behavior. This form of the flat benefit formula implies that providing incentives for early retirement, greater risk for third-party insurers of pension plans, and the potential "backloading" of these pension benefits constitute potential discrimination because women have higher turnover rates.

Peter Orazem, Peter Mattila, and Sherry Weikum concentrate on the public sector in which the spread of comparable worth is perhaps *the* most important innovation to beset this sector's compensation systems since the rise of public-sector collective bargaining. These authors suggest, however, that the economic impact of this innovation has scarcely been analyzed. The wage-setting implications of comparable worth should arguably affect major demographic groups, including union members. Thus, they examine the pay effects of statutory "factor point systems" on state government jobs, which are disproportionately occupied by women, minorities, and union members.

The authors estimate regressions where the dependent variable is the relative points for the ith job, and they also estimate a model where the dependent variable is the point spread as well as the wage of the ith job in a given state. The data used to estimate these alternative specifications are from 14 states, averaging 67 jobs per state, for a total of 940 observations.

Their results provide important insights into the operations of equity-based pay plans in the public sector. For example, the factor point analysis is greatly influenced by market forces despite the often-stated desire to separate the two. Factor point systems do not benefit heavily unionized jobs, and they do not cause equality in pay. They may, however, reduce the pay dispersion across states for the same job relative to systems that match the market. Overall, the authors conclude that comparable plans do lower the importance of relative market wages and that these plans do not raise the wages of women more than other factor point plans. Further, heavily unionized and disproportionately minority jobs tend to lose in both proposed pay and actual pay.

Future Research Agenda

These symposium papers and related discussions on the decline of the American labor movement, unions as an institutional form of worker representation, and the impact of specific public policy reform suggest several topics warranting further research.

1. On balance, do labor market regulations, such as WARN or proposed "termination for cause" legislation, substitute for collectively bargained benefits? If large union wage premiums are responsible for managements' resistance to unions, then public policy interventions should reduce these premiums and, therefore, employers' resistance to unions. There are two effects at work here. On the one hand, legislation may reduce workers' demand for union representation, and, on the other hand, it may reduce employers' resistance to unionization. Which of these two effects is dominant?

2. Unions gain and lose members for several reasons. A careful study of the precise number of new members needed annually to achieve precise net density target gains is an area of unmet research. With estimates like these, evaluating the organizing productivity of union organizers will be better directed.

3. What is the annual non-NLRB net organizing gain (loss) attributed to accretions and expansions in union employment (decertifications, plant closings, or reductions in the quantity of union labor demanded)?

4. To what extent does anti-union animus account for the decline in union membership, controlling for the economic effects of unions? Is a free, democratic society better off with or without unions as a principal industrial relations actor?

5. Is the wage premium smaller among union firms with negotiated ESOPs—where stock values are tied to future investments, growth, and firm profitability—or with union firms with negotiated profit-sharing plans—where value is tied to past investments, growth, and profitability? (Hirsch anticipates that it is smaller among the first set of union firms.)

6. ILUs played a significant role in America's labor history, yet less is known about them than is known about European works councils. This gap in knowledge needs to be bridged.

7. Firms are embracing EIPs, but they do not encourage an ILU "voice." Are firms reluctant to embrace ILUs because they fear 8(a)(2) suits or because they fear they may become *genuinely* independent unions?

8. Why are there conflicting results of the impact of advance notice on unemployment duration? Is this a function of data, estimation technique, or timing? For example, Daniel Mitchell pointed out in his comments on the Addison and Portugal paper that about one out of eight workers who knew or expected termination actually left before termination occurred. How does this analysis fit into the cost/benefit analysis of employers losing and workers winning through advance notice legislation?

9. To what extent do unions exhibit self-interest versus altruistic behavior regarding public policy issues?

10. To what extent can firms afford to pay for pension plans and other fringe benefit plans and stay in business, relative to firms with no pension plans or other less costly fringes? To what extent do pension plans lead to different kinds of age and productivity profiles within the firm?

11. Why do unions generally support comparable worth in the public sector when they do not generally yield pay benefits for their members? To what extent do union interests in reducing wage dispersion and issues of wage equality influence union support for both comparable worth or other factor point systems?

Conclusion

We believe that this symposium advanced our knowledge about the declining role of unions vis-à-vis employers and the role of government in the labor market. Hypotheses accounting for the labor movement's diminishing private-sector role were presented and tested. New models of worker representation were suggested. A practical union-side rejoinder to much of this research and to its policy derivatives was also heard. Further, broad-based papers were presented casting unions into a definitive future role along with government and business but within a context of the social, political, and economic changes needed to keep the United States on the leading edge of economic success.

An agenda for future research was also formulated. Hopefully, students of industrial relations will meet the research challenges it poses. Clearly, the relationships among industrial relations' main institutional actors are in transition. With our limited knowledge, in the event that present industrial relations trends continue, we are poorly positioned even to speculate how employees, businesses, the economy, and society at large may be affected by a largely nonunion America.

U.S. Union Membership in Future Decades: A Trade Unionist's Perspective

CHARLES McDONALD*

THE COLLECTIVE WISDOM OF MOST ACADEMICIANS is that the labor movement in the private sector is dying. Trade unions, they argue, have been in a steady and alarming decline to the present 12.4 percent of the private-sector workforce. Only the growth in public employee unionism has kept union density for the entire workforce at the barely respectable 16.5 percent level. The long-term prognosis, according to this consensus, is worse: By the year 2000 private-sector union membership will be 5 percent of the private-sector workforce if current trends continue.

This scenario is usually bolstered by the following arguments.

1. There is a major economic incentive for U.S. employers to oppose unions bitterly and successfully; the United States has the largest gap in pay between union and nonunion workers among the developed nations.

2. Capital investment policies by employers with both union and nonunion plants lean greatly in favor of the nonunion side; union plants are allowed to age and are ultimately closed as their only hope for survival—modernization—is reduced.

3. Statutory protections for nonunion workers and greater attentiveness by enlightened employers to the needs of their workers reduce the demand for unions.

---

*Assistant to the Secretary-Treasurer, AFL-CIO. The views expressed herein represent the opinions of the author and not necessarily those of the AFL-CIO.

4. Union organizing, which has already dropped precipitously, will continue at its low rate; the numbers needed to offset membership losses far exceed current or predicted levels of organizing success.

Contrary to this academic view, recent events in Eastern Europe, the Soviet Union, China, and South Africa remind us that a strong and free labor movement is an essential bulwark of a decent democratic society. Offering advice to the labor movement, some theorists argue for a *new* labor movement, one marked by a spirit of cooperation with employers. Unions should embrace worker participation, the argument continues, and greater productivity in a changing workplace and be less preoccupied with increasing workers pay and benefits. This *new* labor movement would offer management some deals that are just too good to refuse, opposition would ease, and employees would be able to organize without fear of retribution. It is questionable, however, whether union members will buy into the new model and whether the interest of workers would be adequately protected.

The decline in the labor movement's private-sector representation is well documented. However, according to both objective indicators and the union response, the decline will not be as great as forecast. In fact, there are some encouraging signs of an abatement and, eventually, a reversal of the trend. Much of this turnabout will occur without a major shift of union mission. American unions will remain vigorous advocates of their members' interests. To the extent present trends continue, the solution lies not just in reform of trade unions but in legislative changes that will provide a more hospitable climate for free labor unions to flourish.

Estimates of Union Decline

First, let's tackle the proposition that there will be a 60 percent drop in private-sector union density by the year 2000, that is, from 12.4 to only 5 percent. Projecting private-sector workforce growth of 11 percent in the 1990s, this prediction means that private-sector membership will be less than 5 million by the year 2000, a decline of some 5.3 million from today. Even with the remarkable confluence of circumstances that has caused us to decline to the current 12.4 percent,[1] it took 20 years for union density to decline the same 60 percent projected for the 1990s.[2] In the 1970s, the drop

---

[1]The 12.4 percent figure as well as all typically quoted figures on union density seriously overstate the percentage organizable under the NLRA as distinct from the total wage and salaried workforce. If supervisory personnel were excluded, the private-sector labor movement's percentage organized would be 15.4 percent.

[2]In 1970 unions represented 31 percent of the private sector; today's 12.4 percent represents a 60 percent decline.

was 36 percent, caused by a stunning employment payroll growth of over 27 percent. During the 1980s, a period of uniquely catastrophic conditions for workers and for the labor movement, there was a drop from 20 percent to just 12.4 percent, a decline of "only" 38 percent in private-sector union density.

No reasonable forecaster is predicting for the 1990s a repeat of the events that caused union density to decline so sharply over the past 20 years. First, and of particular importance, private, nonfarm employment will grow only 1.1 million per year instead of the 1.8 million annual rate of the 1980s. Second, while the current administration can hardly be described as a champion of organized labor, at least it is not charting a Reagan-inspired course for all private-sector management to follow toward a union-free environment. In 1981, President Reagan constructed a union-avoidance theme when he annihilated the air traffic controllers and their union, refusing to permit their return to work, at a cost of billions of dollars to businesses and consumers. When he appointed government officials, such as NLRB Chair Donald Dotson, to key labor posts, unabashed advocates of union-free workplaces, he sent a clear message that anti-unionism was "in."

Finally, the most precipitous drop in NLRB organizing since enactment of the NLRA and in private-sector membership took place during the 1981–83 recession. Huge employment losses in auto and other well-organized heavy industries, wrenching structural shifts caused by deregulation of trucking and airlines, a monetary policy that created a massive manufacturing trade deficit and large employment surpluses in the construction industry—all the handiwork of the early Reagan presidency—caused much of the membership decline. There are no serious projections for the 1990s that call for a massive recession or economic restructuring like those of the early 1980s. Much of our unionized industries have already been deregulated by the Reagan administration. A relatively tight labor market is predicted for well into the 1990s, and it will be conducive to union growth. Union membership has typically expanded during tight labor markets such as during the two world wars, the Korean War, and the early and mid-1960s. On the other hand, the recession years of 1958–59 and the early 1980s were hard on union membership.

It is difficult to accept then that even *if* the present trend continues, it would produce a 5 percent density figure in the year 2000. Exactly what that figure will be requires careful consideration, because the environment for union growth will not stagnate and the current trend will not be operative for the next decades.

The factors that most observers feel will determine the outcome include:

1. The attitudes of employees both organized and unorganized toward their work, their employer, and the idea of unionization.

2. The current and future posture of employers toward unions and their employees.

3. Most important, the government's will to protect employee rights at the workplace and to reestablish and enforce the right to organize and bargain collectively.

Employee Attitudes

The sine qua non for union growth is, of course, a workforce that values representation. If employees do not feel the need for such representation, then nothing unions can do and no legal changes are likely to make much of a difference. However, recent Gallup polls show an increase in union popularity since 1981, revealing a pattern that bodes well for union growth: Hispanics, blacks, and young workers, all groups which will grow in the 1990s, register a markedly higher level of union approval than the 61 percent norm in the Gallup poll of all citizens.

Apart from the issue of union approval, Gallup registered an overwhelming sentiment for collective representation at the workplace. Ninety percent of those surveyed supported the proposition, "Employees should have an organization of co-workers to discuss and resolve legitimate concerns with their employer." By a 54 to 33 percent margin employees agreed that they feel more comfortable raising workplace problems through an employee association than as an individual, a broad recognition that employees have distinct interests and that they need and deserve a vehicle for expressing them. At the same time, employees do not have very positive feelings about their employer and their job, important factors in determining the impulse to unionize. According to the Roper Organization, satisfaction with key job elements fell substantially between 1976 and 1988.

Very recent NLRB election results, while not a particularly accurate barometer of employee attitudes, provide some additional good news for labor. For 1989, a nine-year high was reached in the number of employees organized via the NLRB. The win rate of 49.5 percent was a 14-year high. Significantly, the overall win rate was eclipsed by a 60 percent win rate in specific sectors of high employment growth, such as health care and other services. Manufacturing, where the employment decline is expected to continue, remains the toughest sector to win NLRB elections but is still the sector with the highest number of NLRB elections.

Employer Attitudes

Almost as important in determining union success as employee attitude is the response of employers to organizing efforts. Unlike the laws of most other industrialized nations, U.S. labor laws give employers virtually carte blanche to resist efforts by employees to organize.

It has become an article of faith for most private-sector employers that unionization must be avoided at all costs. Business schools teach their students that if employees form a union, the management is weak. Most organizers will testify that employers have become extremely effective both in thwarting an incipient union-organizing drive and in opposing a well-established organizing campaign at all stages from the prepetition stage to the election. Even when employees vote for a union, employers have become adept at avoiding bargaining agreements.

From the employees' standpoint, the employers' position and their methods for enforcing it have greatly affected the organizing outcome. The AFL-CIO, its affiliates, and academic observers have established the importance of employers' response to unionization efforts. In the public sector, union membership has grown dramatically; in most developed countries, none of which tolerates serious employer opposition to union organizing, union density has kept pace with the changing industrial picture.

It is not just in the organizing field that employer opposition affects union membership. The number of employees lost through decertification elections have quadrupled since the early 1960s. While these can be a function of employee disaffection with the union, employers are the catalysts and often the architects of the effort. Management and employee consciousness of this device as a way out of union representation has expanded.

Is there reason to believe that union bashing will be less common among employers in future decades? The answer depends in large part on why employers engage in these tactics in the first place.

If, as many believe, employer opposition reflects an unwillingness on the part of employers to lose any control over the workplace, then no change can be expected in employer behavior. Blanchflower and Freeman (this volume) suggest another explanation, that this opposition is attributable to the ability of unions to increase wages, which drive up labor costs, that is, the union-nonunion wage gap helps explain the decline in union density. This thesis is questionable, however. In recent years, union settlements have not kept pace with nonunion employer compensation, yet employer opposition has not diminished. Furthermore, employer opposition exists even when economic analysis supports a more benevolent posture. For example, Cooke (1990) concludes that employers who collaborated with their unions achieved an 18 percent improvement in added value per employee, whereas employers that were adversarial with their union showed a decline of 15 percent. Nonetheless, many employers elect the latter course.

In addition, it is noteworthy that employer opposition has mushroomed in an era when legislative and judicial activities have extended to nonunion employees at least some of the rights union employees have secured for themselves through collective bargaining. The impact of the Employee Retirement Income and Security Act (ERISA), the Occupational Safety and Health Act (OSHA), minimum wage adjustments, and judicial restrictions on termination-at-will should be greater on nonunion firms and should reduce the union-nonunion wage gap. Nonetheless, no amount of government regulation can alter the management vision of unionization as a pariah of efficient business operation.

If, notwithstanding these contrary indications, Blanchflower and Freeman are right in arguing that employer opposition is closely related to the union-nonunion wage gap and given that employer opposition is an important determinant in employees' efforts to unionize, then it is important to understand where that gap is headed.

In recent years, union settlements, after decades of exceeding nonunion adjustments, have not kept pace with nonunion employers' compensation adjustments. Union membership and leadership are frustrated and, in many instances, pressing more insistently for substantial wage and benefit adjustments. The compensation gap—wages and benefits—in labor's traditional strongholds may begin to widen again.

But the field over which this battle is being fought, for the most part, is in the high-visibility but low-employment growth sectors—manufacturing, transportation, and construction. These are *not* where labor's struggle to stop the decline in union density will be won or lost. The battleground will be in the service sectors, in retail and wholesale trade and in health care. The union presence in these sectors is not enough to establish a union-nonunion gap, which, under the Blanchflower and Freeman analysis, could dictate the intensity of employer opposition.

I am not suggesting that employers will roll over in these growth sectors. In fact, current experience suggests that they will be as tough as many manufacturing employers, but the minimal union penetration and the more limited mobility of much of the local market-based service industry restrict one's confidence in predicting the size of the union-nonunion gap. In manufacturing, production can be moved and new plants built in low-wage areas to escape union compensation and thus exacerbate the gap. The unionized store, bank, or hospital must remain in the same geographic area; the employer cannot move to a union-free haven to maximize his compensation savings. Nonunion employers may have to keep compensation near union levels, and union negotiation outcomes may be affected by competitive pressures within the local labor market. Thus, if one accepts the Blanchflower and Freeman thesis, we don't yet know how vigorously employers will oppose union organization.

It is difficult to be optimistic about the course of employer acceptance of the right to organize and bargain collectively. Anti-unionism is so thoroughly ingrained in the American business culture that even with increased examples of successful labor-management cooperative ventures, sharply reduced strike activity, and concession bargaining, employer opposition to unionization has been increasing. Maybe it would have been worse if unions had been inflexible, but that is pure speculation.

Labor's Adjustments to the Changing Situation

A third determinant of union success is the ability and willingness of unions to help themselves. Will they adapt to change and become more effective in helping employees to organize? In 1985, the AFL-CIO issued a report, "The Changing Situation of Workers and Their Unions," containing a prescription for unions to confront change successfully.

There are at least two major developments over the past 30 years that have crystallized the challenges confronting union organizers. First, there is a sharply different and more complex workforce, one that does not automatically assume that unions are the answer to its problems. Today's workers do not typically have a homogeneous set of problems that an organizer can readily identify and use to develop a mass movement in the workplace, culminating in an NLRB election victory. Even where such problems can be identified, employers are far more attuned to methods for dissuading workers from acting on those feelings.

Second, today's growth sectors and occupations are different from past private-sector union membership. The American trade union movement became a major force in society by organizing workers at vast numbers of large manufacturing, mining, trucking, shipping, railroad, and construction worksites between the mid-1930s and mid-1960s. Leadership and staff personnel reflected this basic membership picture, and as membership and union density grew in these sectors, employee support for unionization was taken for granted. During much of this period, training and supervision of union organizers were not major priorities of the labor movement.

Organizer positions were filled with members or officers from organized shops; some jobs were given as political rewards with little attention paid to the ability of the individual to organize, under the assumption that anyone who was an organizer would succeed where they were most comfortable and without interference. Supervision, training, and accountability were foreign concepts. Successful NLRB election results justified this view.

Sometime in the late 1960s and early 1970s, organizers began to be challenged. Greater skills, more diversity, and greater intensity of effort were needed. However, since overall membership continued to climb for most unions, little was done to begin the internal staff and managerial changes necessary to streamline organizing the future workforce. Given the utility of organizer staff selections and activity as a means of helping solidify political support, there was little motivation to study more deeply the role of the organizer or to manage organizers' time and work practices to maximize organizing performance. The decentralized nature of most union structures also meant that the impetus to organize was in the hands of local leadership. Some leaders viewed new organizing as a potential threat to their ability to be reelected. Other local leaders, more secure and more interested in growth, may not have had the resources and/or knowledge to proceed with organizing in the most effective way.

When Reagan ushered in the 1980s and membership declined, the burden of negotiations, servicing laid-off people, and fighting further cutbacks consumed the attention of union leadership, all at the expense of organizing. Organizing staff often bore the brunt of staff cutbacks. As a result, the labor movement has suffered for its inattention to organizing and for its acceptance of the norms of the 1950s and 1960s. Much of the explanation for the 60 percent drop in the number of NLRB organizing elections can be found at our own doorstep. While the percentage of union victories in NLRB elections has fluctuated only modestly, the 1970s and 1980s witnessed a sharp decline in the number of elections and particularly the average size of the contested unit. Organizers typically did not initiate campaigns but went to the leadership to be organized. There was no need to reach out for targets. Organizers, on their own or under instructions, understandably stuck to employers within their union's jurisdiction, even though such employers might have been the toughest targets, which were fewer each year. Two important factors in maintaining this organizing focus were a relatively high comfort level in dealing with the unorganized in their own industries and membership concerns that their industry should be the prime source of organizing efforts. Methods for organizing did not address effectively the tactics of a well-run, anti-union campaign by consultants. The success of these consultants persuaded employers to rely on them for more aggressive bargaining strategies and more determined opposition to organizing attempts.

We seem to be emerging from this period of organizing neglect with a will to elevate the status of organizing and to reach into unfamiliar terrain. While little has been done to track this trend systematically, recent NLRB figures and evidence from a number of unions suggest that there is an increased appreciation of the need to change and a will to do so.

Beginning in the late 1970s and increasingly through the 1980s, affiliates began to share more of their experiences working through the AFL-CIO's National Organizing Committee. More regional cooperative efforts were created, and the Industrial Union Department and the AFL-CIO found affiliates more willing to coordinate organizing with specific employers. Organizer training programs, in existence for many years, expanded from two-day, ad hoc affairs to week-long efforts, developed by the Meany Center, the AFL-CIO Organizing Department, and individual affiliates.

In 1989, the AFL-CIO created the Organizing Institute with a mission to elevate the status of union organizing by—concentrating on the recruitment and training of organizers in an unprecedented fashion. The recruitment net has been cast broadly—rank-and-file membership, colleges, law schools, and VISTA are but a few institutions providing the recruits. The institute has recognized that it takes a special talent to organize, particularly with our system of representation elections and in the face of extreme employer opposition. The institute is also helping unions tackle the managerial problems inherent in being a union organizer. There is a serious shortage not only of talented organizers but also of lead organizers who can administer large campaigns that require a big staff and who can supervise organizers' activities on a daily basis on more routine campaigns.

The open and enthusiastic response from many AFL-CIO affiliates to the creation of the Organizing Institute and to its initial work reflects an intense drive to improve organizing capability. The institute was structured to require a major investment of federation and affiliates' resources, and both are making a sizable investment. Twenty years ago the proposition that unions would accept, let alone eagerly solicit, recruits from nonlabor sources and allow them to be trained by participation in other unions' campaigns would have been ridiculed.[3]

---

[3]In the 1930s through the early 1950s, organizers often came from outside the trade union ranks and moved from one union to another.

Can the improvement of organizer quality and management, when coupled with changing employee attitudes, make a serious difference? Of course, even the best organizers cannot do much if employees do not desire representation. But, as we have seen, there is reason to believe that a substantial number of employees—particularly young, black, and Hispanic workers—are receptive to the message of trade unionism. But experience teaches that it takes the catalyst of a professional organizer to help unorganized groups come together and form effective organizations. Thus, the skill of the organizers will be very important.

The task we face is formidable. Just to match workforce growth of 1.1 million per year and remain at 12.4 percent of the private sector, we must have a yearly net gain of 136,000 new members, but the opposite is occurring. That means new organizing must carry the brunt of the load. We are now organizing 90,000 employees annually through NLRB elections. In addition, a number of affiliates, particularly in the service and construction industries, are organizing substantial numbers outside NLRB election procedures. We secure an agreement for only 75 percent of those we win elections for, and because of right-to-work laws in 20 states, we don't have 100 percent membership even when we get a contract. At the same time, each year we are losing 10,000 members through decertification. Thus, we have to nearly *double* our current victories to achieve a gross addition of 136,000 new members per year through NLRB processes. To account for plant closings and other sources of membership losses that are not replenished by accretions or expanded employment in unionized settings—that is, to achieve a *net* annual gain of 136,000—we probably need to quadruple employee wins to 360,000 annually or increase proportionately our non-NLRB organizing successes.[4]

There are several reasons to believe that over time, with sustained attention and dedication of adequate resources, we can do just that. One AFL-CIO survey in 1986 by the Department of Organization and Field Services revealed that currently on average an organizer gains representation rights for 60 employees a year. That figure comes as a shock, for it means that we would have to field the impossible number of 6,000 full-time organizers to achieve the target of 360,000 employees just to remain at 12.4 percent of the private-sector workplace. Obviously, the labor movement cannot afford to hire that many organizers, but some increased hiring will be possible. Improved hiring and training practices will be major factors in making

---

[4]A careful study of the precise organizing number needed to stabilize membership is overdue. In addition, non-NLRB organizing gains have never been systematically tracked. This increasingly important area of activity should be more intensely scrutinized.

gains in organizing, such as the example of organizers from the Organizing Institute, who exceeded the average figure sevenfold. We need more of these talented and successful organizers to help employees who desire unionization.

Another positive is that we are just beginning to penetrate the economy's employment growth sectors, such as the service sector. As we represent more people in this area, we will learn the methods and issues for organizing varying types of service-sector employees, who will look increasingly to the labor movement as their representative. The same can be said for professional and technical occupations. The movement away from our basic manufacturing strength is as inevitable as it is necessary.

NLRB statistics may be signaling another positive trend. The number of employees engaged in organizing campaigns and victory percentages is rising. Decertification losses have stabilized at a level well below the peaks of the early Reagan years. Further, figures from a 1990 AFL-CIO Department of Organization and Field Services survey indicate a substantial gain in converting election wins to first contracts—from 63 percent in the early 1980s to 75 percent in the late 1980s.

The impressive consumer benefits and associate membership program, inspired by the AFL-CIO's 1985 report, is just beginning to have an impact on union membership. It will take time to develop these benefits and to use them as a complement to membership growth, but the movement will occur. We have just begun to conduct experiments in the area of associate membership.

Several unions have developed techniques for successfully pressuring employers to ease their opposition to employees' organizing attempts. Affiliates are augmenting grass-roots organizing with strategies that include the use of consumer boycotts, demonstrations, employee rights legislation (e.g., OSHA, minimum wage), environmental laws, and appeals by popular public figures to sympathetic boards of directors. Unions are also beginning to use their pension funds and Employee Stock Ownership Plans (ESOPs) both to thwart or moderate union employment reductions and to counter actual or planned opposition to organizing efforts. The potential for these strategies to produce major gains is underscored by the greater vulnerability of retail, insurance, banking, and health care employers to these tactics. One final development—whose effect on growth is yet to be determined—is the union advertising campaign begun by the AFL-CIO in 1988. This campaign focuses on the benefits of collective representation and how unions can be relevant to the workforce of the 1990s. Even with budget restrictions that do not allow for massive advertising, the results from our initial efforts have been promising.

The Legal Climate

Ultimately, any attempt to predict union density over the next decades must consider the legal climate in which organizing efforts take place. What type of labor standards will be established by law and how will those standards affect organizing? Will the laws governing labor-management relations be reformed in order to give real meaning to the right of self-organization?

Employee rights legislation. Labor's legislative efforts in the employee rights arena will remain undiminished. Basic worker rights are fundamental to AFL-CIO policy, both internationally and at home. Our massive support of Solidarity—since its fledgling days in 1981 when American labor unions were under unprecedented attack domestically—showed that we will pursue goals, spend resources, and devote our emotional energy to causes not immediately or apparently beneficial to our own prosperity but simply because they are "right."

Second, there *may* be institutionally beneficial reasons for our continuing efforts to establish minimum labor standards through legislation and regulatory action. Nonunion firms must not be allowed to widen their cost advantage, a possible outcome if workplace protection were allowed to slacken. Employee protection legislation, as it affects nonunion employers, may not work as well as it should, but that may be due to ineffective enforcement. A government more sympathetic to working people may someday assume power and the cost advantages of operating without a union will narrow, as long as the legislation remains on the books.

A broad and effective statutory rights framework can become the structure on which union growth will be fabricated. If we assume that union firms achieve greater adherence to employee protection laws, we can build on our success in the organized shop and use it as a basis for building union support in the nonunion setting. A good organizer steeped in the knowledge of statutory rights and with the help of the union's legal and research departments can build a deep and durable reservoir of support for a union by helping unorganized workers know and use the protections conferred by law.

Of course, there is some risk that if unions offer nonunion employees help in exercising their legal rights, the employees will use its advice and then say good-bye. Even then, the union will have built a base for future efforts, reduced the nonunion operator's competitive advantage, and helped a group of workers.

There are some who take the opposite view and ascribe—*incorrectly*—

the decline in union density to increased statutory protection for employees, for the United States legislates far fewer protections and benefits for employees than do other developed countries; yet with the exception of France, our union density, is far below those countries. Unions thrive abroad even though employees may see less direct *economic* advantage to being a union member. The U.S. labor movement will continue to press for broader workplace legislation, such as parental leave, just-cause discharge, health care, and employee privacy, just a few of the items that continue to be on our agenda.

Two prescriptions for union growth. Although unions may reverse the current trend and hold their own during the next decades—or even lose some ground—still our society needs a strong and vibrant labor movement, not one struggling to tread water. Fundamental changes in our labor laws are essential if unions are once again to grow. What can make a difference? What will survive the legislative labyrinth? What about the European systems? Do we overhaul the American model or develop something new?

Given a supportive political climate, the unions are calling for legislated card-check recognition, immediate or five-day elections, employer neutrality in organizing efforts, first-contract arbitration, severe and immediate penalties for anti-union discrimination, and elimination of the permanent replacement of strikers. Most of these have been the centerpiece of labor's thwarted attempts to restore fairness to the organizing and collective bargaining process since the mid-1970s.

In the years since the Committee on the Evolution of Work issued its 1985 report, the AFL-CIO has heard from several sympathetic but objective observers, who have argued that there should be a serious rethinking of the industrial relations fabric that Senator Robert Wagner wove in 1935. American industry has undergone profound changes: Tinkering or even overhauling a system designed to deal with the workplace of the 1930s is not enough for the workforce of the future.

These observers were motivated by a desire to see substantive broadening of employee representation, and labor union policymakers listened carefully because of their appreciation of the immense political obstacles confronting an effort at any major overhaul of the way in which workers choose unions to be their exclusive representatives. Perhaps an entirely new method for achieving representation in the United States is needed, one that might prove more politically feasible.

Inevitably, one must look at other developed countries, all of whom (France excepted) have a much higher level of union representation and have shown a greater resilience to workforce and industrial evolution than has the United States. There are several important caveats, however, when viewing comparative union density figures and drawing conclusions on their current state of health: U.S. figures are generally more precise; other countries typically count a significant number of members who are ineligible for U.S. union membership, such as supervisors and managerial employees; more significantly, workforce growth in most of these countries has not been as explosive as U.S. growth in the past 20 years. Germany's workforce, for example, grew during the 1970s and 1980s by 1.6 percent and 1.8 percent, respectively, the equivalent of *one year*'s U.S. workforce growth during the same time.

Data in Blanchflower and Freeman (this volume) reflecting overall union density understate the gap in the breadth of union penetration. The percentage of business *establishments* that have some degree of union representation reflects an even greater differential in favor of the Europeans. Unions in organized U.S. firms probably have a higher average percentage of membership than the typical European firm. U.S. unions are the exclusive representative at the worksite, representing members and nonmembers alike, and unions and employees know that wages and benefits are always on the line at the bargaining table. In Europe, much of the wage and benefit structure is established on a broader industrial or even national basis, and the union shop agreement is not a major feature of European agreements, except in Great Britain.

Why the large gap? First, there are cultural differences in the unions' role in the countries' political and social life. The absence of significant employer resistance to employees' unionization efforts is a primary explanation, and also the fact that European unions have a big hand in the welfare distribution system. There are also major differences in the way unions are established and the scope of collective bargaining at the worksite, which make it easier for workers to form a union and which discourage employers from destroying or preventing unionization.

In most developed countries, including Japan, Australia, and Europe, employee representation is a right, with little formality and no real contest. It often happens as easily as having a group of employees who want a union approach their employer informally and the employer respecting their wishes and beginning discussions. A significant proportion of union membership in European countries is in worksites where less than a majority of employees are union members. By contrast, in the United States, support for a union by a critical mass of employees only marks the beginning of a protracted struggle between the employer and the employees. In most cases, majority support for a union through a secret ballot election must take place before the employer has any obligation to deal with the union.

This means that in other developed countries union density is so high that the nonunion sector is economically insignificant; consequently, the conflict between union and nonunion firms does not exist or is not a serious factor. Furthermore, wages and salaries set by union negotiations are typically applied to or adopted by all employers—union and nonunion alike. The temptation to deunionize is much lower because the "rewards" are less. Where unions are organized in the United States, the relative strength of employee voice in the union setting is much greater than in European countries, and the union-nonunion differential in most conditions of employment will be greater.

Union organizing in the United States is a high-stakes game. Given current employer conduct, employees risk a lot of time, money, and emotional energy. Their jobs are on the line throughout the process and a victory is not so much a money proposition as significant leverage for bargaining for major improvements.

What can be done to lower the risk for employees and create a less hostile environment for those employees who wish to be represented? Two prescriptions are obvious. First is the traditional program for labor law modification, last attempted in 1978, to take away some of the employer's advantages in the representation process by adopting many of the procedures prevalent in Canada. The problem with this approach as an *exclusive* remedy is that the titanic legislative battle that will ensue may very well compromise the remedial provisions and organizing may not be affected greatly. Even if we can improve the procedures, there is a very real possibility that employers and their consultants will eventually establish methods for evading their responsibilities. Organizing and bargaining rules may still be putty in the hands of the legal fraternity.

Furthermore, even if organizing improves, there is no reason to expect that the ongoing "union divestiture" by corporate America will not continue. The problem of a minuscule union share of the millions of business establishments will not be fundamentally altered.

A second prescription is to lower the stakes of the organizing game legislatively by creating a minority representation system to supplement the current model. Under such a system, employee representation could be achieved with less than majority support and without a serious contest, but also without requiring the employer to negotiate a comprehensive bargaining agreement. A nonmajority union will have less bargaining strength, but if large numbers of establishments are organized as a result, there should be broader improvement in conditions and less pressure for individual firms to eradicate their employee representatives to meet the nonunion competition.

The bargaining or discussion process generated by such a system may not result in comprehensive collective bargaining agreements, but that process should produce workplace improvements in the areas of greatest concern to most workers. It may also become a more facile group for developing employee involvement programs (EIPs) and for improving the employer's competitive position. The outcome of discussions with a minority representative will rarely produce as dramatic a conclusion as the contract that now results from the exclusive representation process. Of course, exclusive recognition would be an option in either the unorganized or minority-represented site.

There is precedent for this system not only in other developed countries but in the U.S. government of the early 1960s; it established "formal," "informal," and exclusive recognition for unions, depending on their level of support, ranging from 10 to 50 percent. Most state and local governments without comprehensive bargaining legislation have an ad hoc system that functions along these lines. These systems are not as effective as exclusive representation collective bargaining in protecting employees' interests, but they do have value and can lay the foundation for full-fledged collective bargaining.

A serious question remains: Given the anti-union posture of private-sector American business, can minority representation work? All my examples have been systems where the employer does not oppose unions. Won't private-sector employers engage in the same manipulation and opposition to frustrate the process, and won't they use this minority representation system to co-opt any future unionization attempt for exclusive recognition?

Many employers have not been vigorous in their opposition to minority representative because full control and comprehensive agreements are not the near-term product. Co-opting will not occur in all cases, but even if it does, at least the previously nonunion firm will not have the same competitive advantage over fully unionized operations, since that co-optation will come at the price of improvements in working conditions.

For a minority representation system to work, there must be legislative protection for union activists. Just-cause legislation or a special arbitration mechanism for the minority representation worksite would have to supplement current NLRB discrimination provisions. Another legislative solution is mandated employee representation committees at worksites with more than a specified number of employees. It introduces the idea of collective representation to the huge number of worksites that do not have it, providing a voice for employees even if it is not that of a skilled union professional. This solution contains the same obstacles to union growth that exist with minority representation but with an added one: At least as a minority representative the union has membership; this system may never produce a union member.

One must point again to Europe and Canada, where in most cases these committees coexist with relatively healthy labor unions. The danger that these could become company unions is not necessarily a serious impediment and may be a blessing: The company unions of the 1920s and 1930s helped lay the groundwork for trade union growth. Most organizers prefer organizing the key leadership and members of an independent union for affiliation to the much more difficult task of working with a totally unorganized group.

The labor movement is in a better position to retain and build membership in either an employee representation committee or minority union setting. The new AFL-CIO membership benefit program—credit cards, legal services, life insurance, associate memberships—offers organizational tools that are especially suited to attracting independent unions or associate members in an open shop or employee committee situation.

Whether the AFL-CIO develops these as solutions to the problem of declining union density is a wide-open question. But when the politically opportune time comes, political leaders as well as labor officials and the working population will have to fashion something that promises to overcome the virtual elimination of workplace democracy at nearly 90 percent of private-sector firms. There is a clear demand by working Americans that will only increase if union presence diminishes in the private sector.

Conclusion

Academic observers have, in general, done a thorough job of tracking the decline in private-sector trade unions,[5] absent radical reconstruction by a combination of governmental and internal union action.

What is missing in these observations is a careful analysis of the effect that the projected demise will have on employees, the economy, and American society in general. There is an impressive and lengthy list of current laws that protect American workers, especially those without a union contract, that would never have emerged even from a congressional

---

[5]Less tracked is the growth in public-sector unionism, where, in the absence of employer opposition, employees who are free to decide opt into the system, especially at the state and local levels. Legislated employer neutrality may be the single most important feature of any effort to make changes in private-sector labor law effective in promoting union growth.

committee but for the efforts of organized labor. To say that our work is done, that these rights are in place, never to be rolled back in the future, is to ignore the realities of American political history. Even without direct repeal, dilution through amendments and half-hearted enforcement would be the inevitable outcome in a nonunion America.

Beyond that, if free trade unions have been the cornerstones for the movement to democracy in Eastern Europe and if they are the source of hope for evolution toward true democracy in other parts of the world, then any decline in the United States would represent a threat to our democratic system.

Internal union actions may stem the decline and even begin to increase union growth. However, absent governmental action to augment these efforts, the success of our internal efforts is problematic. There must be convincing public and academic opinion that supports independent and strong unions as an important part of our democratic system.

It is time to begin serious academic study about the conditions (legal, moral, and economic) that must be created if the current trend is not to continue and if the nation's democratic system is to continue to be bolstered by an effective trade union movement.

The Future Role of Government in Industrial Relations

RAY MARSHALL*

THIS PAPER EXPLORES the following hypotheses:

1. Basic U.S. industrial relations policies are rooted in the mass production/natural resource economy that made the United States the world's leading industrial nation during the first quarter of the century. These policies were reinforced by Keynesian macroeconomic policies, which were basically designed to sustain the mass production system and make it more equitable.

2. Mass production and its supporting Keynesian policies have become anachronistic because of changing technology and the globalization of economic activity. In a more competitive global economy, economic viability requires much greater attention to quality, productivity, and flexibility, all of which were much less important to, if not ignored by, mass production systems.

3. These changes require that companies or countries that wish to be high-income, world-class players adopt very different industrial relations and human resource development policies.

4. The United States is losing its status as a high-performance country because its economic and industrial relations systems and policies have been slow to adjust to this more competitive world. A failure to adapt

*LBJ School of Public Affairs, University of Texas at Austin.

31

implies economic decline, growing inequalities in wealth and income, and declining real wages, even though corporations based in the United States might be able to maintain their profits—at least for a while—by continuing their traditional production systems and shifting employment to lower-paid workers overseas and in the United States. Thus, a restoration of high-performance systems will require radical changes in U.S. economic and industrial relations policies. In a more competitive global economy, countries with active consensus-based national goals and strategies have important advantages over countries, such as the United States, that follow passive policies.

The Changing Economy

Traditional labor-management relations are deeply rooted in the economic policies and institutions that made the United States the world's strongest economy during the first half of the century. The most important factors in the country's economic success were abundant natural resources and the mass production system, which made it possible to achieve relatively rapid improvements in productivity through economies of scale and reinforcing interindustry shifts.

The mass production system organized work so that most thinking, planning, and decision making were done by managerial, professional, and technical elites. Line work was simplified so that it could be done by relatively unskilled workers. The assumption was that there was "one best way" to perform a task. It was management's responsibility to discover that one best method and to impose it on the system through detailed regulations, enforced by supervisors and inspectors. Assuming that workers would loaf unless they were closely supervised, management sought to gain control of the workplace by standardizing work processes and transferring ideas, skills, and knowledge to managers and machines.

Monotonous and degrading working conditions were made more bearable by wages that were much higher than that earned by farm labor or in the home countries of the immigrants who flocked to North American factories, mills, and mines during the early part of the century.

The system's major weaknesses were gradually eliminated by the 1940s. A major problem for mass production companies was to control markets and prices in order to be able to justify the large investments required for these systems. Oligopolistic arrangements were worked out to avoid price competition and to handle change mainly by varying output and employment while holding prices relatively constant.

Another problem, however, was that once they stabilized the prices of their products, the mass production companies experienced cyclical instability because production tended to outrun consumption at administered prices. The industrialized market economy countries fixed this problem through so-called Keynesian monetary-fiscal policies, which manipulated government spending and interest rates to generate enough total demand to keep the system operating at relatively low levels of unemployment.

Industrial relations and welfare or income maintenance policies reinforced these macroeconomic and administered price policies. Unions, collective bargaining, unemployment compensation, and Social Security were all justified as ways to sustain purchasing power. Although brought into it reluctantly, oligopolistic companies could see the wisdom of providing purchasing power, especially when it became clear that unions and collective bargaining were not going to really challenge their control of the system—they were merely going to codify workforce practices and protect workers from some of the most arbitrary company practices. The unemployment compensation system also helped companies maintain their workforces by, in effect, supplementing wages during layoffs.

Unions and their supporters had the same aversion to competition in labor markets as the oligopolists did to competitive product markets. Early unions learned that competition forced employers to depress wages and working conditions. Therefore, workers in industrial countries organized not only to extend democracy to the workplace but also to remove labor from competition through collective bargaining and government regulations. Labor theorists, such as the Webbs (1897), argued that removing labor from competition through collective bargaining and government regulations increased efficiency by preventing companies from depressing labor standards, thus forcing them to compete by becoming more efficient. The Webbs reasoned that employers who paid less than the living wage were being subsidized either by workers and their families or by society. Such subsidies therefore generated inefficiencies and made it difficult for countries to develop their human resources.

Both the mass production system and demand management policies were justified by the U.S. economy's remarkable performance during World War II. After the war, the combination of economies of scale, abundant natural resources, strong global demand, and a backlog of technology (much of it, including the computer, developed by the military) ushered in the longest period of equitably shared prosperity in U.S. history. Progressive government policies and collective bargaining counteracted the market's natural tendency to produce inequality. This whole system was reinforced by fixed exchange rates, international trade rules, and supportive financial institutions, all of which aided the expansion of America's mass production system.

The System Erodes

Toward the end of the 1960s, the foundations of the U.S. traditional economic system began to crumble. The main forces for change were technology and increased international competition, which combined to render much of the traditional mass production system and its supporting institutions anachronistic. These changes also dramatically altered the conditions for economic viability. In a more competitive world dominated by knowledge-intensive technology, the key to economic success became human resources and a more effective organization of production systems, not natural resources and traditional economies of scale. Indeed, as the work of Theodore Schultz and other economists demonstrated, the process of substituting knowledge and skills for physical resources had been the main source of improved productivity for at least since the 1920s (Carnevale, 1983; Schultz, 1981).

Technology not only contributed to the globalization of markets but also made the mass production system and traditional economies of scale less important. Although the traditional assembly line can be automated, that probably is not the most efficient use of the new technology. Computerized technology makes it possible to gain many of the advantages of economies of scale through flexible manufacturing systems, which have enormous advantages in a more dynamic and competitive global economy. The new technology provides economies of scope as well as scale because the same technology can be used to produce different products.

Technology makes new organizations of production *possible*, but competition makes them *necessary*. This is so because a competitive internationalized information economy has very different requirements for national, enterprise, organizational, and personal success than was true of largely national goods-producing systems. One of the most important changes for public policy purposes is that national governments have less control of their economies. Therefore, it is no longer possible for a single country to maintain high wages and full employment through traditional combinations of monetary-fiscal policies, administered wages and prices, and fixed exchange rates. In the 1970s and 1980s, internationalization weakened the linkages between domestic consumption, investment, and output that formed the basic structure of the traditional Keynesian demand management system. The weakening of these Keynesian linkages became very clear when U.S. tax cuts in the early 1980s increased consumption and also greatly stimulated imports and therefore produced much smaller increases in domestic investment than had resulted from earlier tax cuts in less globalized markets.

It would be a mistake, however, to conclude, as some have, that this more internationalized environment requires less government involvement. In an internationalized economy, national government policies must be more selective both as to function and economic sectors, but they are at least as important to successful economic performance as they were in more national goods-producing systems. In fact, careful research by Aschauer (1988, 1989a, 1989b) at the Federal Reserve Bank of Chicago has demonstrated that a major cause of the decline in productivity growth in the United States since the 1960s has been the decline in *public investment* for infrastructure, not, as many conservatives believe, because of a decline in private investments. These matters will be explored at greater length after a discussion of how internationalization and technological change have altered the conditions for economic viability.

The Basic Choice: Low Wages or Higher Quality and Productivity

These altered economic conditions do not just change the *magnitude* of the requirements for economic success—they fundamentally alter the *necessary structures* and *policies*. This is so because in the more competitive global information economy, economic success requires greater emphasis on some factors that were much less important in traditional mass production systems. These new factors are quality, productivity, and flexibility.

Defined as meeting customers' needs, quality becomes more important for two reasons. First, as the mass production system matured and personal incomes rose, consumers became less satisfied with standardized products. Second, the more competitive environment of the 1990s is largely consumer-driven; the mass production system was more producer-driven, especially after governments and oligopolies "stabilized" prices. In the more competitive environments of the 1970s, oligopolistic pricing became anachronistic; and flexible prices become more important. Furthermore, the mass production system depended heavily on controlling national markets; with internationalization U.S. companies have much less market control.

Productivity and flexibility are closely related to quality. The difference is that now productivity improvements are achieved through using *all factors of production* more efficiently, not, as in the mass production system, mainly through economies of scale and compatible and reinforcing interindustry shifts. Indeed, in the 1970s and 1980s interindustry shifts lowered productivity growth because they were, on balance, from more productive manufacturing activities to less productive services.

Flexibility enhances productivity by facilitating the shift of resources from less to more productive outputs; it improves quality through the ability to respond quickly to diverse and changing consumer needs. Moreover, flexibility in the use of workers and technology improves productivity by reducing the waste of labor and machine time.

Firms and economies can compete in more global knowledge-intensive markets either by lowering their incomes or by becoming more productive. Since the early 1970s, U.S. companies have been competing mainly through reducing domestic wages and by shifting productive facilities to low wage countries. This is one of the reasons why real wages were lower in the United States in 1990 than they were in 1970, and why in 1989 U.S. wages were about tenth among the major industrialized countries (U.S. Bureau of Labor Statistics, 1990).

Worker Participation and Higher-Order Thinking Skills

The fundamental issue, of course, is how to arrange production in order to achieve quality, productivity, and flexibility. The answer appears to be to restructure production systems and to develop and use leading-edge technologies. Productivity is improved by work organizations that reduce waste of materials through better inventory control, promote the efficient use of labor, and develop more effective quality controls to prevent defects. High-performance systems have a high degree of employee involvement in what would have been considered "management" functions in mass production systems. Indeed, in more productive and flexible systems, the distinctions between "managers" and "workers" become blurred.

A number of features of high-performance production systems encourage worker participation. For one thing, these systems require workers to have more knowledge and skill, and skilled, educated workers are less tolerant of monotonous, routine work and authoritarian managerial controls. Second, quality, productivity, and flexibility are enhanced when production decisions are made as close to the point of production as possible. Mass production managerial bureaucracies were designed to achieve quantity, managerial control, and stability, not flexibility, quality, or productivity in the use of all factors of production. Mass production systems are based on managerial information monopolies and worker controls; high-performance systems require that workers be free to make decisions. To accomplish this balance, information must be shared, not monopolized because in high-performance systems, machines do more of the routine, direct work and people do more indirect work. One of the most important skills required for indirect work is the ability to analyze the flood of data produced by information technology. Workers who can impose order on chaotic data can use information to add value to products, improve productivity and quality, solve problems, and improve technology.

Indirect work also is more likely to be group work, requiring more communication and interpersonal skills. These skills are necessary because productivity, quality, and flexibility require close coordination among what were formerly more discrete components of the production process (e.g., research and development, design, production, inspection, distribution, sales, services). These functions were more linear in the mass production system but are more interactive in dynamic, consumer-oriented production systems.

Another very important skill for high-performance systems is the ability to learn, which is more important here than in mass production systems and is also very different. The simplification of tasks and the standardization of technology and productivity in the mass production system limit the amount of learning needed or achieved. More learning is required in a dynamic, technology-intensive workplace, and more of that learning must be through the manipulation of abstract symbols. For line workers, mass production systems stressed learning almost entirely by observation and doing.

Learning in more productive workplaces is also likely to be more communal and cooperative. The mass production system's adversarial relationships impeded the sharing of information among workers, managers, and suppliers. A high-performance system, by contrast, encourages the sharing of information and cooperative efforts to achieve common objectives. In addition, communal learning becomes more important as a means of building the kind of consensus needed to improve the performance of more highly integrated production processes. High-performance workers are not only required to be self-managers, but also to be able to perform a greater array of tasks and adapt more readily to change. This requires a reduction of the mass production system's detailed job classifications and work rules. Well-educated, well-trained, highly motivated workers are likely to be much more flexible and productive, especially in supportive systems that stress equity and internal cohesion. Indeed, humans are likely to be the most flexible components in a high-performance system.

Other features of high-performance workplaces require greater worker participation. One feature is the need for constant improvements in technology—what the Japanese call "giving wisdom to the machine." Technology is best defined as how things are done. The most important fact about technology is not the physical capital itself, but the ideas, skills, and knowledge embodied in machines and structures. Technology becomes standardized when the rate at which ideas, skills, and knowledge can be transferred to a machine or structure diminishes. Standardized technology requires fewer ideas and less skill and knowledge than leading edge technology. High-performance organizations emphasize developing and using leading edge technologies because standardized technologies are highly mobile and are likely to be employed mainly by low-paid workers. Some U.S. companies have responded to competitive pressures by attempting to combine high technology and low skills through automation. This combination has not proven to be more productive than standardized technology with low-skilled workers. The most productive systems therefore have highly skilled workers who can develop and use leading edge technology. The shorter life cycle of poducts and technologies in a more dynamic and competitive global economy provides important advantages to continuing innovation and creativity. The more mobile technologies become, the more critical participation by highly skilled workers becomes to competitiveness.

The need to pay more attention to quality control and productivity is another reason high-performance systems work better with more worker involvement. In cases where direct contact with customers is required, flexible, highly skilled employees can provide better customer service than is true of highly specialized mass production workers, who can provide only their specialized service. Moreover, in manufacturing systems, even the most sophisticated machines are idiosyncratic and require the close attention of skilled workers to adapt them to particular situations. With the smaller production runs permitted by information technology and required by more competitive markets, workers must control production and be able to override machines; the mass production system usually made it impossible for people to override the equipment. The mass production system's long production runs made it possible to amortize start-up defects over those long runs. Systems with short production runs cannot afford many start-up defects. They must have workers who override the machines if the latter start producing defects. Quality-driven systems also must provide for more self-inspection by workers, which must often be on the basis of visible observation to *prevent* defects rather than by inspections to *detect* them at the end of the production process. Quality control is facilitated by just-in-time inventory and other mechanisms that make defects more visible or detectable early in production processes. Productivity and quality are enhanced by early detection; otherwise those defective components become invisible when they enter the product, and they are discovered as the products malfunction when used by customers.

Incentive Systems

The explicit or implicit incentives in any system are basic determinants of the outcomes. High-performance organizations ordinarily stress positive incentive systems. Mass production incentives tend to be negative—fear of discharge or punishment; they also tend to be more individualistic and implicit. Process and time-based mass compensation systems, for example, often tend to be unrelated to productivity or quality and to even be counterproductive, as when workers lose their jobs if productivity improves or when "incentives"—especially for managers—bear no relationship to objective performance or equity and therefore create disunity within the work group. Moreover, expressed incentives are sometimes to improve productivity, whereas the operative implicit incentives stress stability and control or some component of the production process (e.g., reducing shipping costs or the cost of supplies), which often has negative effects on the whole system. By contrast, high-performance incentives are more likely to be communal, positive, explicit, based on measurable outcomes, and directly related to the enterprise's stated objectives.

Positive incentives enhance flexibility as well as productivity and quality. Group incentives and job security encourage flexibility by simultaneously overcoming resistance to the development and use of broader skills and by providing employers greater incentives to invest in those skills. Similarly, bonus compensation systems simultaneously provide greater incentives for workers to improve productivity and quality and create a more flexible compensation system. Participative systems in themselves create positive incentives.

It would be hard to overemphasize the importance of internal unity and positive incentives for high-performance, knowledge-intensive workplaces, partly because all parties must be willing to go "all out" to achieve common objectives. In traditional mass production systems, workers are justifiably afraid to go "all out" to improve productivity for fear they will lose their jobs. This is the reason job security is one of the most important incentives a high-performance company can offer. Similarly, the fragmentation of work within mass production systems gives workers little incentive to control quality—quality is somebody else's responsibility. A high-performance system, by contrast, makes quality control everybody's responsibility. In addition, positive incentives are required because the effective use of information technology tends to give workers greater discretion (Zuboff, 1988). It is difficult to *compel* workers to think or even to tell whether or not they are doing it. It also is very hard to compel workers to go all out to improve quality and productivity.

Effect on Traditional Systems

Globalization has strengthened employers relative to unions in several important ways. Unions received considerable public support during the 1930s because they were necessary to protect workers from arbitrary treatment in Tayloristic management systems and also because they reinforced Keynesian economic policies. In advanced democratic countries, most people continue to recognize the need for unions to protect and promote workers' interests in the polity and society as well as in the workplace. But they increasingly question the economic value of collective bargaining because the reduced efficacy of Keynesian policies has caused a perception that unions are no longer needed; the functions they performed in maintaining purchasing power and stabilizing wages and prices are viewed as no longer as critical as they were in the 1930s. For the main problems confronting more competitive global economies—the control of inflation and competitiveness—unions and collective bargaining are often seen as negatives. Similarly, many employers who valued collective bargaining's stabilizing functions see less need to cooperate with unions since traditional collective bargaining processes are less effective in taking labor out of competition. On the other hand, internationalization gives employers greater market, resource, and production options, thereby strengthening companies relative to unions. Reduced public support for unions and pro-employer biases in U.S. laws and policies have enabled employers to intensify and expand their anti-union activities.

Unions have also suffered because their appeal has been mainly to skilled manual and mass production workers and less to workers in the rapidly growing service and technical occupations. Most industrial unions have been more adept at administering contracts under largely adversarial relationships than they are at establishing cooperative relationships and improving productivity, flexibility, and quality. Exceptions include unions in the highly competitive garment and clothing industries, which have always had to give greater attention to productivity in order to sustain a wage advantage over nonunion competitors. Another exception is in areas such as construction, where unique customer needs made mass production difficult, thus requiring more highly skilled workers and cooperation to meet customers' needs.

Some people interpret the relative decline of union strength in the

United States to mean that unions are anachronistic, like their related oligopolistic mass production and regulated industries. I disagree. The fact that the relative strength of U.S. unions has declined much more than their counterparts in other countries (especially Canada, where union strength has increased since the 1960s) suggests that their problems are due to unique U.S. factors, not to the obsolescence of trade unions per se. In fact, a case can be made that unions continue to have a vital role, though their methods, like those of mass production companies, must be adapted to a more competitive global economy. Genuine worker participation in high-performance enterprises, for example, is unlikely unless workers have independent sources of power to represent their interests. Indeed, unions are an integral part of high-performance companies in Sweden, Germany, and even in Japan. Independent sources of power are essential in more national high-performance economies for two major reasons. First, workers are not likely to exert themselves unless they are protected from the adverse consequences of doing so. Second, it is very difficult to have effective participatory, cooperative arrangements between parties who have unequal power. This is so because the stronger party will be inclined, ultimately, to exert unilateral control, thus destroying cooperation and internal unity and causing the weaker party to seek countervailing power. This happened, for instance, during the 1920s and 1930s, when management's unilateral actions encouraged workers to form or seek independent unions.

I am not arguing that effective nonunion systems are impossible, but I do believe that they are hard to maintain in the long run. It is especially difficult for these systems to work when management's main motives are to avoid unions or to reduce labor costs. There can be little question that the workers' ability to freely organize and bargain collectively has been an important check on arbitrary and discriminatory actions by companies. The right of self-organization has been sufficiently diluted in the United States so that it no longer provides adequate safeguards to workers.

I have argued elsewhere (Marshall, 1987) that under modern conditions labor organizations are at least as essential for the economy, society, and polity as they were in mass production systems. However, the methods used to protect workers must change to reflect a very different economy. For one thing, unions must play a more active role in strengthening high-performance production systems. They can do this by strengthening such noncollective bargaining participatory processes as labor-management safety and health committees and joint programs to improve productivity. Unions also could encourage or force companies to develop global strategies that compel managers to take longer time perspectives, develop leading edge technologies, and adopt more positive incentive systems. Unions should continue to challenge elitist management perquisites and unfair compensation systems, which not only create disunity but also have little or nothing to do with individual or company performance.

It is particularly important for unions to challenge management practices that produce short-run profits but which are contrary to the interests of workers, communities, and the country as a whole. Examples include company policies to compete by reducing wages and employment rather than by improving productivity. Other countries promote high-performance management practices through collective bargaining or regulations that require consultation with workers representatives or justifications to public bodies before plants can be closed, wages cut, or workers laid off.

Finally, unions should continue to champion public policies designed to make the United States a high-wage, equitable, full-employment economy. Above all, this will require developing more democratic institutions, effective public schools, school-to-work transition processes, and on-the-job learning systems for line workers. Learning systems for workers are at least as necessary to high-performance systems as managerial training, which now consumes an inordinate share of corporate resources. The joint programs in the construction, automobile, and communications industries are good beginnings, but they are only a fraction of what they should be. According to the American Society for Training and Development, 15,000 firms—less than one-half of 1 percent of all companies—account for over 90 percent of all workplace training in the United States. In addition, the Commission on Skills of the American Workforce (1990) reported that U.S. companies were far behind their principal Asian and European competitors in both training and organizing for high performance.

What is required, of course, is for unions and their supporters to develop the modern intellectual equivalent of Keynesian economics to show that unions are good for the economy as well as for the polity and society. Although unions must modernize their policies, methods, and structures to make them more responsive to their members' needs, stronger public support requires a rationale that shows that unions are an essential economic institution; they are not narrow special interest groups because their activities strengthen the entire economy.

Evidence

Greater worker participation will improve productivity, quality, and flexibility. Unfortunately, the evidence for this proposition is difficult to establish because worker participation processes have different meanings, are qualitatively different from place to place, and never occur in isolation from other factors.

However, there is growing evidence that worker participation and work reorganization are important factors in improving productivity and economic competitiveness (Dertouzes et al., 1989). This should not be surprising, of course, since labor accounts for at least 70 percent of total costs. Small improvements in labor productivity can have a much greater impact on total productivity than larger increases in physical capital. A Brookings Institution study edited by Alan Blinder acknowledged the positive contribution of worker participation, though Blinder considers such productivity improvements to be "transitory" although potentially "impressive" (Blinder, 1989–90, 1990). Blinder, like most economists, believes that "the best way to raise productivity growth, and perhaps the only way to do so permanently, is to speed up the pace of technological innovation" (Blinder, 1989–90, p. 33). The trouble with this view, of course, is the implied assumption that technological innovation is external to the production process and not an integral part of it. This view also fails to recognize that high-performance production systems with positive incentives, skilled workers, and a high degree of worker involvement have the capacity for *continuous improvements* in productivity and technology. The Brookings study shows, nevertheless, that incentive compensation systems raise wages about 11 percent an hour more than it does for workers under other systems, and this increase happens without reducing fringe benefits or hourly wages (Blinder, 1989–90). Blinder concludes that "worker participation apparently does help make alternative compensation plans . . . work better—and also has beneficial effects of its own. This theme was totally unexpected when I organized the conference [that led to the study]" (Blinder, 1989–90, p. 38).

In 1987, David Lewin and others at Columbia University studied the relationship between the financial performance of 500 publicly traded companies and the degree of employee involvement. Analyzing the data, they concluded that the mere presence of an employee involvement process was not significantly related to positive improvements in any of the financial indicators. However, the further a firm moved up the employee involvement index (measuring degrees of employee involvement) and the more employees were involved in decision making, the greater the magnitude of financial performance. What appears to be critical is the scope or comprehensiveness of employee involvement and participation programs.

High employee involvement is associated with better financial performance, particularly on the return on investment and the return on asset measures (Economic Policy Council, 1990).

In addition, there is abundant evidence from case studies on the relationship between worker participation and improved quality and productivity. Perhaps the most clear-cut and compelling evidence is from the New United Motor Manufacturing Co., Inc. (NUMMI), a joint venture between Toyota and General Motors in Fremont, California. This was a plant that GM closed in 1982 because its managers could not make it competitive. Toyota reopened the plant as NUMMI in 1984 with a new management system, most of the same UAW members, and essentially the same equipment, which was much less automated than in GM's most modern plants. One of the most important changes NUMMI made was to guarantee workers a high level of job security. Other changes included a reduction in job classes from about 100 to four; the elimination of such management perks as private dining rooms, parking lots, private offices, and separate dress codes; and the establishment of work teams of five to 10 people who set their own work standards, laid out the work area, determined the workload distribution, and assigned workers to specific tasks.

NUMMI's key managerial concept is a commitment to high-quality standards by workers and managers. Quality control is built into the production process. The company uses a modified "just-in-time"[1] inventory system to reduce costs and improve quality by immediately identifying faulty parts. It also imposes very high-quality standards for suppliers and works closely with those companies to solve quality problems. The inspection function is largely decentralized to line workers.

From a production standpoint there can be little doubt that NUMMI, which makes Toyota Corollas and the GEO Prism (Chevrolet Novas were discontinued in 1989, and the plant started producing light trucks in 1991), has been a success. Productivity at the plant is 50 percent higher than at the former GM plant, and in 1989 NUMMI ranked first among all GM plants in the United States. A 1988 MIT study reported that productivity was about 40 percent higher than in traditional GM plants and was about equal that in Toyota's Japanese plants. Also in 1989, *Consumer Reports* judged NUMMI's Chevrolet Nova to be the highest quality of any American-built car (Krafcik, 1989). As a result of these successes, there has been strong interest in NUMMI among American managers. GM uses the plant as a managerial training center, and other companies have hired NUMMI managers.

Toyota's main objectives at NUMMI were to establish a U.S. production and marketing center and to ascertain whether or not that company's

---

[1]Supplies or parts that are delivered "just in time" for their use, thus eliminating the need for large inventories, which not only are expensive to maintain but also conceal defects.

management system could be successfully used with U.S. workers and unions. There is no doubt that Toyota succeeded in demonstrating that this could be done. It has improved on the NUMMI experience with its Camry, produced in its newer plant in Georgetown, Kentucky. In 1990, J.D. Powers & Associates ranked the Corolla ninth among the highest quality U.S.-built cars (the Camry was third); Toyota's Cressida was ranked first. What makes the Corolla and Camry performance so impressive is that they are lower-priced subcompacts whereas almost all the other ranked cars were luxury vehicles (White, 1990).

General Motors' main objective at NUMMI was to learn more about the Japanese management system. GM managers had relied more heavily than Toyota or Ford on automating to improve productivity and competitiveness. NUMMI taught GM that workers were not the problem; GM also learned that machine technology alone was not the answer. The NUMMI experience helped GM to produce even better results at its Saturn plant in Tennessee and at its truck plant in Shreveport, Louisiana, than at NUMMI.

Saturn was originally designed to leapfrog the competitive advantage enjoyed by Japanese auto companies. In many ways the Saturn agreement improves on NUMMI's. Saturn uses the team concept, but the union participates at every level in the management system, not just on the shopfloor as is the case at NUMMI. As at NUMMI, job classifications have been greatly reduced to one for production workers and three to five for skilled workers. Like NUMMI, Saturn dispenses with management perks, but goes further: All workers are on salary equal to 80 percent of average UAW wages in other U.S. auto plants. The other 20 percent varies according to such factors as productivity, profits, and quality. Saturn, unlike NUMMI, assigns relief workers to each work team, and the work is more self-paced than at NUMMI. Moreover, the team leaders at Saturn are elected by members of their work units or through an election designed by the UAW; at NUMMI they are determined by management. Saturn also follows NUMMI's lead in giving workers job security by providing no layoffs for 80 percent of workers except for severe economic conditions or unforeseen catastrophic events.

Critics argue that NUMMI has subjected workers to "management by stress" by speeding up the production line and by eliminating easy jobs and slack time. Some workers have been very critical of NUMMI's very strict absentee policy, which calls for firing workers with four "offenses" in a one-year period. Examples of offenses range from three absences in a 90-day period to not reporting in absent before the shift begins. Personal and family illnesses are not allowable absences (Parker and Slaughter, 1989). Others argue that some NUMMI managers have regressed to their former authoritarian ways and criticize the "team" concept for weakening union solidarity (Parker and Slaughter, 1989).

Despite these criticisms, the UAW and the overwhelming majority of the plant's workers strongly support NUMMI's participatory processes. As the Saturn agreement demonstrates, however, improvements are needed in the NUMMI system. Indeed, the management systems in Sweden and Germany are much better than Japan's because their systems are more pervasive and give workers control at every level. The Japanese system actually applies to only 15–20 percent of workers; the Swedish and German systems are more universal.

The evidence strongly supports the conclusion that restructured production systems emphasizing worker participation can greatly improve productivity and quality as well as the quality of work life. In a more competitive global economy, firms can compete either by reducing wages or improving productivity and quality through worker reorganization and improving workforce skills. There also is strong evidence, however, that *genuine* worker participation is much less pervasive in the United States than in Japan or Western Europe. How do we account for this? Several hypotheses might be advanced:

1. The mass production system was more successful and more entrenched in the United States, so unions and management are more reluctant to abandon the adversarial and authoritarian systems that it produced than are their Japanese or European counterparts.

2. Most American employers are not convinced that participatory systems are more effective than traditional mass production systems and authoritarian management procedures. There appears to be enough uncertainty about these new approaches that most American managers apparently believe the risks outweigh the potential benefits.

3. Government policies in the United States encourage companies to follow low-wage strategies. This country, for example, has been extremely reluctant to restrain managerial decision making, either by requiring the kind of worker participation processes that exist in almost all other major industrial countries or by strengthening the workers' right to organize and bargain collectively, which has been greatly diluted since the 1940s and 1950s. U.S. polices also have been reluctant to interfere with the "employment at-will" doctrine, which made it easy for American companies to shift the cost of change to workers and communities through layoffs and plant closings. Indeed, tax and tariff policies actually encourage companies to shift employment to low-wage countries. Unlike other advanced industrial countries, the United States has not adopted a high-wage, full employment strategy. It has, for example, encouraged the perpetuation of industries that

are viable only through low wages; most other industrialized countries actively discourage such industries through high minimum or negotiated wages and other restrictions.

Perhaps the most serious limitation of U.S. policy has been its failure to have a human resource development strategy to produce the skilled workers needed for high-performance work systems. The mass production educational system and the absence of policies to educate and train the 75 percent of frontline workers who are not college-educated seriously limit the country's future potential. Major economic competitors have policies to provide strong basic education and work training for those skills that do not require four years of college. U.S. secondary school graduates, by contrast, consistently score near the bottom on international math and science assessments—even below many developing countries, and the country has almost no postsecondary skill training programs for most non-college-bound youths. A recent report, for example, found that in mathematics 95 percent of Japanese high school students outperform the top 5 percent of U.S. students (Council on Competitiveness, 1990). Without higher-order thinking skills, dropouts—and even most high school graduates—are increasingly condemned to a lifetime of low wages and joblessness. The United States' principal competitors see to it that all young people acquire basic thinking skills by the time they are 15 or 16 years old. These basic academic skills provide the foundation for further education, professional and technical job training, or work. These countries also have a variety of technical training and education programs for those who do not elect to go on to technical college immediately. However, higher education remains an option even for those who elect technical training or work options after completing their basic education.

The provision of high-quality basic education followed by apprenticeship or other technical training reinforces a high-wage strategy in two ways. First, highly skilled workers are not content with low-skill work. Second, workers with higher-order thinking skills are equipped to handle high-performance work organizations.

Conclusions

If we want to develop high-performance production systems, the role of government in industrial relations must include the following:

1. To develop a consensus that our national economic goal is to remain a world-class, high-income, democratic country.
2. To develop strategies to achieve these objectives, including:
    a. Supportive macroeconomic policies to encourage adequate eco-

nomic growth to achieve low levels of unemployment and to develop means other than unemployment and low wages to combat inflation.

b. Active policies to include labor standards as part of the rules governing all international transactions. These rules would simultaneously protect labor standards in the developed countries and make it possible for Third World workers to participate more equitably in the economic development of their countries, thus enhancing global demand.

c. Measures to strengthen human resource development for workers who do not attend college. These include:

(1) National performance standards for all high school graduates

(2) Alternative high-quality, postsecondary education and job training systems. These systems should be open-ended and make it possible for workers who wish to do so to attend college.

(3) An entitlement program to provide at least four years of education and training beyond high school for everyone.

(4) Professional standards developed by tripartite groups (labor, management, and government) for occupations that do not require four years of college.

(5) A refundable training and education tax on all employers. Companies that conduct acceptable training would not have to pay the tax. Part (e.g., 25%) of the funds created by this tax could be used for work reorganization.

d. *Strengthen workers' right to organize and bargain collectively.* It is particularly important to correct the pro-employer biases in U.S. industrial relations policies. This can be done by prohibiting companies from permanently replacing striking workers (which greatly weakens the right to strike and therefore the effectiveness of collective bargaining), strengthening the present very weak penalties for violating workers' collective bargaining rights, providing unions equal access to employees during organizing campaigns, and streamlining NLRB processes to prevent tactical delays in both representation and unfair labor practice cases. Special attention should be given to facilitating first contracts for newly organized workers. This might be done by making it possible for workers to help one another by waiving secondary boycott restrictions for first contracts, specifically outlawing employer boycotts and mutual assistance activities during strikes over first contracts, or requiring binding arbitration over first contracts. Similarly, government should either provide food stamps and unemployment compensation to strikers on the same terms as for workers who have been laid off, or terminate all government assistance to companies during strikes.

e. Strengthen worker participation by:

(1) Removing or clarifying antitrust and other legal barriers to labor-management cooperation at every level (including corporate boards), except where these are subterfuges to violate workers' rights to organize and bargain collectively.

(2) Mandating joint labor-management committees to promote such objectives as the administration of occupational safety and health programs and pensions and welfare funds.

(3) Strengthening research and development on genuine worker participation programs and provide technical assistance to workers and employers who wish to improve noncollective bargaining labor-management activities.

Above all, we must recognize the need to integrate economic, labor market, human resource development, and industrial relations policies. The key to our economic future is an educated, healthy, motivated workforce, along with high-performance production systems. These will not be achieved by passive policies and dependence solely on market forces. Markets are necessary institutions for economic efficiency, but under present conditions market forces and unrestrained managerial choices will produce lower wages and more unequal income distributions. Without public strategies to alter these outcomes, the United States is unlikely to remain a world-class, high-wage country.

The Challenge of Human Resources Development

JOHN T. DUNLOP*

SINCE THE FUTURE ROLE OF UNIONS, government, and industry in industrial relations can be interpreted many different ways, it is essential to be clear about the following questions: (1) What are the trends in these roles? (2) What is the forecast for future roles? and (3) What ought to be these roles in the future? The first question is historical, the second projective, and the third is normative. These three questions and their answers should not be confused.

Industrial Relations Systems

In 1958, when my *Industrial Relations Systems* was first published, I listed four objectives of the volume, all of which are still relevant to our subject.

1. *Facts have outrun ideas*. Integrating theory has lagged far behind expanding experience. The many worlds of industrial relations have been changing more rapidly than the ideas to interpret, to explain, and to relate them (Dunlop, 1958). Any such theory has as its ambitious objective a general theory of industrial relations—to provide tools for the analysis,

---

*Lamont University Professor Emeritus, Harvard University.

interpretation, and understanding of the widest possible range of facts and practices. Central to such an interaction are the dynamic changes within the environment—technological, market or budget, and the locus and distribution of power in the larger society—and changes within and among the actors and the impact of these developments on the output or rules of the system. All the actors consist of hierarchies with their own internal interactions at varying levels of these organizations (Dunlop, 1985).

2. *Comparative research depends on the scope of the system.* It provides a basis for further studies among enterprises, industries, and developed as well as developing countries (Jensen, 1964; Walker, 1970).

3. *There are other outputs to the system than industrial warfare or labor-management peace.* Prior to the late 1950s, most discussions of industrial relations classified arrangements along a continuum from warfare at one end to cooperative policies at the other (Selekman, 1947; Harbison and Dubin, 1947).

4. *One must try to make one world of direct experience in industrial relations and the realm of ideas.*

The industrial relations systems framework yields a fairly simple and efficient format to identify and describe the changes in any general system as well as in particular sectors. The internal organization and governance of unions, government, and industry are themselves changing as well. Technological changes—such as the computer, miniaturization, communications, biotechnology; changes in markets and budgetary constraints such as globalization, regional shifts, demography, and governmental regulatory policies; and shifting power relations and values in the larger community as reflected in law and public opinion—all are operating on these three actors and creating substantive changes in the outputs of the system. While these interactions are complex, the model provides an agenda and a framework to organize data and insights. The model also provides an analysis to guide intervention to resolve practical problems.

I will concentrate here on the most controversial of the three questions raised at the outset, namely, the normative one. What ought to be the roles of labor organizations, government, and industry in the U.S. industrial relations system in the future, particularly with regard to human resources development?

Productivity and Human Resources

Among the major problems the United States faces is its relatively poor performance in productivity. We probably have, by a small and decreasing margin, the highest average productivity in the world, but in many sectors we no longer lead the listings. Our national annual rate of increase in output per hour in manufacturing in the period 1960–88 was 2.8 percent per year compared with 7.8 percent in Japan, 4.4 percent in Germany, and even 3.7 percent in the United Kingdom (U.S. Bureau of Labor Statistics, 1988). During 1979–88, gross domestic product per employed person in the United States grew at the average rate of 1.0 percent per year compared with 1.5 to 2.5 percent per year in the major European countries (Terleckyj, 1990).

Economic growth and improvement in productivity depend on four basic factors: research and development, investment in plant and equipment, investment in infrastructure (Munnell, 1990), and investment in human resources development. Human resources development and the creation of a more productive, skilled, and adaptable workforce in turn depend on six factors: (1) the education system, particularly K-12, (2) health care, (3) training and retraining, (4) family policy, (5) labor-management policies at the workplace under collective bargaining or without labor organization, and (6) the general health of public service in the country, a point stressed by Paul Volcker and his National Commission on the Public Service (National Commission on the Public Service, 1989). Any analysis of the future role of unions, government, and industry in our industrial relations system needs to start with these six problem areas.

The Current Situation

The current state of human resources development in these six areas is, unfortunately, discouraging, as is also its consequent impact on productivity, economic growth, and international competitiveness.

In the age group 10–17, with about 3.5 million in each cohort year, 10 percent are at very high risk and another 15 percent are at serious risk. Such risks include teen-age pregnancy, drug abuse and alcohol addiction, criminal activity and incarceration, and absenteeism and school dropouts. More than 20 percent of youth under the age of 18 live in single-parent homes, and more than half of these live in poverty. According to New York Superintendent of Schools Joseph Fernandez, "We have created a Third World country in our midst." Despite the growing average education attainment of the workforce—measured by the number of college graduates— education in K-12 is recognized to be in disarray.

Second, our health care is in a shambles—31.8 million people are without health insurance; counting dependents, that number rises to 49.3 million. There are major deficiencies in child care and prenatal care. Despite the 11–12 percent of gross national product expended and the many centers of high-quality care, we are reinforcing problem areas. Insufficient housing might well be added to this list of problem areas.

As to training and retraining, 20 percent of the labor force is functionally illiterate with inadequate skills in reading and arithmetic to hold a job, much less a good job today or one in the future. Despite more than 20 years of public policies aimed at employment and training, we have made little headway in the extraordinarily turbulent markets we have been experiencing (Doeringer, 1990).

Family policy measures are largely nonexistent, despite a growing recognition of the decisive impact of changes in family structure, demography, and working patterns on the labor force and, ultimately, on productivity.

Our national labor policy is in a disastrous state in many respects: in its bias toward conflict and against cooperation and joint problem solving; in its artificiality, legalism, and delays; in its failure to encourage mediation and negotiated rule making; and in the lack of a serious major role for labor and management representatives in industrial relations policy-making and administration (Dunlop, 1987).

Morale in the public-service sector—federal, state, and local—is at a low ebb, with dire consequences for the public weal. In sum:

> It is my sincere conviction that it is the failure to develop appropriate institutions to educate, to train and retrain, to maintain health, to manage and elicit productive and cooperative services from its workforce that is our country's most critical failure. Our poor performance with human resources cannot in the long term be offset or compensated for in the test of international competition by location, natural resources, history, capital structure or our political democracy. (Dunlop, 1989, p. 25)

The ideology in vogue in the United States allows us to allocate responsibility for performance in only three ways—first, to the market and self-interested exchange; second, to the government as a device for coordination and directing resource; and, third, to voluntarism and its thousand points of light. But my colleague Raymond Vernon rightly tells us that "many governments are learning how to create partnerships across the public-private frontier that are more flexible and more pragmatic than they have tended to be in the past. . . . The United States faces the prospects of a world increasingly peopled by enterprises of ambiguous identity, part public, part private, operating in ways that are foreign to the U.S. experience" (Vernon, 1988, p. 56).

Future Directions

Since the 1980s, a number of large-scale businesses and groups of local businesses have begun to play a new role in each of the six areas of human resources, with the quality in part of a public good. In a few situations, labor organizations and even universities have been involved. A few examples are business-education partnerships, health care coalitions, training programs for employees scheduled to leave the enterprise, family policy measures, joint labor-management problem solving apart from the legal framework of collective bargaining, school-based management, and so on. In general, these experiences have taught us that past ideology—based on barriers between private and public, business and government—is not helpful. In fact, it has been an impediment to problem solving, institutional reform, and social intervention. New forms of organization and new structures and partnerships are developing that cut across old boundaries. These new departures, of course, reinforce the debate on the nature and responsibilities of business corporations and their management in a global economy.

We are also observing a change in roles among labor, government, and business on some issues and problems—a real change in their relationship. We see governments less as regulators and more as catalysts and mediators. We see the growth of negotiated rule making rather than the use of the Administrative Procedures Act for successful regulation. We see business engaged in a variety of public good activities and community roles apart from a direct impact on the bottom line.

I am pleased to report that the Business and Government Center at Harvard University's John F. Kennedy School of Government made the George S. Dively Award to Dayton Hudson Corporation in 1986 for its National Literacy Initiative and to General Mills in 1987 for its program of care for the elderly in the community. On a lesser scale, we see unions engaged in training, education, housing, legal aid, and international roles apart from traditional business unionism.

These development can be illustrated with a few of my own personal experiences in problem solving (Salter and Dunlop, 1989). They include the Joint Labor-Management Committee for Municipal Police and Fire in Massachusetts, which has operated for 13 years by mediation—in contrast to the previous Board of Arbitration and Conciliation; the three-way collective agreements in Northern Ohio and Michigan among processors, farmers, and a migrant farm labor organization outside of state or federal labor-relations statutes; the Textile and Tailored Clothing Corporation $(TC)^2$, a joint effort of labor and management to develop and introduce new technology into these workplaces and facilitate a "quick response" to the consumer in order to enhance the competitiveness of the domestic industry; the enactment of three statutes reforming the pension system for municipal employees in Massachusetts; and the framework of a collective agreement between the Harvard Union of Clerical and Technical Workers (HUCTW) and Harvard University. These are only a few examples of the hundreds of community partnerships dealing with education, health care, and training that have been at work for many years.

These developments do not introduce more central planning or mass displacement of the market system. Rather, they constitute new forms and relationships—partnership, coalitions, and forums—and new boundaries for markets rather than those envisaged in the compartmentalized ideology of the past. These new forms apply particularly to areas of human resources development such as education, training, health, and housing.

This transformation of the relations among labor, government, and industry at the local, state, and national levels is in the direction of development for constructive problem solving. The serious issues of our times cannot rely solely on the market, legislation, and the Administrative Procedures Act. Only less conventional tools will accomplish the results that our society requires. A new set of relationships is required among labor, government, and business, especially for the task of developing trained, productive, and adaptable human resources.

Unionism in the United States and Other Advanced OECD Countries

DAVID G. BLANCHFLOWER and RICHARD B. FREEMAN*

MOST THEORIES OF LABOR IN capitalist economies stress the factors that lead workers to form unions to bargain with management over wages and conditions of work, producing similar labor relations among countries over time (Kerr et al., 1964). Yet far from converging to some modal type, trade unionism—traditionally the principal worker institution under capitalism—developed differently among Western countries in the 1970s and 1980s (Freeman, 1989). The proportion of workers represented by unions fell precipitously in the United States. It also dropped, though to a lesser extent, in Japan, the Netherlands, and the United Kingdom (during the Thatcher years), and France, while increasing or maintaining high levels in most Continental European countries and in Canada and Australia. The divergence in union density occurred despite increased trade, communications, production by multinational firms, and technological transfer and capital flows among countries that ought to have exerted greater pressures for convergence in labor institutions than in earlier decades when there were tighter national boundaries.

---

*The authors' affiliations are, respectively, National Bureau of Economic Research, Dartmouth College and Centre for Economic Performance; and National Bureau of Economic Research and Harvard University.

In this paper we explore the dimensions of the divergence in union representation between the United States and other advanced OECD countries in the 1970s and 1980s and relate these differences in density to differences in the economic effects of unionism across countries during this time. Arguing that the high union wage premium in the United States has contributed to the decline in U.S. density, we suggest that U.S. unions must make major tactical and policy innovations to regain strength in the private sector while the nation will have to develop new industrial relations institutions to guarantee workers a voice in workplace decisions.

The Economic Environment and Unionization in the 1970s and 1980s

The rapidly changing economic and political environment of the 1970s and 1980s placed union movements in the developed world under stress unprecedented since the depression of the 1930s. The following were the major changes:

1. A slowdown in world economic growth and productivity and the increased inflation following the 1970s oil shocks, which created adverse labor market situations in virtually all Western countries: Unemployment rates skyrocketed, particularly in Europe; unemployment consistent with a given level of job vacancies rose; real wages fell for blue-collar workers, particularly in the United States; and unions in several countries took real wage cuts in the 1980s in order to stimulate employment.[1]

2. The composition of employment shifted from traditionally highly unionized to nonunion sectors and workers. The share of employment in manufacturing dropped almost everywhere, while the share of employment in white-collar work grew, producing a labor force for whom many traditional union issues were irrelevant. The female proportion of employment rose; the level of workers' schooling increased; and the age structure of the workforce changed as the baby boom generation entered the labor market. Since the workplace needs of white-collar workers, women, and more educated and younger workers differ somewhat from those of prime-age, male, blue-collar workers, who built most union movements, new tactics and policies were needed to attract these workers to the labor movement.

3. Labor markets became increasingly internationalized, as the trade

---

[1]The United Kingdom is a striking exception, with substantial real wage gains through the 1980s. The gain in real wages of Japanese workers through the 1980s was expected, given the rapid growth of the Japanese economy and low rates of unemployment.

component of the GNP grew sharply, immigration increased, and capital markets became more global (Freeman, 1988a). The United States lost its lead in world technology and productive know-how, eliminating a source of potential economic rents for American workers.

4. Collectivist and socialist ideologies lost favor to individualistic market ideologies. Reagan broke the air traffic controllers' strike in the United States, and Thatcher introduced tough labor legislation in the United Kingdom and defeated the mineworkers' union in a protracted dispute. Indicative of the change in political climate, labor parties in Australia and New Zealand adopted market-oriented economic policies, as did most governments in Western Europe.

Thus, in the 1980s, the social and economic environment became increasingly hostile to unionism and to many traditional union practices and policies. In this environment U.S. unions suffered grievous losses in their representation of workers in the private sector, with density falling to 1920s and 1930s levels. From this scenario, one might expect unions to be in rapid retreat in most other advanced OECD countries as well, but this expectation is erroneous. The available data on union density in developed countries, while far from perfect, show a divergent pattern of change across countries. As Table 1 demonstrates, density declined dramatically in the United States and moderately in Japan and France in the 1970s and the 1980s; fell in the United Kingdom, the Netherlands, and Italy in the 1980s after increasing in the 1970s; but rose in the 1970s and remained at historically high levels in many other countries. The unweighted average level of density for countries exclusive of the United States grew by 5 percentage points from 1970 to 1986–87. The difference in density between the United States and the other countries more than doubled: In 1986–87 U.S. density was 36 points below the average compared with 17 points below the average in 1970. Moreover, the decline in U.S. union density from rough equality with Canadian density to less than half the Canadian rate shows that the divergence represents more than the disparate development of different kinds of unionism. After all, the United States and Canada have similar industrial relations systems, with many of the same employers and unions operating in both countries.

There are, of course, problems with comparing the figures in Table 1. The definition, meaning, and sources of membership data differ across countries (Walsh, 1985; Visser, 1989) in ways that can bias trends as well as levels. The British data, for instance, may understate the 1980s fall in density because some unions exaggerated membership to maintain high representation on the Trade Unions Congress Executive Committee and in the Labour Party. By contrast, the Italian data may overstate the 1980s

TABLE 1

UNION MEMBERSHIP OF NONAGRICULTURAL WORKERS AS A PERCENTAGE OF
NONAGRICULTURAL WAGE AND SALARY EMPLOYEES, 1970–86/87
(percentages)

Country	1970	1979	1986–87	1970–79	1979–86	1970–87
With sharp rises in density						
Denmark	66	86	95	+20	+9	29
Finland	56	84	85	+28	+1	29
Sweden	79	89	96	+10	+7	17
With 1970s rises in density stable in 1980s						
Belgium	66	77	76	11	−1	10
Ireland	44	49	51	5	2	7
West Germany	37	42	43	5	1	6
Australia	52	58	56	6	−1	5
Canada	32	36	36	4	0	4
Switzerland	31	34	33	3	−1	2
Norway	59	60	61	1	1	2
With 1970s rises in density decline in 1980s						
Italy	39	51	45	12	−6	6
United Kingdom	51	58	50	7	−8	−1
New Zealand	43	46	41[a]	3	−5	−2
With declining density						
Austria	64	59	61	−5	2	−3
Netherlands	39	43	35	4	−8	−4
France	22	20	17[a]	−2	−3	−5
Japan	35	32	28	−3	−4	−7
United States	31	25	17	−6	−8	−14
Unweighted average (exclusive of U.S.)	48	54	53	6	−1	6
Deviation of U.S. from un-weighted average	−16	−28	−34	−12	−7	−20

SOURCES: U.S. Department of Labor, Division of Foreign Labor Statistics, "Union Membership," September 1988; additional figures from Centre for Labour Economics, OECD data file, London School of Economics; Visser (1989); and R. Bean (1989), pp. 171, 159.
[a]Data available only for 1985.

drop in density due to increasing membership in autonomous union groups in the public sector and among foremen and lower level management unassociated with the major federations. The U.S. figures mix two opposing trends: a precipitous fall in density in the private sector (to a bare 12.5% in 1989) and growing unionism in the public sector. These and other problems notwithstanding, there is no gainsaying the finding in Table 1 that the United States has "taken a different road" in industrial relations from that of most developed countries. In the private sector, the United States has gone a long way toward the union-free nirvana of the rabid opponents of trade unionism.

International Social Survey Programme Data

To see if U.S. unionism affects economic outcomes in ways that may help explain its extraordinary drop in density, we examine the effect of unions on economic outcomes in advanced OECD countries, using data from the International Social Survey Programme (ISSP). The ISSP is a program of cross-national collaboration, carried out by national research institutes that conduct annual surveys of social attitudes and values.[2] It coordinates national social science surveys to produce a common set of questions asked in identical form in the participating nations. Thus, it permits us to compare union membership and estimate the effects of unions on outcomes from comparable micro files that had not been possible before. In 1990, the group consisted of 11 nations, five of whom provided information on union membership. In addition, in 1987 Switzerland ran an equivalent survey that also contains information on union membership.

As a first step toward analyzing the ISSP data, we calculated unionization rates for workers with different characteristics in the six countries with unionization data[3] (see Table 2). The density figures in the "All" column corroborate the country pattern in Table 1, showing in particular that the United States had by far the lowest rate of organization (18% vs. an unweighted average for the other countries of 44%). Given the problems of

---

[2]The genesis of the survey is as follows. In late 1983, Social and Community Planning Research (SCPR) in London started a social indicator series—the British Social Attitudes Surveys (BSA)—which is similar to the General Social Survey (GSS) of the National Opinion Research Center (NORC), University of Chicago. The Nuffield Foundation funded international contacts with GSS and the Zentrum fuer Umfragen Methoden und Analysen (ZUMA) in Mannheim; ZUMA conducts its own social indicators study, the Allgemeinen Bevoelkerungsumfrage der Sozialwissenschaften (ALLBUS). In 1984 ISSP was formed with an additional member—Australia. The group agreed to: (1) jointly develop topical modules dealing with important areas of social science, (2) carry a module of a 15-minute self-completion supplement to their regular national surveys, (3) include a common core of background variables, and (4) make the data available to the social science community as soon as possible. Each nation agreed to fund its own data collection and bear any costs that it incurred. ISSP's character, then, is shaped by the advantages and limitations of a small module of identical questions added to existing annual or biennial social surveys. By 1989 there were 11 participating nations. Switzerland is not one of the countries participating in the ISSP, but a team at the Sociologisches Institut der Universitat Zurich replicated the 1987 module and has kindly provided us with the data.

The ISSP data are archived with the ZentralArchiv at the University of Koln. For initial analyses of the ISSP data, see "British Social Attitudes: The International Report," in Jowell et al. (1989).

[3]We shall refer to Switzerland as one of the ISSP countries although, as noted, the Swiss are not official participants in the cross-country data set.

TABLE 2
UNION MEMBERSHIP ACROSS COUNTRIES
(percentages)

	Australia	Austria	West Germany	United Kingdom	United States	Switzerland[b]	Unweighted Average	Deviation of U.S.
All	54	49	33	47	18	36	44	−26
Male	56	56	40	52	22	42	49	−27
Female	51	39	21	40	13	24	35	−22
Years of schooling								
10 or less	52	47	37	50	20	35	44	−24
11–12	56	55	26	40	21	36	42	−21
13 or more	49	47	25	52	15	40	42	−27
Age of workers								
18–24	52	37	24	36	9	28	35	−26
25–44	57	53	33	46	17	36	45	−28
45 or more	48	55	38	53	22	41	47	−25
Part time	37	12	9	23	9	d	20	−11
Full time	55	51	34	50	18	36	45	−27
Manual	56	57	44	53	30	n/a	53	−23
Nonmanual	45	44	27	42	13	n/a	40	−27
Manufacturing	43[a]	52	37	48	25	n/a	45	−20
All other	47[a]	49	31	46	16	n/a	43	−27
Public sector	71	74	44[c]	75	20	62	58	−38
Private sector	42	48	33[c]	31	15	26	36	−21
No. of observations	2,195	1,369	2,130	2,011	1,968	512		

SOURCE: Tabulated from International Social Survey Programme data.
[a] 1986 data only.
[b] 1987 data only.
[c] 1985 and 1987 data only.
[d] Small number of observations.

comparability of union figures, the similarity between these data and the figures in Table 1 is reassuring. The ISSP data also show that men, full-time workers, manual workers, and public-sector workers are relatively highly unionized in all countries. By contrast, there are only moderate differences in density between highly educated and less educated workers and between employees in manufacturing and in the rest of the economy. The reason is high unionization in the public sector (included in the "All other" industry grouping), where many educated workers are employed. By the mid-1980s union members in the developed countries were increasingly public sector, educated, and nonmanual (Freeman, 1989, Table 2). Finally, while younger workers (those aged 18–24) are underrepresented in unions in all the countries, their level of unionization in the United States, 9 percent, is exceptionally low compared with a 35 percent average union density in the other countries.

What Unions Do Across Countries

Labor relations differ among countries in ways that go beyond crude unionization rates. In the United States, thousands of local unions bargain over contracts often running to 200 or more pages that typically set local members' wage rates. In Scandinavia, unions often negotiate national wage agreements with employer associations and enter agreements with the government and employer federations that link wage settlements to national economic policies. Australian unions argue wage cases before arbitration tribunals and are the mainstay of the Labour Party. French and West German unions negotiate industry or regional agreements whose terms the Ministry of Labor can extend to nonunion workers. In Japan company unions bargain at the firm level and engage in the Shunto Offensive to determine national wage patterns. We expect differing arrangements to produce different economic outcomes, notably on wages, which in turn can affect the development of unionism.

We assess country differences in union effects on wages by estimating log wage equations and by comparing coefficients of variation for union and nonunion workers from the ISSP *micro* data set. This method of analyzing how national industrial relations affects outcomes differs from studies that link taxonomies of those systems to *macro*economic variables (Crouch, 1985; Bruno and Sachs, 1985; Grubb et al., 1983; Calmfors and Driffil, 1988; Freeman, 1988b). Our major finding is that *U.S. unions have much greater effects on wages than have unions in other countries but have roughly comparable effects on other measured outcomes.* The large union wage effect gives U.S. management an exceptional profit incentive to oppose unions, and is a major reason for U.S. unionism declining more than that for other countries.

Union wage effects. To see if unionism has different effects on wages in different countries, we estimated least squares earnings equations for the six countries. The dependent variable in each regression is the log of gross monthly wage and salary earnings. To maintain comparability across countries, we included regressions with only the most basic control variables: experience (age-schooling-5), experience squared, education, sex, and, in some cases, industry dummy variables. We use least squares because more complicated structural models yield unreliable estimates of union effects that add little to our knowledge (Freeman and Medoff, 1981; Lewis, 1986).[4]

Table 3 presents our estimated union-nonunion wage differentials for each country, the average union differential for all countries except the United States, and the deviation of the U.S. differential from that average. Complete regressions are reported in Table A1 of Appendix A. The first thing to note about the differentials is that they accord well with estimated union wage effects for the limited countries for which union effects have been estimated in other data sets. Our 0.22 ISSP-based estimate for the United States is in the range of Current Population Survey-based estimates of union-nonunion wage differentials for the United States (Freeman and Medoff, 1981; Lewis, 1986); our 0.10 ISSP-based estimate for the United Kingdom is within the 0–10 percent range reported in extant British studies (Blanchflower, 1991; Blanchflower and Oswald, 1988c)[5]; while the 0.08 Australian estimate is in the 7–10 percent range for that country (Mulvey, 1986; Kornfeld, 1990). These similarities validate the ISSP as a survey for

---

[4]The reason is that such models require correct specification of the structure of a complex system, and they yield wildly divergent results depending on the structure chosen. While one can criticize ordinary least squares analyses for failing to take into account such issues as simultaneity in unionization and outcomes, selectivity of union members, etc., these analyses do provide a robust description of the patterns in the data. Moreover, to the extent that selectivity, simultaneity, and related problems are the same across countries, comparisons of union-nonunion differentials across countries may well be valid despite these problems.

[5]As a further check on the validity of the ISSP-based estimates for the United Kingdom, we estimated log earnings equations, using data from the British Social Attitudes Surveys of 1983–87. These provide a much larger sample from which to estimate union wage effects than the ISSP for the United Kingdom, which is a subset of these surveys (see Table A1 in Appendix A). The resulting coefficients on unionism are quite similar to those in our ISSP regressions (full results are reported in Table A1).

TABLE 3

MULTIVARIATE REGRESSION ESTIMATES OF DIFFERENCES IN THE LOG[a] EARNINGS
OF UNION AND NONUNION WORKERS, 1985–87
(standard errors in parentheses)

Country	Regressions Without Industry Dummies	Regressions with Industry Dummies
United States	0.22	0.18
	(.05)	(.05)
United Kingdom	0.10	0.10
	(.03)	(.02)
West Germany	0.08	0.06
	(.02)	(.02)
Austria	0.07	0.05
	(.03)	(.03)
Australia	0.08	n.a.
	(.04)	
Switzerland	0.04	n.a.
	(.05)	
All except U.S.	.08	0.07
Deviation of U.S. from others	.14	0.11

SOURCE: Tabulated from International Social Survey Programme data. See Appendix A, Table A1.
[a]Log refers to the natural logarithm.

assessing the effects of unionism on wages across countries. The estimated wage union effects for Austria, West Germany, and Switzerland (for which we have no other estimates) show only modest union effects.

Given centralized wage-setting procedures in Austria (an exemplar corporatist economy) and in Australia (where arbitral decisions affect all workers) and the extension of union wage agreements to nonunionized workers in West Germany, one may question the plausibility of the estimated relation between unionism and wages in these countries. How do unions win wage advantages for their members in these settings? There are two mechanisms for doing this: wage drift at plant levels, which is potentially more important for unionized workers; and the speed of adjustment of wages toward nationally determined levels, potentially faster where unions are stronger. In Australia, both mechanisms operate: Some unions gain "over-award" pay for members, and the better organized workers lead in the timing of their wage settlements. Wage drift has long been important in Europe and the subject of attention in West Germany, Sweden, and the Netherlands.

The most striking finding in Table 3 is, however, *not* the modest union wage estimates in the European countries and Australia, but rather *the high union-nonunion differential in the United States*. The U.S. differentials of 0.22 in column 1 and 0.18 in column 2 are 2.5 times as great as the unweighted average differential for the other five countries. Moreover, evidence on union-nonunion wage differentials for Japan and Canada, not included in the ISSP data, shows that this pattern also holds true for them. Estimated union wage differentials in Japan are more like those in Europe and Australia than in the United States. In Japan union wage effects are small except for women, presumably because the Shunto Offensive sets wage patterns for the entire country, and union effects on bonuses and severance pay do not come close to producing a differential of U.S. magnitude (Nakamura et al., 1988; Osawa, 1989). Even in Canada, with an industrial relations system similar to the United States', non-ISSP estimated differentials appear to be smaller than comparable estimated differentials in the United States—1970s and 1980s differentials on the order of 10–20 percent (Gunderson, 1982; Simpson, 1985)—compared with 20–25 percent differentials in the U.S. Current Population Survey (Freeman and Medoff, 1981; Lewis, 1986). In short, U.S. unionism produces greater union-nonunion wage differentials than unionism in other advanced countries.

Wage dispersion. Until recently, the direction of the union effect on wage dispersion was subject to controversy because unionism has both positive and negative effects on dispersion. Raising the wages of organized workers relative to otherwise comparable, less organized workers unions increases wage inequality—a point stressed by Milton Friedman (1962). On the other hand, by pushing standard rate wage policies, unions reduce dispersion among organized workers, and by increasing the wages of union manual workers relative to nonunion nonmanual workers, unions also lower inequality. The available micro data sets in the 1970s for the United States showed that the lower dispersion of pay among union workers and between white- and blue-collar workers in unionized settings dominates the increased dispersion because of the union differential on otherwise comparable workers to produce a net reduction in wage inequality (Freeman, 1980a, 1982). Is this a general feature of unionism?

The coefficients of variation in earnings of union and nonunion workers, shown in Table 4, suggest that the reduction in inequality is not unique to U.S. unionism. In each country the coefficient of variation is lower among unionists than among nonunionists and for manual and nonmanual workers. The separate analyses of manual and nonmanual workers are important here, as they allow us to rule out the possibility that the differences in dispersion are due to differing union and nonunion shares of manual and nonmanual employment, as opposed to genuine union effects on pay in-

TABLE 4

Coefficients of Variation in Earnings, Union
and Nonunion Manual and Nonmanual Workers

Country	All Workers			Manual Workers			Nonmanual Workers		
	Union	Nonunion	Diff.	Union	Nonunion	Diff.	Union	Nonunion	Diff.
United States	58	81	−23	52	69	−17	63	83	−19
United Kingdom	53	74	−21	51	77	−16	52	71	−19
West Germany	43	64	−21	38	52	−14	47	66	−19
Austria	43	60	−17	31	46	−15	47	68	−21
Australia	56	65	−9	44	50	−6	48	63	−15
Switzerland	46	85	−39	—	—		—	—	

Source: Tabulated from International Social Survey Programme data.

equality.[6] Moreover, in contrast to the finding of greater union-nonunion wage differentials in the United States in Table 3, the union-nonunion differences in coefficients of variation in the United States are similar in magnitude to those in the other countries, except for Australian manual workers, whose small union-nonunion difference is the exception.[7]

Our finding that unionism is associated with lower earnings dispersion outside the United States is consistent with Metcalf (1990) and Blanchflower and Oswald (1988a), who report lower wage inequality among union than nonunion workers in the United Kingdom. Kupferschmidt and Swidinsky (1989) report a similar result for Canada in cross-section and longitudinal data. Consistent with our small estimated effect of unionism on dispersion in Australia, Kornfeld (1990) reports only modest union-nonunion differences in variances of earnings among young Australian workers. Evidence on modes of wage payments in British firms suggests, moreover, that British unions lower dispersion by reducing merit/indi-

---

[6]For a full analysis, it is necessary to decompose the difference in dispersion of pay into the part due to differences in characteristics in workers, the part due to union effects on the impact of characteristics on pay, and the part due to union effects within groups having the same characteristics. U.S. studies that do a full decomposition find that differences in characteristics account for only part of the total differential (Freeman, 1980a, 1982).

[7]In addition to reducing dispersion of wages for specified groups of workers, unionism in the United States has been found to reduce the effect on earnings of wage-determining characteristics such as education. To see whether foreign union movements also "flatten" earnings equations, we estimated separate earnings equations for union and nonunion workers in the ISSP data set. The estimates in Table A1 in Appendix A reveal a complex pattern. U.S. unionism reduces the effect of education but not the effect of gender on earnings. Unionism in West Germany, Australia, and Switzerland reduces sex but not education differentials.

vidual pay determination just as do U.S. unions. In the United Kingdom, unionized firms are 16 (manual) to 28 (nonmanual) percentage points less likely to use these pay policies than nonunion firms (Blanchflower and Oswald, 1988a). Comparable U.S. figures show a 23-point difference in the use of merit/individual performance pay between union and nonunion firms (Freeman, 1982).

Nonwage effects of unionism. Since the ISSP lacks information on non-wage outcomes that unionism might influence, we rely on other studies to assess country differences in what unions do to employment, provision of fringes, job tenure/turnover, productivity, technical change, and profits. As these comparisons are based on differing data and statistical models, they are subject to more uncertainty than those in Tables 3 and 4, particularly with regard to estimated magnitudes. With this understanding, our reading of other studies supports the generalization that *unions overseas had similar effects on nonwage outcomes as U.S. unions*.

Consider first the effects of unionism on employment and the growth of employment. Consistent with the existence of a sizable union wage effect in the United States, there is evidence that the presence of unions results in a decrease in employment in the private sector.[8] Leonard (this volume) and Freeman and Kleiner (1990a) report negative effects of unionism on employment; Freeman and Medoff (1984) and Allen (1988) find that the firms substitute workers not covered by collective bargaining for union members, reducing employment of those members; and Carter et al. (1990) report slower growth of unionized employment in industries with higher union wage differentials. For the United Kingdom, which ranks second in the estimated union wage effect (see Table 3), Blanchflower et al. (1991) find a substantial negative union effect on employment growth from 1980 to 1984.[9] We are unaware of studies of union employment effects in other countries.

With respect to fringe benefits, virtually all U.S. studies show that when there are unions, fringe benefits increase, particularly pension benefits (Freeman and Medoff, 1984). Studies of other countries yield a similar finding. For Great Britain, Millward and Stevens (1986) and Green et al.

---

[8]The U.S. data show higher employment in unionized settings in the public sector. See Freeman (1986) and Freeman and Ichniowski (1988). This is attributed to the role of unions in raising demand for public services and increasing public-sector budgets for unionized activities.

[9]Whether the U.S. and British union effects on employment growth reflect short-term adjustments or long-term slower growth rates in unionized workplaces is open to question (Wadhwani, 1989; Pencavel, 1989).

(1985) report that unionism raises fringe benefits.[10] For Canada, Kupferschmidt and Swidinsky (1989) find that pensions are more likely under unionism. For Japan, Nakamura et al. (1988) report that the labor costs of bonuses and severance pay are higher in unionized firms. For Australia, Kornfeld (1990) finds greater probabilities of pensions for unionized than nonunion workers.

Turning to job tenure and quits, the cross-country evidence also yields results comparable with those for the United States. Muramatsu (1984) and Osawa (1989) find markedly lower quits in union than in nonunion sectors in Japan. Elias and Blanchflower (1989) report greater tenure among unionists in the United Kingdom than among otherwise comparable nonunion workers. For Australia, Kornfeld (1990) reports union effects on tenure and quits among young workers that appear, if anything, to be larger than those found among young Americans. We know of no study that rejects the union "exit-voice" trade-off for any country.

Estimates of the effect of unionism on productivity are subject to controversy. Most U.S. studies indicate a positive union productivity effect (see the summaries in Belman, 1989, and Freeman, 1990), but there are enough counter-examples (see Hirsch, 1991a) to suggest that it is the *state of labor relations rather than unionism and collective bargaining per se that determines productivity*. Limited overseas studies support this finding. Muramatsu's analysis (1984) for Japan found a positive union coefficient comparable with the Brown-Medoff (1978) estimate for the United States, but it may not have adequately controlled for the effects of firm size on productivity (in Japan unionization is concentrated in large firms). Whether productivity is higher or lower under unionism in the United Kingdom is the subject of debate. Metcalf (1990) interprets early 1980s evidence as indicating that productivity is lower under unionism, but he notes that productivity grew

---

[10]Exceptions to this in the United Kingdom are the provision of company cars (see Green et al., 1985) and of private medical services, as indicated in the following table using data from the 1987 British Social Attitudes Survey:

	All	Union	Nonunion
Public and Private Sectors	18	13	22
Manual	10	12	9
Nonmanual	23	14	31
Private Sector	21	14	24
Manual	11	14	10
Nonmanual	28	15	32

We interpret the negative relation between unionism and the provision of private medical coverage as reflecting the commitment of British unions to the National Health Service.

more rapidly in unionized settings thereafter, potentially erasing the early 1980s productivity gap. Callaghan (1989) and Nolan and Marginson (1990) disagree with Metcalf's assessment. Our reading is that the British evidence is inconclusive, indicating that even in a country whose union structure has long been lambasted as inefficient, it is difficult to find compelling evidence for negative union productivity effects.

Studies of productivity change and technological progress for the United States have yielded three basic findings: (1) productivity growth is modestly and statistically insignificantly slower in unionized settings (see Belman, 1989, for a summary of studies); (2) new technologies are adopted as rapidly in union as in nonunion settings (Eaton and Voos, 1989); (3) R&D and investment spending are lower under unionism (Hirsch and Link, 1987; Hirsch, 1991a). Studies for the United Kingdom and Canada confirm some but not all of these findings. They show that unions do not adversely affect the speed of adaption of new technology (Daniel, 1987; Betcherman, 1988) and that the United Kingdom has lower R&D-to-sales ratios in more heavily unionized industries (Ulph and Ulph, 1989).

By contrast, British evidence that union firms had faster increases in productivity during 1980–84 than nonunion firms (and had similar rates of increase in other years) runs counter to U.S. findings, as does evidence that unionism is unrelated to investment (Wadhwani, 1989). As neither the U.S. nor the British studies contain adequate controls for the age or maturity of union and nonunion plants and industries, we are leery of interpreting the different results as reflecting genuine differences in union impacts. Perhaps they reflect the different development of unionism—the fact that British unions grew rapidly in the 1970s in new industries and plants, whereas U.S. unions failed to organize new firms and sectors and thus were concentrated in parts of the economy facing slow productivity and limited investment. This interpretation is consistent with Hirsch's fixed-effects analysis (1990) of the lower productivity growth and investment in unionized firms in the United States; controlling for "firm effects" in various ways, Hirsch concludes that the observed correlations are due largely to the location of unions in declining sectors.

One of the most important findings from U.S. research has been that unionism is associated with markedly lower profitability (see Belman, 1989). Estimates of the effect of unionism on profits in the United Kingdom (Blanchflower and Oswald, 1988b; Machin, 1988) show a similar pattern. In the United States, the profits effect results from the large effect of unionism on wages, which exceeds the positive effect of unions on productivity. In the United Kingdom, the profits effect results from a moderate effect of unions on wages and no—or possibly a negative—

union effect on productivity. While the estimated profits effects are not sufficiently precise to determine whether unions reduce profitability more in the United States than in the United Kingdom, and while we lack estimates of the effects of unions on profits in other countries, we infer from wage and productivity findings that the profits effect is especially large in the United States. If the standard method of estimating union-nonunion wage differentials is reasonably correct (or biased in a similar way across countries), the 20–25 percent higher wage (and moderate productivity offset) implies that U.S. unionized firms will be at a significant cost disadvantage compared with foreign unionized competitors as well as with nonunion U.S. competitors.[11]

Implications for American Unionism

While economic theory does not predict how a given union wage differential will affect the probability of unionization, it does predict how differentials alter the money incentive to the two players. The welfare calculus of union monopoly wage gains predicts that at any given differential, management has a greater *monetary* incentive to prevent unionization than workers have to organize. This is illustrated in Figure 1. Here, the union

Figure 1. Changes in the Union Wage Premium on the Intensity of Worker and Management Attitudes Toward Unionization

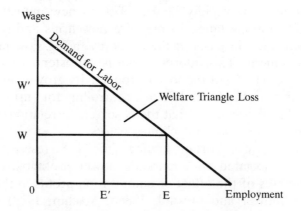

---

[11]As an example of the magnitudes involved, assume that unionized production workers are 20 percent of total cost of production in the United States and overseas. Then a 15-point greater wage impact translates into a three-point difference in costs. As profits are 15–20 percent of costs, the result is lower profitability on the order of 15–20 percent (= 3 ÷ [15 or 20]).

premium WW' increases payments to workers by the rectangle 0EWW' while reducing employer profits by 0EWW' and by the triangle WW'EE'/2. The loss to the employer is greater than the gain to workers because the welfare triangle loss comes out of profits (Freeman, 1986a). In addition, because the fall in employment EE' depends on the wage differential, the welfare loss is a function of the square of the union premium (Freeman and Kleiner, 1990b),[12] so that the dollar incentive for management to oppose unions will rise at an increasing rate as the premium grows. By contrast, for workers considering unionization, the benefit from a greater wage differential should increase at a decreasing rate. This is because higher differentials reduce the probability that the worker remains employed at the organized workplace, lowering the benefit directly, and because the danger of losing the job should raise worker risk aversion.[13] With all else the same, increases in the union differential should eventually reduce density by increasing employer opposition more than they increase the monetary benefits of unionism to workers.

Is there evidence that the high U.S. union wage differential deterred union organizing in the 1970s and 1980s?

Studies of the union wage differential in the United States show that the differential of 15 percent or so in the 1960s and early 1970s jumped to 20–25 percent in the late 1970s and 1980s (Johnson, 1981; Lewis, 1986)— consistent with the fall in union organizing success and in density (Freeman, 1986a). In addition, the adverse economic developments described earlier arguably made union wage differentials more expensive to firms in the 1980s by reducing the economic rents they could share with workers; they also made unionism less attractive to workers by increasing the risk of job loss.

---

[12]If all the variables are measured in log units, $EE' = -h\ WW'$, where h is the elasticity of labor demand. Then the welfare loss is just $h(WW')^2$. With variables measured in absolute units, h is the slope of the demand curve rather than the elasticity.

[13]Formally, the worker will value potential unionization at

$$E'/E\ U(W'/W) + (1-E'/E)\ U(W - C) \tag{1}$$

where E'/E is the probability that the worker remains employed, W'/W is the wage advantage from organizing, W is the nonunion wage, C is the cost of finding a new job when displaced, and U is the workers utility function with $U' > 0$ and $U'' < 0$. By the demand curve $E'/E = -h\ W'/W$, where h is the elasticity of labor demand. Then, differentiating (1) with respect to W'/W, we obtain the impact of changing the differential on the gain:

$$-h\ U(W'/W) + E'/E\ U' + h\ U(W - C)$$
$$= E'/E\ U' + h\ [U(W - C) - U(W'/W)] \tag{2}$$

Differentiating equation (2) with respect to the differential yields the following expression for the change in slope of the gain curve as the differential changes:

$$E'/E\ U'' - 2h\ U' < 0, \text{ as asserted.} \tag{3}$$

Consistent with these findings, Linneman and Wachter (1986) and Linneman et al. (1990) find that union differentials in an industry were positively associated with declines in union density.

The effect of premiums on the incentive to unionize is, however, only part of the story. Unions and management have, after all, to act on their incentives to influence outcomes. Here one must go beyond price theory to consider how legal and institutional arrangements affect the way unions organize and the tactics management uses to prevent organization. These arrangements differ across countries and can change sharply in short periods of time, as Thatcher's 1980s industrial relations laws illustrate (see Freeman and Pelletier, 1990). For present purposes, we simply note that the United States decides union membership through an adversarial electoral process at the plant level, which has evolved into a system where management has a greater say in unionization outcomes than it does in other countries.

Centralized versus noncentralized wage-setting systems. To use cross-country data to test the hypothesis that differences in union wage effects help explain the divergencies in density, we want, ideally, to compare estimated union wage effects by country to changes in density. However, as union wage premiums are available for only a limited number of countries, we follow a cruder procedure here. We contrast changes in union density in countries with centralized wage-setting institutions—where union wage effects are likely to be small—to changes in density in countries with decentralized (U.S. style) wage-setting institutions—where union wage effects are likely to be larger. As there is no accepted typology of national industrial relations systems, we use three classifications of centralization: a corporatist/noncorporatist dichotomy developed by Crouch (1985) and used by Bruno and Sachs (1985); an earlier classification by Blyth (1977); and a classification by Calmfors and Driffil (1988). By using three classifications, our results are independent of the judgment calls of different analysts. Our maintained hypothesis is that countries with centralized wage-setting systems have relatively small union premiums, giving management less incentive to oppose organization.

The results of our analysis, displayed in Figure 2, show that unions did better in countries with centralized as opposed to decentralized wage-setting systems in the 1970s and 1980s. Regression analyses contained in Freeman (1989) show that this finding is unaffected by controls for macroeconomic conditions across the countries. However, since neocorporatist or centralized systems differ in many ways from decentralized industrial relations systems—they are more likely to have a significant labor party, to

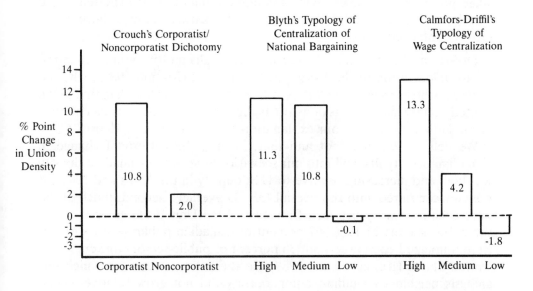

Figure 2. Changes in Union Density of
National Industrial Relations Systems, by Country

SOURCES: Crouch (1985): Corporatist countries include Austria, Denmark, Finland, the
Netherlands, Norway, Sweden, Switzerland and West Germany.
Noncorporatist countries include Belgium, Japan, New Zealand,
United Kingdom, France, Italy, Australia, Canada and the United States.

Blyth (1977): Countries ranked as High include Austria, Norway, Sweden and
Denmark.
Countries ranked as Medium include Finland, New Zealand,
Australia, West Germany and Belgium.
Countries ranked as Low include the Netherlands, Japan, France,
United Kingdom, Italy, the United States and Canada.

Calmfors and (We ranked the countries from their ratings.)
Driffil (1988): Countries ranked as High include Austria, Norway, Sweden,
Denmark, Finland and West Germany.
Countries ranked as Medium include the Netherlands, Belgium,
New Zealand, Australia and France.
Countries ranked as Low include the United Kingdom, Italy, Japan, Switzerland, the United States and Canada.

have favorable legal regulation of unions, and to give unions responsibility for delivering welfare state services, such as unemployment benefits[14]—one cannot conclude that unions have done better solely, or even primarily, because of lower wage premiums. What one can conclude is that differences in the nature of industrial relations systems *associated* with union wage premiums are linked with a country's unionization experience and that from this perspective the drop in U.S. density fits into the broader cross-country pattern.

Objections: The Canadian experience. If a high union premium was inimical to unionization in the United States in the 1970s and 1980s, why did Canada, whose union wage differential is only modestly less than that in the United States, maintain its density? Is the Canadian experience a counter-example that invalidates our explanation of the drop in U.S. density?

We believe that it is not and that, in fact, the pattern of change in Canadian density fits well into our scenario. First, while Canadian density was high and increasing relative to U.S. density in the 1970s and 1980s, it was low compared with the overall OECD average. Second, much of the difference in density between Canada and the United States occurred in the public sector: In 1986, 67 percent of Canadian public-sector workers were unionized compared with 36 percent of public-sector workers in the United States (Kumar et al., 1988). In the private sector, to which our analysis pertains, Canadian union density did not grow relative to the workforce. In manufacturing, density was stable throughout the 1970s but fell from 49 percent organized in 1977 to 42 percent organized in 1986 (Wood and Kumar, 1980; Kumar et al., 1988), suggesting that the high differential may have begun to cut into membership where unionized employers competed with overseas firms, including increasingly deunionized U.S. manufacturers.

Third, Canadian labor law substantially limits what management can do to oppose unions. Canada does not rely on lengthy legalistic adversarial elections to decide unionization; in most circumstances, unions are certified with a simple card check. Canada does not permit management to engage in the massive union prevention campaigns that pervade the United States, and the two major provinces, Ontario and Quebec, have gone a long way to protect unions as institutions. Ontario has first contract arbitration, which limits management's right to replace strikers, and, in general, has taken a pro-collective bargaining attitude. Quebec, where unions have fared especially well, has an extension of contract law by which the provincial Ministry of Labor extends collective bargaining to unorganized workers. Legal insti-

---

[14]These characteristics are prevalent in Denmark, Sweden, Finland, and Belgium.

tutions like these provide a buffer for Canadian unions to maintain density even with a sizable union wage premium. The decline in density in Canadian manufacturing in the 1980s suggests, however, that economic forces may ultimately overpower even this favorable legal environment.

Objections: Reverse causality. Thus far, we have interpreted estimated differences between the union wage differential in the United States and other countries as a "valid" indicator of the exogenous differential that in theory induces employer opposition to union organization. What about the possibility of reverse causation? Maybe the union wage differential is high in the United States because density is low: U.S. unions might be located in sectors where unions "innately" win high differentials, whereas unions in other countries are in sectors where differentials are innately lower. From this perspective the observed high union-nonunion wage differential in the United States is an artifact of sample selectivity: If we ranked workers by the potential for a union differential, the low-density United States would include only those with a high potential, whereas countries with higher densities include workers with lower potential differentials.

We do not believe this is the correct way to interpret the observed differences in our data. First, evidence within the United States tends to reject the notion that union wage effects are large when union density is small. Union wage differentials tend to be greater the greater the extent of unionization in a sector (Freeman and Medoff, 1984; Lewis, 1986), presumably because this gives unions greater bargaining power. Second, if selectivity were the major cause of the estimated large effects of unionism on wages in the United States, we could expect similar differences in other market outcomes, which we did not find. Third, the fact that employers as well as workers affect union density makes the direction of the selectivity effect uncertain. Indeed, one could readily argue that selectivity operates to bias downward union wage effects in the United States, as employers fight hardest against unions that have the most potential for raising wages and accept unions where they have the least potential.[15] Fourth, and in a similar vein, massive employer opposition to unions in the United States but not elsewhere is consistent with the greater demand by unions for higher wages in the United States than in other countries. All of this does not deny the possibility that our estimates may be contaminated by the reverse effects of density on wage differentials. Rather, our claim is that this potential contamination is unlikely to *reverse* our finding that union

---

[15]Our model suggests an even more complex relation. At first, higher potential union wage differentials might induce greater unionization, but as the potential differential rises beyond a certain point, employer opposition should grow more rapidly because of the increasing welfare loss that comes out of profits, reducing union density.

wage differentials are higher for similar workers in the United States than in other countries.

Looking to the future. If our comparative analysis is correct, the decline in U.S. union density is not an aberration—the result of Reagan's breaking the air traffic controllers union, of stodgy, incompetent union leadership, or of the decline in manufacturing in the 1980s—but is structurally rooted in what U.S. unions do on the wage front. Whereas in the 1950s and 1960s the large differentials that U.S. unions gained for their members were probably economically justified given the United States' role as world economic leader, the increased differentials that developed in the 1970s are, in our view, a major liability to the future development of unionism. If private-sector unions continue to pressure for higher wages and if the economic and political environment remains more or less the same, U.S. unionism will continue to decline, with density in the private sector dropping below double digits by the mid- to late 1990s. In this scenario the U.S. industrial relations system will be an even greater exception in the OECD in the 1990s than it was in the 1980s. Unions will be relegated to a few aged industrial sectors and to public and some nonprofit sectors, producing "ghetto unionism" similar to what the United States had prior to the spurt in unionization in the 1930s and 1940s. The U.S. industrial relations system will be effectively controlled by management.

Is there a feasible alternative to this scenario? What might we learn from the experience of unions overseas about other roads the country might take in industrial relations?

At the outset, we rule out as infeasible the most favorable environment for unionism—a centralized or corporatist industrial relations system. Such a system is not only incompatible with the history of U.S. industrial relations but is also unworkable in a large and diverse economy. A small country with some centralized wage-setting history, such as Australia, can seek to emulate the Scandinavians—as the Australian union movement has tried to do. The United States and probably Canada and the United Kingdom cannot.

One feasible step is for unions to develop forms of membership outside collective bargaining, as exists in many European countries where workers are union members even in plants where unions do not have negotiating rights. To do this, U.S. unions would have to provide the new services recommended in the 1985 AFL-CIO report, *The Changing Situation of Workers and Their Unions*—low-interest credit cards, job training and counseling, access to low-cost legal help, etc. British unions, such as the General, Municipal and Boilermakers Union, have taken initiatives in this area, apparently with modest success. Thus far, the U.S. effort has been minimal.

A second possibility is for U.S. public sector, white-collar, and service worker-oriented unions to make a major organizing effort in the private sector. This would require a campaign based on improving working conditions, job flexibility, workers' right to independent judgment on the job, fairness in promotion—the collective voice aspects of unionism stressed in *What Do Unions Do?* (Freeman and Medoff, 1984)—rather than one based on gaining huge wage increases, which would result in battles with management. However, experience overseas suggests that such drives are more likely to succeed under the aegis of a separate labor federation. In highly unionized Scandinavia, blue-collar, white-collar, and university graduate workers have separate federations. In the United Kingdom, the Electricians and Plumbers Union left the Trade Union Congress to pursue its own single-plant/single-union negotiating program. And spurts in U.S. unionism in the past have generally involved major organizational changes in the union movement, such as the development of the CIO in the 1930s.

At the national level, one aspect of foreign experience deserves attention. These are plant/firm-level elected committees that give workers representation independent of union status and of negotiating rights over wages. In Western Europe, such committees—called works councils—seem to work reasonably effectively. Canada has instituted works committees to deal with occupational health and safety issues. The growth of quality-of-working-life councils in nonunion as well as union settings in the United States shows that management recognizes the value of worker participation in the workplace. Accepting that most U.S. workers are unlikely to have collective bargaining in the foreseeable future, it seems logical to consider legislation to provide incentives to create elected employee committees to deal with workplace problems. Legislation could, for example, link the tax breaks associated with employee stock ownership plans—instituted to encourage worker participation but which have not, in general, done so (Blasi, 1988)—to the establishment of employee representation committees. If the elected committees operate effectively, they can deliver a "collective voice," while avoiding the monopoly wage differentials that have, by our analysis, led U.S. employers to fight vehemently against unions.

In sum, our analysis has shown that the monopoly wage effects of U.S. unions have exceeded those of unions overseas and probably have contributed to the precipitous fall in U.S. union density. To recover in the next decade, U.S. unions will have to emphasize their collective voice role, drawing on international experience, experimenting with new initiatives, and developing a new brand of unionism.

Appendix A

TABLE A1

COMPLETE REGRESSION ESTIMATES OF DIFFERENCES IN THE LOG EARNINGS OF UNION AND NONUNION WORKERS
(standard errors in parentheses)

Explanatory Variables	West Germany		Austria		Australia	Switzerland[a]
	(1)	(2)	(3)	(4)	(5)	(6)
Experience	.0367	.0385	.0497	.0519	.0377	.0442
	(.0022)[b]	(.0022)	(.0045)	(.0046)	(.0056)	(.0035)
Experience$^2 \times 10^3$	−.4740	.5022	−.8107	−.8477	−.4906	−.4597
	(.0401)	(.0403)	(.0947)	(.0965)	(.1065)	(.0405)
Schooling	.0607	.0664	.0750	.0855	.0939	.0707
	(.0037)	(.0037)	(.0070)	(.0068)	(.0086)	(.0060)
Male	.4452	.4578	.3436	.3369	.4276	.3835
	(.0233)	(.0225)	(.0304)	(.0279)	(.0387)	(.0541)
Union	.0555	.0758	.0467	.0734	.0817	.0395
	(.0230)	(.0236)	(.0282)	(.0277)	(.0363)	(.0476)
Married	.0372	.0307	−.0202	−.0259	−.0220	−.0104
	(.0232)	(.0236)	(.0322)	(.0329)	(.0415)	(.0555)
Part time	−.5937	−.6178	−.6864	−.6771	−.8029	−.7244
	(.0576)	(.0584)	(.0762)	(.0767)	(.0668)	(.1705)
1986 dummy	.1171	.1243	.0212	.0176	.0128	
	(.0253)	(.0253)	(.0327)	(.0332)	(.0439)	
1987 dummy	.1099	.2257	.2588	.2698	.2078	
	(.0589)	(.0313)	(.0342)	(.0346)	(.0443)	
Industry dummies	27	No	30	No	n.a.	n.a.
Constant	6.0733	5.8718	7.5785	7.4226	1.0858	6.3190
	(.0809)	(.0639)	(.1052)	(.0962)	(.1296)	(.1062)
Adjusted R^2	.4483	.4242	.4378	.4018	.2306	.4289
N	1,855	1,855	1,047	1,047	1,971	481
F-test	44.0	152.8	22.4	79.1	66.61	52.51

[a]Only 1987 statistics are available.

(Table A1 cont.)

Explanatory Variables	United States		United Kingdom[b]		United Kingdom[c]	
	(7)	(8)	(9)	(10)	(11)	(12)
Experience	.0439	.0522	.0313	.0284	.0362	.0365
	(.0050)	(.0051)	(.0038)	(.0038)	(.0021)	(.0021)
Experience$^2 \times 10^3$	−.5042	−.6549	−.5119	−.4787	−.5902	−.5983
	(.0949)	(.0969)	(.0732)	(.0733)	(.0395)	(.0401)
Schooling	.1191	.1164	.1504	.1398	.1226	.1255
	(.0074)	(.0069)	(.0095)	(.0087)	(.0050)	(.0047)
Male	.4630	.5335	.5070	.5668	.4084	.4283
	(.0408)	(.0382)	(.0265)	(.0240)	(.0157)	(.0148)
Union	.1840	.2189	.1010	.0957	.0704	.0914
	(.0488)	(.0484)	(.0256)	(.0231)	(.0146)	(.0133)
Married	.0867	.0844	.0506	.0639	.0560	.0611
	(.0380)	(.0388)	(.0297)	(.0299)	(.0166)	(.0170)
Part time	−1.2013	−1.2874	−1.0970	−1.1428	−.9964	−1.0584
	(.0731)	(.0745)	(.0400)	(.0392)	(.0201)	(.0198)
1986 dummy	−.0148	.0219	.1730	.1769	+4 year	+4 year
	(.0494)	(.0503)	(.0272)	(.0273)	dummies	dummies
1987 dummy	.0702	.0922	.2337	.2337		
	(.0480)	(.0489)	(.0277)	(.0279)		
Industry dummies	46	No	60	No	60	No
Constant	7.1536	6.9986	6.3694	6.3968	6.4141	6.5064
	(.4639)	(.1232)	(.1780)	(.1119)	(.0965)	(.0625)
Adjusted R^2	.4183	.3752	.6072	.5022	.6523	.6333
N	1,922	1,922	1,843	1,843	4,986	4,986
F-test	27.08	129.2	44.8	295.7	132.7	783.4

[b]Calculated from International Social Survey Programme data.
[c]These data are taken from the 1983–87 British Social Attitudes Surveys. The ISSP data used in columns (9) and (10) are subsets of that used in columns (11) and (12). For further details of the BSA data and variable definitions, see Blanchflower (1990).

Unions and Employment Growth

JONATHAN S. LEONARD*

TO STAND STILL IS TO DIE. Unions in the United States face an uphill battle for existence. Even if they had continued to organize and win elections at the high rates of the 1950s, the proportion of the workforce unionized would still have declined (Dickens and Leonard, 1985). The dynamics of the workplace are crucial in this scenario. The vast majority of jobs are born nonunion, and union jobs have a higher death rate. Employment continues to grow, particularly in new establishments and industries. It is the unusual industry in which existing contracts are extended to cover new plants. In consequence, new establishments rarely begin operations under a collective bargaining agreement. The failure of union organizing to maintain pace with the growth of the labor force is well known and dramatically highlighted in lost elections. But there is another channel of union decline that is more subtle, less dramatic, but just as important: Ground once won in the battle to organize begins to slip away as employment erodes.

Although a great many studies examine unions' impact on wages, none has studied unions' impact on employment at the plant level, despite their logical connection in microeconomics and importance in understanding the context of industrial relations. Both types of studies are essential to under-

---

*Haas School of Business, University of California at Berkeley. I thank Jeffrey Zax, William Dickens, and Mario Bognanno and seminar participants at Berkeley and MIT for their comments, and the Institute of Industrial Relations for its support.

standing the nature of the challenge facing unions and the decisions unions and management have made.

This study examines two fundamental questions in industrial relations. First, do unions save or destroy jobs? The charges on each side of this issue are part of nearly all organizing campaigns. Job instability provides fertile ground for union organizing among those fearful for their jobs. At the same time, management commonly paints unionization as leading to greater rigidity and higher costs that will jeopardize employment. Except in situations in which unions are engaged in pure rent redistribution or productivity enhancement, union wage gains will generally come at some cost in terms of employment.[1] If we assume that the schedule of labor demand does not shift because of unionization itself, evidence on employment growth in union and nonunion plants can yield insights into the elasticity of the labor-demand constraints that unions face, as well as into the decisions unions make in trading off employment for wages. More competitive product markets imply more elastic labor demand and so greater employment loss at the establishment level for a given wage increase. A distinct question is whether management destroys and disinvests from union jobs faster than from similar jobs because they are unionized, and whether such behavior can be distinguished from profit maximization. A pure anti-union animus implies a downward shift in labor demand at every wage level.

This study breaks new ground by testing for differences in employment growth between union and nonunion manufacturing plants and by distinguishing this difference from vintage effects. Three competing hypotheses are addressed. First is the accepted neoclassical model of unions: Unions raise wages and costs; therefore, in competitive markets unionized plants suffer declining employment and eventually go out of business.[2] The second is the positive alternative advanced by Brown and Medoff (1978), that unions raise productivity in addition to wages; therefore, union plants need not differ from their nonunion counterparts in terms of employment growth.[3]

---

[1]Unions may also attempt to increase the demand for goods and services produced in the unionized sector, and hence the derived demand for union labor. This shift in labor demand is conceptually distinct from movements along a given demand schedule.

[2]I ignore models in which the ex ante probability of unionization is used to discount expected returns on investment in new plants (Baldwin, 1983).

[3]Other explanations have been offered for the survival of unions that raise costs. Lazear (1983b) develops a model that explains the coexistence of union and nonunion plants by assuming that all firms must pay some random cost to keep unions out. On the margin, the cost of allowing the union in equals the cost of keeping it out, and some firms will be unionized with no cost difference on the margin. The union threat effect does not by itself explain the coexistence of union and nonunion plants in competitive markets so long as the union wage effect is positive. Freeman and Medoff (1982) estimate that the union wage effect increases with the percentage of the workforce organized, which suggests a relatively weak threat effect.

The third hypothesis is that unions operate in noncompetitive product or labor markets and engage in pure rent distribution without affecting employment.

All three hypotheses are tested by comparing the rate of growth of employment over time across individual union and nonunion manufacturing plants. First, I derive the properties of cost functions for unionized plants, allowing both union wage and productivity effects; and I establish conditions for the coexistence of union and nonunion plants in competitive long-run equilibrium. Next, I present the main empirical results, a comparison of employment growth rates within regions and industries in union and nonunion plants. This analysis is refined by comparing the effects of plant aging and unionization. The major finding is that employment growth is significantly slower in union plants. Union wage effects are then not, in general, counterbalanced by union productivity effects; nor are unionized plants generally immune from competitive pressure; nor do unions engage solely in the redistribution of rents. The slower growth of employment within union plants in turn plays a major role in explaining the ongoing decline in the proportion of the workforce organized. The faster employment decay in the unionized sector could be offset only by an organizing campaign of a scale and vision not seen since before 1950.

Past Studies

Although many union wage studies have followed Lewis's landmark empirical analysis (1963), there have been no systematic studies of union employment effects at the plant level. The available measures of union employment effects are at the industry level and focus on substitution rather than scale effects. Comparing aggregate employment growth in union-intensive sectors (mining, construction, manufacturing, transportation, communications, and public utility industries) with that in the remaining relatively nonunion sectors, Lewis (1963) reports an elasticity of relative employment with respect to relative wages of -1, that is, a union wage effect of 10 percent reduces union employment by 10 percent. However, since Lewis controls for relative output in the two sectors, this is in the nature of an elasticity of substitution.

More recent estimates of the union effect through substitution on man-hours worked indicate that it is difficult consistently to find significant negative effects. In a useful and rare appraisal of the union employment effect, Pencavel and Hartsog (1984) conclude, "Even when negative man-hour effects are calculated, our estimated standard errors do not permit us to make any useful confident statements, and quite often we cannot reject the null hypothesis that unionism has not had any effect on relative man-hours worked" (p. 217). Since relative output in the union sector compared with the nonunion sector is controlled for in the regressions, this finding suggests a low elasticity of substitution of other factors for union labor and cannot preclude substantial scale effects of unionism on employment.[4]

Tangential issues to ours have attracted more research attention, for example, the union wage effect. Parsley (1980) and Lewis (1963) report union wage gaps on the order of 15 to 25 percent, while Mitchell (1972) reports effects in the range of 25–30 percent. Brown and Medoff (1978) report a union productivity effect in manufacturing that is of comparable magnitude with the wage gap reported by Lewis. Clark (1985), Connerton, Freeman, and Medoff (1983), and Boal (1984) found union productivity effects at various times in various industries, ranging from −20 percent to +38 percent (Freeman and Medoff, 1984, Table 11.1). If the union productivity effect really is of a magnitude comparable with the union wage effect, that would help explain the continued existence of union plants in competitive markets, though as Freeman (1983) and Clark (1984) show, the effect on profits is best measured directly.

A related issue is explored by Dickens and Leonard (1985), who develop a measure of employment growth within union plants as the residual from total union membership less flows from the NLRB election process. Their analysis suggests that the difference in the rate of employment growth between union and nonunion plants is substantial and may account for at least 35 percent of the decline in the percentage of the workforce organized between 1950 and 1980.[5]

Union Cost Functions

In competitive markets, unionized plants can compete with nonunion plants in the long run only if long-run minimum average cost in the union sector equals that in the nonunion sector. The parameters of the production function in the union sector cannot be identical to those in the nonunion sector if factor prices are not identical. Consider a constant returns to scale Cobb-Douglas cost function:

$$C(W,R,Q) = A\alpha^{-\alpha}(1-\alpha)^{\alpha-1}W^{\alpha}r^{1-\alpha}Q \tag{1}$$

---

[4]In seven out of eight specifications, Pencavel and Hartsog (1984) find an elasticity of relative employment with respect to relative output that is significantly less than 1, as did Lewis (1963). While neither paper discusses this result, whose correct interpretation is not clear, it may reflect a higher capital/labor ratio in the union sector.

[5]Blanchflower, Millward, and Oswald (1991) have presented similar results for Britain: Employment grows 3 percent per year slower in union than in nonunion plants.

where W = cost of labor, R = cost of capital, Q = output, and A,α = technological parameters. Now let union wages be λ times nonunion wages, with $\lambda > 1$. Then the ratio of union to nonunion costs, conditional on output, is λ^α. The union cost function is always above the nonunion cost function, and the minimum point on the nonunion long-run average cost curve is below that on the union cost curve. A union plant can survive in competitive markets only when its productivity is higher, either by raising α in some cases or by decreasing A by at least λ^α.

If these conditions are not met, we expect union plants to grow more slowly and to go out of business faster than comparable nonunion plants, assuming, of course, that unions do raise quality adjusted wages. If union plants do not grow significantly slower than nonunion plants, we may infer either a union productivity effect that balances the union wage effect or the absence of competition in the product market. If union plants do grow significantly slower than do nonunion plants, we may infer that whatever the union productivity effect may be in this sample, it is not great enough to offset the union wage effect and that unions do not simply redistribute rents.

Union and Employment Growth Within Manufacturing Plants

Sample characteristics. Estimates of employment growth rates based on a sample of California manufacturing plants (see Data Appendix) reveal growth rates significantly higher in nonunion plants.[6] Between 1974 and 1980 employment in the average union plant increased slightly from 512 to 521, while employment in the average nonunion plant increased by 19 percent from 244 to 290 (see Table 1). It needs to be emphasized that employment is not decreasing in union plants; on the contrary, it is increasing[7]; it is just not increasing as fast as in nonunion plants.[8]

---

[6]The distinctive feature of this data is that it combines data on the presence of a collectively bargained contract with data on plant level employment over time.

[7]The growth rates used here come from a longitudinal sample of plants and must be interpreted in this light. In particular, they may be subject to truncation bias. Small plants are underrepresented in the sample, and plants in which employment falls below 25 may drop out of the sample. The sample does not include plants that were born or died during the sample period. If union plants were more likely than nonunion plants to go out of business during this period, then the union effect on growth will be relatively understated.

[8]Such slower employment growth in union plants can help explain the decline in the proportion of workers who are union members, but it cannot account for the decline in the absolute number of union members. Between 1974 and 1980, the California Department of Industrial Relations (CDIR) reports that the proportion of manufacturing wage and salary employees unionized fell from 36 to 25 percent. In this sector, the absolute number of union members fell by 7.5 percent, while total employment grew by 32 percent. The CDIR reports union membership only in odd-numbered years, so the data for 1974

TABLE 1

Variable Definitions and Means in Complete Samples and in Union and Nonunion Subsamples

| Variable | Complete Sample | Means | | Definition |
		Union	Nonunion	
SIZE80[a]	363.5	520.5	289.5	Total employment, 1980
SIZE74[a]	329.5	512.2	243.5	Total employment, 1974
(SIZE74)^2	960,020	2,346,639	306,426	Total employment squared, 1974
GROWTH[a]	.236	.158	.273	Growth rate of total employment
SINGLE	.203	.120	.242	=1 if one-plant company
PWC[a]	.265	.235	.230	% nonclerical white collar
SIC20		.111	.177	.079 food, except SIC203
SIC203	.041	.049	.037	Preserved fruits and vegetables
SIC22	.011	.005	.014	Textiles
SIC23	.027	.005	.037	Apparel
SIC24	.039	.050	.034	Lumber
SIC25	.028	.026	.029	Furniture
SIC26	.051	.085	.034	Paper
SIC27	.055	.050	.056	Printing
SIC28	.076	.057	.084	Chemicals
SIC29	.014	.026	.008	Petroleum
SIC30	.043	.040	.044	Rubber and plastics
SIC31	.005	.005	.005	Leather
SIC32	.051	.063	.045	Stone, clay, and glass
SIC33	.041	.047	.038	Primary metal
SIC34	.107	.097	.111	Fabricated metal
SIC35	.073	.063	.078	Machinery, except electrical
SIC36	.113	.073	.132	Electrical and electronic machinery
SIC37 SIC372	.038	.047	.034	Transportation equipment, except aircraft and parts
SIC372	.025	.026	.025	Aircraft and parts
SIC38	.038	.005	.053	Instruments
SIC39	.017	.003	.023	Miscellaneous
Los Angeles	.453	.406	.475	Los Angeles SMSA
San Francisco	.128	.178	.105	San Francisco SMSA
San Diego	.168	.118	.192	San Diego, Anaheim-Orange, Riverside-San Bernardino SMSAs
San Jose	.062	.054	.065	San Jose SMSA
N. California	.054	.082	.041	Other Northern California
S. California	.135	.162	.122	Other Southern California
N	1,798	576	1,222	Sample size

[a]Continuous variable; all others are dichotomous.

This is consistent with unions that raise costs in imperfectly competitive markets.

Employment growth is concentrated in smaller plants in both the union and nonunion sectors in our sample. Weighting all plants equally, the average growth rates across plants were .27 and .16 in the nonunion and union sectors, respectively. Total employment grew by much less in each sector, .189 and .016, respectively. Since the average nonunion plant is roughly half the size of the average union plant, the regressions that follow correct for initial employment level so as to separate union from size effects on growth.[9] Without conditioning on size, the difference in employment growth in union and nonunion plants would be even greater. Union plants are not only larger, but they are also more likely to be part of a multiplant company. Such large companies may have more experience with collective bargaining. They also tend to have more rigidly bureaucratized personnel procedures and higher pay, which may tend to reduce union differentials.

Regression results. Union plants do not grow as fast as their nonunion counterparts. Table 2 presents the major results, which are regressions across California manufacturing plants of 1980 employment on 1974 employment, the square of 1974 employment, corporate structure, proportion nonclerical white-collar, 20 industry dummies, and five area dummies. Separate equations are estimated for the complete sample and for the union and nonunion subsamples. The key result in the first equation is that the coefficient on union status is negative and significant. This indicates that unionized plants grew 9 percent slower than nonunion plants, ceteris paribus, between 1974 and 1980.[10]

Over time, this has a substantial cumulative effect. Equations (3) and (4) of Table 2 estimate growth rates separately in the nonunion and union subsamples between 1974 and 1980. These are found to be 0 percent and −18 percent, respectively, when evaluated at the mean initial size in each

---

and 1980 are the averages of the two neighboring odd years, which should also reduce measurement error.

[9] Union plants also have a lower proportion of nonclerical white-collar workers. This is not surprising in view of the number of studies (see, e.g., Farber, 1978) showing that white-collar workers are less likely to be union members.

[10] The finding here that employment grows more slowly in union than nonunion plants is probably not fully explained by the substitution of other factors of production for union labor. Freeman and Medoff (1982) estimate that the elasticity of substitution of other factors for production labor is very low in unionized manufacturing. Such a substitution effect could explain a one-time movement along an isoquant. A continuing decline in union employment could imply long adjustment lags or rising union wage differentials.

TABLE 2

EMPLOYMENT GROWTH IN UNION AND NONUNION PLANTS
(dependent variable = total employment, 1980; standard errors in parentheses; all
equations include 20 industry dummies and 5 area dummies)

Sample Equation	Full (1)	Full (2)	Union (3)	Nonunion (4)
SIZE74[a]	1.001	1.025	.833	1.027
	(.017)	(.034)	(.029)	(.030)
$(SIZE74)^2$	.0000018	.000025	.0000094	.000025
	(.0000010)	(.000005)	(.0000016)	(.000004)
UNION[b]	−30.9	27.5	—	—
	(16.5)	(26.7)		
SINGLE[c]	56.4	62.2	36.6	61.3
	(18.7)	(20.0)	(49.8)	(17.7)
PWC[d]	129.0	91.8	122.1	91.2
	(38.4)	(41.8)	(93.3)	(37.6)
UNION × SIZE74	—	−.175	—	—
		(.040)		
UNION × $(SIZE74)^2$	—	−.000017	—	—
		(.000005)		
UNION × SINGLE	—	−38.3	—	—
		(42.7)		
UNION × PWC	—	84.4	—	—
		(76.7)		
R^2	.91		.94	.85
Mean of the dependent	363.5	363.5	520.5	289.5
N	1,798	1,798	576	1,222

[a]Total employment in 1974.
[b]Dichotomous variable set to 1 if the plant was covered by a collective bargaining agreement.
[c]A dochotomous variable set to 1 if the plant was not part of a multiplant company.
[d]Proportion of nonclerical white-collar employees.

sector. They correspond to annual growth rates of 0 percent and −4.3 percent, respectively.[11] With this differential in plant growth rates and no new plants, certifications, or decertifications, it takes 26 years (starting from 35.8% in 1974) for the proportion of the California workforce organized to fall below 15 percent.[12] Average annual growth rates are 4 percentage points lower in union than in nonunion plants.

---

[11]These equations do not correct for selection, although they do directly control (linearly) for variables such as union status and initial size that could be expected to affect survival. Evans (1987) reports that growth equations for manufacturing firms similar to those estimated here are insensitive to a selection correction, although he does not investigate union effects. Both growth and exit rates typically fall with age and size (Evans, 1987; Dunne, Roberts, and Samuelson, 1989).

[12]After only 10 years, the proportion unionized would fall from 25 percent in 1980 to 18 percent in 1990. Compare this with recent experience in the private U.S. nonconstruction industry as a whole, where union density dropped from 28 percent in 1970 to 24 percent in 1980 (Pencavel and Hartsog, 1984).

These estimates imply that the proportion unionized would fall from 35.8 percent in 1974 to 29.2 percent in 1980, compared with the actual 1980 level of 25 percent. That is, differential employment growth within plants between the union and nonunion sectors accounts for 61 percent of the decline in percentage unionized in California manufacturing. Thus, slower employment growth in union plants is of central importance in understanding the decline in the proportion of the workforce unionized.

Corporate structure is surprisingly important. It is not clear why the growth of a plant should depend on whether or not it is part of a larger corporation. With perfect capital and labor markets and constant returns to scale and scope, size should not matter. However, we observe that plants that are not part of a larger corporation have significantly faster growth rates. This holds even when conditioning on initial period size. White-collar intensive plants also grow faster, as do those outside major metropolitan areas.

The impact of unions on employment growth may depend on the initial size, corporate structure, or skill composition of the plant.[13] For example, with imperfect or costly capital markets, union plants that can temporarily rely on cross-plant subsidization within a multiplant corporation may be able to maintain employment relative to single-plant companies. If the latter face greater and more immediate competitive pressure, they may not differ greatly from small nonunion plants. The interactions in equation (2) in Table 2 indicate that the impact of unions on growth does not depend significantly on corporate structure or occupational composition, but it does depend significantly on size. Unions do not have a negative impact on growth until the plant exceeds 155 employees. At very small plants, unions have an insignificant positive effect on employment growth. This is consistent with the argument that the union wage effect is smaller in smaller plants and that during the 1970s large plants faced a substantial reduction in their market power as international competition increased.

Equations (3) and (4) of Table 2 allow for full interactions by estimating the employment relationships separately in the union and nonunion subsamples. F-tests reject the identity of coefficients across union and nonunion sectors. Looking at the coefficients on 1974 employment and its square, we see that while employment decreased by 18 percent, ceteris

---

[13]A union stands to gain little or nothing from organizing a plant that will soon be closed, so unionization may depend on expected growth. By itself, this would lead to underestimates of the impact of unions on employment growth as unions target plants in which labor demand is inelastic and employment is expected to increase. However, the average union plant in the sample is 36 years old in 1982. Growth prospects today could scarcely have been credibly forecast two or three decades ago when most of these plants were organized.

paribus, in the average union plant, it was stable in the average nonunion plant. Corporate structure seems to make a difference only in the non-union sector. Thus, unionized plants are more like nonunion plants that are part of multiplant companies than like single nonunion plants.

Since the 1940s debate between Dunlop (1944) and Ross (1948), the question of how unions trade off employment and wages has drawn little attention. In Pencavel's (1984) model, the union picks a wage-employment combination from a known labor demand curve. This curve will, of course, differ across industries, and one expects union preferences (if we may speak of such a thing) to differ across unions. If all plants in an industry have identical labor demand schedules, then we can use different unions' choices of wage-employment combinations to identify the labor demand schedule. Unions that suffer the greatest employment losses should also have the highest wages. Similarly, if all locals of a given union have the same preferences (which is unlikely), then we can use the variation in the elasticity of labor demand across industries to identify the marginal rate of substitution of wages for employment along a union indifference curve.

Regressions not shown in Table 2 suggest that the data do not identify these effects. These equations estimate employment growth rates in the union sector, controlling individually for the largest unions and for 20 industries. In general, the unions' effects on employment do not significantly differ from one another. A probable explanation is that the identifying assumptions are unsupported: There is just as much variation within as across industries and unions.

Vintage Effects on Employment Growth

The great burst of union organizing during the 1930s and 1940s created a baby boom in the age distribution of union plants. These cohorts have now aged 40 or 50 years. Since union organizing and success rates have not kept pace with employment growth nationally, we would expect union plants to be older on average than nonunion plants. This raises the specter that the union effect (measured above) is really an age effect. As the fixed capital in plants depreciates and becomes obsolete, employment growth may slow.[14]

The subsample of plants in the San Francisco SMSA that we tested was asked the question: "In what year did you begin operations in your current location?" As expected, the union plants are older by about five years, but

---

[14]We use data collected on the age of manufacturing establishments in the San Francisco SMSA to test for the effect of aging on plant growth and to isolate this effect from union effect.

the difference is not statistically significant. Union plants were on average 36 years old in 1982 while nonunion plants were 31 years old.

The number of years a company has been operating a given plant has no significant effect on employment growth in this subsample. Table 3 replicates Table 2 with the addition of the age variable. There are no significant cohort effects, perhaps because of selection effects.

Equation (1) shows that while both unionization and age hinder employment growth in the San Francisco subsample, neither does so significantly. This is not because the age effect is collinear with the union effect, but because neither effect is statistically significant in the subsample.

Some evidence of significantly slower employment growth in union plants can be seen in equation (2). Evaluated at the mean 1974 size of 262.2, a union plant shrinks by 1.5 percent by 1980 while a nonunion plant

TABLE 3

VINTAGE EFFECTS ON EMPLOYMENT GROWTH
(dependent variable = total employment in 1980;
all equations include 17 industry dummies)

Equation	(1)	(2)	(3)
SIZE74	.976	.843	.698
	(.113)	(.130)	(.192)
$(SIZE74)^2$	.000040	.00029	.00035
	(.000055)	(.00007)	(.00010)
AGE[a]	−.539	−.163	−.299
	(.6400)	(.526)	(.835)
UNION[b]	−13.33	−2.53	−4.57
	(29.7)	(37.8)	(27.5)
SINGLE	76.21	22.2	47.2
	(40.0)	(33.4)	(37.3)
PWC[c]	−3.84	−8.14	19.9
	(84.5)	(69.2)	(78.0)
UNION × SIZE74	—	.179	—
		(.176)	
UNION × $(SIZE74)^2$	—	−.00036	—
		(.00009)	
AGE × SIZE74	—	—	.0039
			(.0039)
AGE × $(SIZE74)^2$	—	—	−.0000054
			(.000020)
R^2	.87	.92	.90
Mean of the dependent	289.2	289.2	289.2
N	168	168	168

[a]Number of years the current business has been in operation at a given plant as of 1982.
[b]Dichotomous variable set to 1 if the plant was covered by a collective bargaining agreement.
[c]Proportion of nonclerical white-collar employees.

shrinks by 0.5 percent, ceteris paribus. While union plants below 248 employees grow faster than their nonunion counterparts, union plants do grow significantly slower in the larger size classes. Equation (3) shows that the age effect itself is also significantly negative in the larger plants.

Conclusion

This paper determines the impact of unions on employment growth by estimating it directly. This fundamental question concerning unions and the conditions under which they operate has not been systematically analyzed before. The results are central to determining the extent to which unions depend on imperfectly competitive product markets or balance wage increases with productivity increases. In a sample of California manufacturing plants, employment grows significantly slower in union than in nonunion plants by 2 to 4 percentage points per year. The slower growth of employment within union plants accounts for 61 percent of the decline in the proportion of the California manufacturing workforce organized. It is essential to understand the union employment effect in order to understand the decline of unions and of unionized employment. Unionized plants face substantial competitive pressure.

This result is not robust to estimation in a small subsample for which age of plant is measured, which may be a peculiarity of the subsample. However, there are two other ways to think about this result. The first is to treat age as exogenous. In the subsample that conditions on age, the union effect on employment is insignificant.

It is, however, no accident that union plants are older. This second view reinforces the position that unions are in decline because they have not kept up with organizing new plants. This leaves unions with a stock of older plants in which employment decays faster.

Either way, the policy implications for unions are clear: Given the decay of employment in previously organized plants, unions cannot grow—and indeed they face steeper declines—unless they achieve better organizing success than they have had since World War II. Given the high mortality rates of new establishments and the poor economies of scale for unions in administering small ones, unions would be well advised to wait for new plants to mature a few years before investing scarce resources in organizing attempts.

This frame of reference also suggests a subtle attraction of public-sector organizing: Since these jobs are less likely to disappear, there is a longer and less risky return on organizing efforts. Indeed, recent evidence indicates faster employment growth in union than in similar nonunion departments in local governments and suggests that in the public sector, unions have been able to shift out labor demand (Zax, 1989).

Our current labor law bars threats to close a plant out of anti-union animus and requires bargaining over the effects of plant closure, and of partial closure in some cases. But decisions involving capital investment—or disinvestment—are generally left in management's hands. The NLRB and the courts have been loathe to second-guess what they view as business decisions regarding capital. It is difficult to envision a practical alternative. If we accept that in most cases unions raise labor costs and that the normal management response to cost increases is not known with precision, then the practical difficulties of differentiating profit maximization from disinvestment in union plants—not because they are more costly but because they are unionized—become daunting.

The clearest tests would be offered by cases in which unions lowered unit labor costs, but such cases appear to be unusual. It may be unwise to amend labor law to prevent management from doing what might have been done even in the absence of unions, and it may be difficult to implement requirements that the NLRB differentiate acts taken in response to unions as distinct from the union impact on costs.

If unions cannot expect much recourse from the law, then their direct relations with management are extremely important, especially union involvement in corporate strategic decision. In some cases (e.g., in the automotive industry), unions may even be in a position to trade with management for restrictions on plant shutdowns and the movement of work, as well as for management noninterference in organizing campaigns at new plants.

Unions retain major long-run roles in the redistribution and creation of rents and the political representation of workers. Pure rent redistribution does not imply the employment losses observed here under unions. A traditional approach to rent creation has been to erect barriers to competition, as, for example, in recent restrictions on automobile and steel imports. Where such attempts can be justified in terms of the provision of some public good, government regulation may be warranted. Some view such government regulation as a substitute for unions, reducing unions' relative attractiveness to workers. Our results suggest that government regulation that reduced the union cost differential would have the added benefit to unions of reducing the disparity in growth rates, at least in the short run. However, some union growth differential remains, even given the existence during the sample period of the Occupational Safety and Health Act (OSHA), the Employee Retirement Income and Security Act (ERISA), the Fair Labor Standards Act (FLSA), the Age Discrimination in Employment Act (ADEA), and Title VII statutes at the federal level, along with significant erosion of employment at will at the state level. Moreover, government regulation that limits competition in the domestic labor market but ends at the water's edge will be of declining utility as international trade increases.

In the wake of the massive employment disruptions of the early 1980s, some evidence suggests increasing union attention to creating quasi rents through productivity enhancements. Gain sharing, profit sharing, and information sharing may under some conditions lead to efficiency gains that ameliorate the rate of employment loss estimated here for union plants.

A union's strength depends in part on its size. National unions have often given greater weight to this fact than locals, which helps explain investments in costly and risky organizing campaigns. The battle over unionization does not end, however, with a certification election, but continues through the channel of erosion of employment growth in union plants.

Data Appendix

A new and detailed set of information at the plant level of disaggregation was assembled for this study. The union status of each plant was determined by examining the 1982 collective bargaining contract collection of the California Department of Industrial Relations, which has more than 3,400 private-sector agreements on file and makes intensive efforts to obtain all contracts covering 50 or more employees. In 1982 this file included 1,364 contracts in the manufacturing sector, covering 450,310 employees. Since unions never achieve contracts in many plants in which they are certified as exclusive bargaining agents, only plants with collective bargaining agreements are referred to here as unionized.

The coverage of this file is extensive, especially for contracts with more than 50 employees. According to the U.S. Department of Labor (1981, Table D.2), there were 2,001,000 employees in California manufacturing in 1980. Applying the 1977 California average of 35 percent nonproduction workers in manufacturing yields 1,300,650 production workers (U.S. Bureau of the Census, 1977). In a pooled 1973–75 CPS sample of 6,022 private-sector production workers in California, Freeman and Medoff (1982) estimate the proportion unionized at .35, close to the national average of .36 (Freeman and Medoff, 1979, Table 4). Nationally, Freeman and Medoff (1982) report that 49 percent of production workers in manufacturing were union members. On this basis, we would expect to find 637,320 union members among production workers in California manufacturing.

Eighty-eight percent of all employees covered by collective bargaining agreements with at least 100 workers in California manufacturing are subject to union shop or modified union shop security clauses (California Department of Industrial Relations, 1982, Table 1). The contract file includes about 396,000 union members, or 62 percent of the number we would expect to find by applying the Freeman-Medoff estimates of percentage unionized to BLS totals. Part of this discrepancy may be due to the striking decline in unionism in California. Union members as a proportion of all production workers in California manufacturing dropped from .56 in 1975 to .42 in 1979 (California Department of Industrial Relations, 1980, Table 1). If we adjust Freeman and Medoff's 1973–75 benchmark downward by the same 25 percent to .37, then we would expect 481,240 union members of California manufacturing. On this basis, the contract file includes 82 percent of all union members in California manufacturing. The remainder are likely to be in establishments of less than 100 employees. To the extent that some unionized establishments are still not identified as such, this measurement error will bias our results against finding any difference between the union and nonunion sectors.

Data on plant occupational structure, employment growth, industry, location, and contractor status come from a longitudinal file based on Equal Employment Opportunity (EEO-1) reports. This longitudinal file includes 1,869 California manufacturing plants, 1,273 of which have more than 100 employees. California also accounted for 8.9 percent of all U.S. manufacturing employment in 1977. For comparison, the *U.S. Census of Manufactures* (U.S. Bureau of the Census, 1977) counted 3,278 California manufacturing plants with at least 100 employees. Since these plants are required by law to file EEO forms, the undercount is significant. Roughly half the EEO sample is lost in the construction of the longitudinal file. A case study of similar sample attrition by Ashenfelter and Heckman (1976) concludes that nonmatches were largely random. The remaining undercount is unexplained. While one might imagine that plants with poor EEO records simply do not report, this in itself should not bias our union-nonunion comparison.

Firm Investment Behavior and
Collective Bargaining Strategy

SUSTAINED GROWTH IN PRODUCTIVITY, employment, and output requires regular infusions of physical capital and periodic product and process innovations. Who controls the returns emanating from such tangible and intangible capital is a crucial determinant of investment activity. If unions appropriate a share of the quasi-rents[1] accruing to long-lived capital, then union coverage, bargaining power, and strategy are likely to influence firm investment behavior. Unions and management may develop incentive-compatible, long-run bargaining protocols so that collective bargaining coverage has a relatively small impact on factor mix and investment behavior. On the other hand, noncooperative behavior and incentive incompatibility between unions and management are likely to increase the

---

*Department of Economics, Florida State University. Financial support from the W.E. Upjohn Institute for Employment Research is gratefully acknowledged. Elizabeth Gregory provided assistance with the union coverage survey. Helpful comments were received on an earlier version of the paper from seminar participants at Harvard University, the University of North Carolina, and the University of South Carolina.

[1]Quasi-rents are the returns to capital exceeding its opportunity costs; they provide what are largely the normal returns to previous R&D and capital investment.

negative effects of unionization on investment and may also undercut the already dwindling power of unions in the workplace.

This paper presents a model of union rent seeking in which collective bargaining coverage acts as a tax on quasi-rents accruing to long-lived, firm-specific capital. Assessing the effects of collective bargaining on investment behavior requires empirical evidence. Previous empirical studies, however, have been seriously limited by the absence of a firm-level measure of the extent of union coverage. This study overcomes that problem by using firm-specific, union coverage data collected by the author. The study then examines investment behavior on the part of 706 publicly traded U.S. companies over the 1972–80 period. In addition to estimating the effect of collective bargaining coverage on physical capital and R&D investment, the analysis delineates direct and indirect union effects, examines the stability of union-nonunion investment differences over time, and identifies differences in union investment effects across broad industry categories.

Following an outline of the theoretical framework, the data, descriptive evidence, and empirical model are presented. Regression results provide evidence of union effects on capital and R&D investment. Union investment effects persist even in equations estimated separately by year and industry group. The implications of these findings for collective bargaining strategy are discussed.

Union Rent Seeking, Bargaining, and Investment Behavior

When a union and management bargain over the level and mix of pecuniary and nonpecuniary compensation, work conditions, and workplace governance structures, management can be assumed to be striving to maximize the value of the firm (the discounted stream of future earnings). The union maximand is less clear; presumably, the union seeks contract provisions that will provide compensation-employment combinations more highly valued by its members than those available in alternative jobs.[2] Since each party has some degree of monopoly or monopsony power, short- and long-run bargaining outcomes are indeterminate. The parties engage in repeated bargaining (typically, every three years) and may arrive at either cooperative (i.e., jointly maximizing) or noncooperative bargaining outcomes. In either case, investment decisions are likely to differ between union and nonunion companies.

---

[2]This section is based on discussion in Hirsch (1990a). Potential principal-agent problems between shareholders and management and between union leaders and the rank and file are deliberately ignored. On the latter, see Faith and Reid (1983).

Union monopoly power derives from a combination of the rights granted to workers by U.S. labor law, and the costs a union can impose on a firm through a strike or other systematic reduction in labor input. Management must bargain in good faith with a union that has won recognition in an NLRB representation election, but neither side is required to arrive at a contractual agreement. To the degree that it is costly for a firm not to reach an agreement or to substitute a nonunion workforce, monopoly power accrues to the union. The union's bargaining power is constrained, however, by the level and elasticity of labor demand (although settlements need not be on the demand curve) and by the legal rules and enforcement surrounding the NLRB union representation process. The firm accrues monopsony power to the degree that its employees possess firm-specific skills not easily transferred to other firms and because workers face fixed costs associated with job changes.

Union rent seeking will be distortionary in the long run if firms respond to union demands by altering their investment in tangible and intangible capital. Recent studies have provided diverse theoretical models of the union bargaining process in a dynamic setting.[3] Here, a game-theoretic, rent-seeking model is presented. The model assumes the following:

1. The firm cannot, without cost, substitute nonunion for union labor (or plants).

2. The firm has (or would have, without the union) long-lived intangible or physical capital providing quasi-rents. Stated alternatively, once in place, the costs of capital are partly fixed and capital is relationship-specific.

3. The time horizon over which the union rank and file evaluates its utility is shorter than the horizon over which shareholders evaluate earnings. Or, similarly, the union discounts future returns more highly than do shareholders.[4]

Such assumptions are reasonable. Substitution of nonunion for union labor is costly, owing to the union's strike threat and workers' possession of firm-specific skills. The productive life of innovative or physical capital (often emanating from past R&D) typically exceeds the life of a union contract, and such capital cannot be transferred without cost. The union

---

[3]See Baldwin, 1983; Grout, 1984; Bronars and Deere, 1988; van der Ploeg, 1987; and Tauman and Weiss, 1987. Empirical evidence bearing on these models is provided in Connolly, Hirsch, and Hirschey, 1986; Hirsch, 1990a, 1990b; Bronars and Deere, 1988; Bronars, Deere, and Tracy, 1988; Abowd, 1989a; and Wadhwani and Wall, 1989.

[4]The possibility of opportunistic behavior in which firms appropriate worker rents associated with relation-specific skills is ignored because such behavior is typically limited by reputational effects. For an analysis of this issue, see Williamson, Wachter, and Harris (1975), Klein, Crawford, and Alchian (1978), and Crawford (1988).

(or rank and file with median preferences) is also likely to have a more limited time horizon than do shareholders. Whereas the shareholders should have an unlimited horizon because ownership shares are transferable (the future, of course, may be highly discounted), union members are unable to sell or transfer their positions in the union.

Noncooperative bargaining outcomes. In the case of noncooperative bargaining outcomes, once long-lived capital is in place, the union can appropriate or tax some share of the quasi-rents deriving from that capital. As long as the union maintains a credible strike threat and the firm can recover its variable costs, the firm will "voluntarily" share with the union its returns on capital rather than severely curtail production. The union can appropriate a larger share of the quasi-rents the more firm-specific is the innovative and physical capital and the longer is its productive life. The union places a wedge between the private and social rates of return so that in response to the union tax, the firm reduces its investment in long-lived capital until the postunion marginal rate of return is equal to the opportunity costs of funds. Investment in all forms of vulnerable capital will decrease; in the most extreme case, the firm ceases investment and eventually shuts down its union operations. Baldwin (1983) suggests an alternative scenario: Union firms maintain some inefficient capital (or plants) in order to mitigate high union wage demands by shutting down low-productivity plants, thus decreasing union employment.[5]

As long as there are a limited number of bargaining periods, noncooperative bargaining outcomes are likely and investment activity will be restricted. To encourage the firm to invest in long-lived capital, a union could announce a low future wage demand. This wage commitment would be neither credible nor binding beyond the contract period, however, because once the capital was in place, the union could increase wage demands in the final bargaining period. Knowing this, the firm would not commit to a nonunion investment level. The union could make its wage commitment credible by offering a "bond" or "hostage" that it would forfeit if it reneged on its promise. But unless the bond is held by a third party, the firm would have an incentive to default on the bond and could not make a credible commitment to the union. Such bonds do not have obvious real world counterparts.

---

[5]Baldwin's model implicitly assumes that the contract wage is similar across all the firm's union plants and that the firm is free to vary employment. Hence, union wage demands based on productivity at a firm's efficient plants would lead to layoffs or shutdowns at the firm's inefficient plants.

Cooperative bargaining outcomes. Because collective bargaining is characterized by repeated bargaining, current behavior by both the firm and the union will affect each party's reputation and credibility in future bargaining rounds.[6] This limitation on the scope for opportunistic behavior increases the likelihood of cooperative bargaining outcomes. A cooperative outcome is defined here as one that maximizes the joint value of the firm and the union.[7] This joint value is the sum of the firm's market value (the present value of future earnings to shareholders) and the present value of union members' rents.

Holding the capital stock fixed, the possibility of cooperative outcomes from repeated union-management bargaining implies that union representation has no distortionary effects on output, price, or factor usage. This is the strong efficiency or vertical contract curve case (Brown and Ashenfelter, 1986; Clark, 1984) in which the firm and the union maximize the size of the pie and bargain over the distribution of returns to labor and to shareholders.[8] In the long run, however, union rent seeking will be distortionary relative to an otherwise similar nonunion environment. Specifically, union rent seeking is likely to lead to reduced investment in long-lived, relation-specific capital.[9] Such underinvestment results from the limited time horizon over which a democratically controlled labor union evaluates its future returns and the nontransferability (i.e., incomplete property rights) of union membership. Union leaders respond to rank-and-file members with median preferences. Typically, these are relatively senior members with a relatively short expected remaining tenure at the firm. Moreover, senior workers may make relatively high wage demands if they face relatively low probabilities of permanent (seniority-based) layoff and perceive little threat to their pension payments.[10] Largely un-

---

[6]An exception occurs when a firm is expected to shut down operations. Initially, union wage demands and the union-nonunion wage differential may increase in a *declining* industry with long-lived specific capital. For similar arguments, see the analysis of the U.S. steel industry by Lawrence and Lawrence (1985).

[7]Abowd (1989b) refers to this joint value as the value of the enterprise.

[8]Strong efficiency implies that the firm's employment level is a function of the opportunity cost wage, and not the "own" wage as implied by settlements on the labor demand curve. This prediction has formed the basis for empirical tests of on-the-demand curve versus off-the-demand curve bargaining models (Farber, 1986).

[9]Crawford (1988) argues that governing long-term relations with short-term contracts will, in general, lead to inefficient contracts and underinvestment in relation-specific, fixed-cost capital. The argument here is that even if efficient (jointly maximizing) contract settlements obtain, there still will be lower investment by union than by similar nonunion companies.

[10]Government pension guarantees may worsen union myopia. Unionized companies, on the other hand, have an incentive to underfund their pension plans as a means of making the union more forward looking; on this point, see Ippolito (1985).

weighted in the union calculus are preferences of relatively junior members, or of unobserved workers who could be future union members were the union's compensation demands lower. Thus, the union will attach great weight to current rents, while heavily discounting potential future rents.

Although efficient (cooperative) contracting in this situation maximizes the sum of owner and union member "wealth," rational union myopia results in lower investment than obtains in a nonunion firm, shifting returns more heavily toward the present and away from the highly discounted future. There are few obvious mechanisms for making union goals more fully incentive-compatible with those of the firm.

Impact on investment. The rent-seeking model predicts that collective bargaining coverage changes investment decisions because firms respond to a rationally myopic union by decreasing investment in vulnerable capital. In contrast to the prediction of the conventional on-the-demand-curve model, firms facing a rent-seeking union may decrease both the capital level and the capital-labor ratio. Firms will decrease investment most in long-lived, relation-specific capital whose returns are most easily appropriated, while either increasing or decreasing investment in capital whose returns are less easy to appropriate. Even the prediction that unionized firms will invest relatively more than nonunion firms in labor-saving capital need not follow. If the union can retain its preinvestment strike threat with a reduced workforce (e.g., through the ability to shut down a plant), then the returns from labor-saving capital are no less appropriable than those from factor-neutral investment. On the other hand, if the union's strike threat and bargaining power are functions of the size of the organized workforce, then the prediction of labor-saving investment more readily follows.

Returns from investment in R&D and non-R&D innovative activity may accrue over a shorter time span than returns from physical capital, but such capital may still be relatively long-lived and appropriable. Relatedly, knowledge about products or processes emanating from R&D projects may lead to investment in physical capital whose returns in turn face a high union tax rate. That is, the decision to lower future investment in physical capital may decrease current investment in R&D. For these reasons, unionized firms are less likely to invest in innovative activity than are similar nonunion firms. This decrease in innovation is likely to be most notable for relatively factor-neutral product or process innovation. Labor-saving process innovation may be less affected since the substitution effect of a wage increase may heighten the relative importance of labor-saving innovation.[11]

The union rent-seeking model presumes that union coverage will have both direct and indirect effects on capital and on R&D investment. Union firms in general experience lower rates of profit than do otherwise similar nonunion firms.[12] Because current profits provide a primary (and possibly low-opportunity cost) source for funding investment, decreased profitability leads "indirectly" to lower rates of R&D and capital investment, independent of any direct union effects. The "direct" effect of unionization results because the union tax is likely both to be distortionary and to decrease investment in capital whose returns are most vulnerable to union appropriation, even in the event of cooperative or efficient long-run contracting between firms and unions. Union companies reduce investment until the postunion marginal rate of return equals the opportunity cost of funds. Lower investment by union firms in physical capital and R&D will be observed, unless offset by particularly strong wage (substitution) effects.

Because high union wage rates in part reflect a tax on the returns to tangible capital investment, it is not possible to observe relative factor prices facing union firms. It is therefore difficult to estimate a labor demand curve for union firms since the observed wage rate overstates the cost of labor relative to capital. The finding that unions have relatively little effect on the capital-labor ratio (Clark, 1984), commonly interpreted as implying efficient bargaining outcomes off the labor demand curve, may in fact result because unions have little effect on relative factor prices. That is, union firms may use factor mixes similar to what they would use if they were nonunion, but still be operating on their labor demand curves (unions are more likely to be organized in capital-intensive firms). Union rent seeking has an output effect, leading to lower investment and employment, but may have little effect on factor mix.

Data and Descriptive Evidence

A few empirical studies have examined the effects of union coverage on the investment behavior of firms. These studies have been hampered, how-

---

[11]Lach and Schankerman (1989) provide evidence that R&D "Granger-causes" capital investment, but investment doesn't Granger-cause R&D. Most company-financed R&D expenditures are for product rather than process innovations, although product innovations by companies selling intermediate products make up a major source of process innovations to purchasers.

[12]Unions may capture profits associated not only with quasi-rents but also with those emanating from product market power or from disequilibrium. For more detailed information, see Hirsch (1990b, 1991b) and Becker and Olson (1987).

ever, by the limited availability of company-specific information on union coverage. Past research has relied on the industry as the unit of observation (Abowd, 1989a) or has matched three-digit industry union membership figures to individual firm data (Connally, Hirsch, and Hirschey, 1986; Bronars and Deere, 1988). Both approaches fail to account for the considerable intraindustry variation in unionization, and both necessarily entangle union and industry effects on investment.

The information on company union coverage used here is drawn from the author's survey (conducted during late 1987 and 1988) of firms included in the National Bureau of Economic Research's *R&D Master File*. The NBER file consists of all publicly traded U.S. manufacturing-sector companies operating in 1976 that were included on Compustat tapes during 1976–78.[13] Beginning with the 1,904 companies listed in the *File*, all that could be located were contacted by phone and/or mail. Representatives at the largest 1,100 firms received a follow-up questionnaire if they did not respond initially. They were asked to respond to the following question for 1977 and 1987: "To the best of your knowledge, approximately what percentage of your corporation's total North American workforce is covered by collective bargaining agreements?"[14]

A measure of 1977 union coverage was obtained for 723 firms; 578 of these firms supplied usable 1977 union coverage data. Coverage was estimated for 20 additional firms that reported figures for 1987 but not for 1977.[15] Coverage figures for another 125 firms were estimated based on data from an independent 1972 Conference Board Survey. Among all of the companies for which union coverage data were available, 706 had sufficiently complete information on other variables to be included in subsequent empirical analysis.[16]

Means and standard deviations of firm-level union coverage by manufacturing industry category are presented in Table 1. Company union coverage in 1977 averaged 33 percent among this sample of firms. The substantial

---

[13]Cummins et al. (1985) describe the *R&D Master File*. Access to these data was kindly provided by Zvi Griliches.

[14]Union data for 1977 correspond to the firm as it existed in 1977. In cases where firms had merged, efforts were made to acquire union figures for the operating units as they existed in 1977.

[15]Estimates were derived by multiplying the 1987 figures by 1.21, based on the ratio of 1977-to-1987 coverage figures among the 567 firms for which both years of data were available. The correlation between 1977 and 1987 coverage was 0.87.

[16]No obvious response bias is evident. Investment intensities in capital and R&D are highly similar among those companies that responded to the survey and those that did not respond. The 1972 union data were kindly provided by David C. Hershfield, who developed the figures from data collected in a 1972 survey by the Conference Board. For an analysis of companies in the Conference Board Survey, see Hirsch (1990a). Details on the conversion of the 1972 figures to 1977 values are available from the author on request.

TABLE 1

COMPANY UNION COVERAGE BY INDUSTRY GROUP, 1977
(unweighted)

Industry Group	N	$\overline{\text{UN}}$[a]	Standard Deviation
Total	706	.331	(.280)
Food and kindred products	71	.419	(.271)
Textiles and apparel	39	.233	(.296)
Chemicals, excluding drugs	43	.286	(.195)
Drugs and medical instruments	38	.138	(.181)
Petroleum refining	29	.281	(.188)
Rubber and misc. plastics	25	.381	(.248)
Stone, clay, and glass	24	.444	(.256)
Primary metals	41	.613	(.222)
Fabricated metal products	39	.316	(.280)
Engines, farm, and const. equip.	25	.384	(.226)
Office, computers, and acct. equip.	22	.043	(.073)
Other machinery, not electrical	48	.369	(.284)
Electrical equipment and supplies	47	.081	(.164)
Communications equipment	27	.456	(.243)
Motor vehicle and transp. equip.	43	.523	(.260)
Aircraft and aerospace	11	.305	(.235)
Professional and scientific equip.	31	.116	(.195)
Lumber, wood, and paper	55	.387	(.300)
Misc. manuf. and conglomerates	48	.343	(.255)

[a]UN is the proportion of a firm's North American workforce covered by a collective bargaining agreement in 1977.

interindustry and intraindustry variation in coverage evident in the table underscores the importance of measuring unionization at the firm level to obtain reliable estimates of union effects on firm investment behavior. Except for the primary metals category, all industries have at least one non-union firm, while all categories except office, computers, and accounting equipment have at least one firm with union coverage above 60 percent. The least highly organized industry categories are office, computers, and accounting equipment; electrical equipment and supplies; professional and scientific equipment; and drugs and medical instruments.

The data set was constructed by matching firm and industry data with the firm-level union coverage survey information. The investment behavior of the 706 companies from the *R&D Master File* is analyzed for the years 1972–80. Complete data are available for all firms in 1976; missing observations increase as one moves away from 1976. The data set includes information on annual capital investment and the gross and net capital stock, R&D investment and stocks, patents, sales, employment, debt, and advertising expenditures. Data on company age (years since incorporation) were obtained from *Ward's Business Directory* or *Moody's Industrial Manual*. Four-digit industry data on shipments and payrolls were drawn from the Bureau of Industrial Economics' tape-consolidating data from the Annual Survey of Manufactures. Four-digit data on industry concentration (adjusted for imports and regional concentration) and import penetration for 1972 and 1977 were taken from data assembled by Weiss and Pascoe (1986). Industry union coverage data for 1976–78 at an approximate three-digit level was obtained from Kokkelenberg and Sockell (1985), based on estimates from the May Current Population Survey (CPS) tapes. Industry data are matched to the firm at the two-, three-, or four-digit level, based on Compustat's SIC-code designation of the firm's principal industry in 1976.

Descriptive evidence. Table 2 presents evidence on differences in firms' rate of return on capital, capital investment intensity, the ratios of capital

TABLE 2

Mean Outcomes by Union Category, 1972–80

Variable[b]	Nonunion[a]		Low Union		Medium Union		High Union		All Firms	
	N	Mean	N	Mean	N	Mean	N	Mean	N	Mean
UN	1,320	0.000	1,473	0.138	1,632	0.452	1,416	0.709	5,841	0.333
π_k	1,320	0.101	1,473	0.084	1,632	0.073	1,416	0.068	5,841	0.081
INV/S	1,320	0.065	1,473	0.063	1,632	0.055	1,416	0.060	5,841	0.060
K/S	1,320	0.859	1,473	0.971	1,632	1.034	1,416	1.182	5,841	1.014
INV/K	1,320	0.079	1,473	0.064	1,632	0.054	1,416	0.054	5,841	0.062
L/S	1,320	0.033	1,473	0.031	1,632	0.029	1,416	0.029	5,841	0.030
CAPAGE	1,320	5.744	1,473	6.778	1,632	8.066	1,416	8.600	5,841	7.346
R&D$_1$/S	975	0.045	1,075	0.021	1,261	0.015	865	0.011	4,176	0.023
R&D$_2$/S	1,320	0.033	1,473	0.015	1,632	0.012	1,416	0.007	5,841	0.016
PAT/S	1,117	0.189	1,406	0.133	1,548	0.118	1,356	0.061	5,427	0.122
ADV$_1$/S	749	0.029	738	0.032	740	0.025	636	0.019	2,863	0.027
ADV$_2$/S	1,320	0.017	1,473	0.016	1,632	0.011	1,416	0.009	5,841	0.013
AGE	1,320	42.560	1,473	58.387	1,632	60.494	1,416	62.509	5,841	56.398

[a]Nonunion (UN=0); Low Union ($0<UN\leq.30$); Medium Union ($.30\leq UN<.60$); High Union ($UN\geq.60$).
[b]Variables are defined as follows: UN: proportion of firm's workforce covered by collective bargaining agreement; π_k: gross rate of return to capital and gross cash flow earnings divided by the value of the gross inflation-adjusted capital stock; INV/S: annual capital investment expenditures, divided by sales; K/S: gross inflation-adjusted capital stock (current dollars) divided by sales; INV/K: annual capital investment, divided by the gross capital stock; L/S: employees per \$1,000 (constant 1972) of sales; CAPAGE: average age (years) of capital stock, gross book value of plant minus net book value of plant, divided by current year depreciation; R&D$_1$/S: R&D expenditures divided by sales (R&D-active firms only); R&D$_2$/S: R&D expenditures divided by sales (all firms); PAT/S: stock of patents granted (with assumed 15% depreciation rate), divided by millions of 1972 dollar sales; ADV$_1$/S: advertising expenditures divided by sales (advertising-active firms only); ADV$_2$/S: advertising expenditures divided by sales (all firms); and AGE: company age, years since incorporation.

stocks to sales and employment to sales, the average age of capital, R&D investment intensity, the ratio of the patent stock to sales, advertising intensity, and company age, all cross-tabulated by union status over the nine-year 1972–80 period. Total sample sizes are less than nine times 706, however, owing to missing data in years other than 1976. "Nonunion" is defined as firms with no union coverage; "low" union as covered firms with less than 30 percent coverage; "medium" union as firms with coverage of at least 30 but less than 60 percent; and "high" union as firms with coverage 60 percent or higher.

The rate of return to capital, π_k, measured by earnings divided by the gross inflation-adjusted capital stock, decreases as one moves from the nonunion to the high union categories. Unionized companies are more capital-intensive and less labor intensive than nonunion companies, as seen by the ratios of the capital stock, K/S, and employees to sales, L/S. Although unionized companies have larger capital stocks, investment intensity (measured by the ratio of investment to sales, INV/S, and investment to the capital stock, INV/K), is lower among highly unionized than among nonunion companies. Consistent with these figures is the finding that the average age of capital, CAPAGE, proxied by accumulated depreciation divided by annual depreciation, increases with respect to unionization, ranging from an average of 5.7 years in nonunion companies to 8.6 years among high-coverage companies.

Table 2 also includes measures of R&D intensity (company-financed R&D expenditures divided by sales) for two samples of firms. $R\&D_1/S$ includes R&D-active firms, that is, those reporting positive R&D expenditures. The second measure, $R\&D_2/S$, includes not only R&D-active firms in the sample, but also nonreporting firms, which are assumed to have zero R&D expenditures (see Bound et al., 1984, for a discussion of this issue). Both measures of investment intensity decrease markedly with union coverage. The drop is particularly sharp between the nonunion and low union groups. Patent intensity exhibits a pattern similar to R&D intensity. The stock of patents granted per dollar of (deflated) sales, PAT/S, declines sharply with union coverage. The ratio is about three times higher among the nonunion than among the high union companies. Among those companies that reported annual advertising expenditures, advertising intensity, ADV_1/S, is about 3 percent of sales among the nonunion and low union sample of firms, as compared with about 2 percent among the high coverage firms. Finally, nonunion companies are significantly younger than are union companies, averaging 43 years since incorporation, as compared with an average of about 61 years for unionized companies.

The descriptive data presented in Table 2 are suggestive, but they do not allow reliable inferences regarding partial correlations or causal effects. Subsequent analysis therefore examines in detail the relationship between company-level union coverage and firm investment behavior during the 1970s.

Union Effects on Capital and R&D Investment

Model specification. Profit-maximizing firms invest in physical and R&D capital in order to obtain capital stocks that provide optimal flows of capital services. Investment is thus determined by factors influencing product price, output, production technology, and relative factor costs. Physical capital and R&D investment equations are estimated here for companies over the period 1972–80. The following general form of an investment equation is estimated:

$$I_{it} = \alpha + \Sigma\beta_j X_{jit} + \Sigma\gamma_k Z_{kit} + \Sigma\delta_m YEAR_{mt} + \psi UN_i + e_{it} \qquad (1)$$

where I_{it} is investment of firm i in year t, measured alternatively by the log of annual capital investment, $\ln(INV)$, and by the log of annual R&D expenditures, $\ln(R\&D)$. The coefficient α is an intercept; X_j represents j firm-specific variables, and β_j are the attaching coefficients; Z_k represents k industry variables, and γ_k are the attaching coefficients; $YEAR_m$ represents m year dummies, and δ_m are the corresponding coefficients; UN_i measures union coverage in firm i during 1977, and ψ is its coefficient (measurement of unionism is discussed below); and e_{it} is a random error term assumed (at this stage of the analysis) to have zero mean and constant variance.

Optimal investment is a function of output (and thus product price) and relative factor prices, *inter alia*. To account for output (or scale), an investment-intensity equation can be estimated by dividing both sides of the equation by sales or, alternatively, by including output on the right-hand side (a log-intensity equation is equivalent to a double log levels model in which the log output coefficient is constrained to equal unity). Here, double log models are estimated in which input variables measuring employment and the capital stock (and the R&D stock in the case of R&D investment) are included on the right-hand side. Output is some linear combination of the included input variables. Product price should vary little between union and nonunion companies competing in the same market. (The inability of union companies to fully pass forward higher costs is evinced by the substantial union-nonunion differential in profitability.) Firm-specific price differences owing to, for example, demand shifts, are accounted for by firm profitability and growth rate variables. Industry differences in price are accounted for by industry sales growth, industry dummies, and other industry-level variables.

Since firms in a cross section face similar investment costs, a direct measure of the capital costs facing individual firms is not essential and is not used here (such a measure is not available). Year dummies can account for differences in costs over time, while industry dummies may capture industry-specific cost and price differences. To the extent that retained earnings provide a lower cost source of funds, investment should be positively related to current firm profitability, which is included as a regressor. A direct measure of the labor costs facing most firms in the sample is not available, but a measure of industry labor costs is included. The industry wage provides a measure of the opportunity cost wage facing the firm, which is more important than the firm's own wage in determining investment if cooperative bargaining outcomes obtain. Moreover, to the extent that union appropriation of firm quasi-rents takes the form of higher wage costs, inclusion of a firm-specific wage variable might capture much of what is in fact a union effect on investment.

The Data Appendix provides definitions for all variables used in the regression equations. The control variables differ slightly between the ln(INV) and ln(R&D) equations. Included among the firm variables X in the ln(INV) equations are firm profitability, π_k, measured by the company's gross rate of return on capital; firm size, ln(L), measured by the log of employment; the current capital stock net of new investment, ln(K)(−1), measured by the log of the inflation-adjusted capital stock minus current investment; company age, AGE, measured by years since incorporation; and company-specific sales growth, GROWTH, measured by annualized logarithmic growth in sales between years t and t − 2 (firm years with GROWTH less than −1.0 or greater than 1.0 are excluded from the sample). Industry variables are matched to firms at the two-, three-, or four-digit level, depending on the firm's designated primary industry code in Compustat. Included among the industry variables Z are industry sales growth, I-GROWTH, measured by the annualized logarithmic growth in constant dollar shipments between years t and t − 4; industry average earnings, I-EARN, measured by the log of the average compensation per worker in the industry; industry concentration, I-CR, measured by the four-firm concentration ratio adjusted for regional markets, imports, and exports; foreign competition, I-IMPORT, measured by the share of imports in total domestic sales; industry union coverage, I-UN; and industry dummies IND at an approximate two-digit level.

Included in the ln(R&D) equations are the current capital stock, ln(K), and a variable measuring the R&D stock minus current R&D expenditures, ln(R&D stock)(-1). All other variables are identical to those included in the ln(INV) equations. The R&D investment equation includes only R&D-active firms, that is, company-years with positive reported R&D expenditures.

Union rent seeking is likely to have both direct and indirect effects on firm investment behavior. The union tax on the returns or quasi-rents to nontransferable capital will directly decrease capital and R&D investment, as firms adjust investment to equate their marginal postunion tax rate of return with their marginal financing cost. Marginal rates of return for union and nonunion firms will be equivalent only if firms face identical and perfectly elastic marginal supply of funds schedules. Union rent seeking will also have an indirect effect on investment. By lowering current company profitability, the unionized company will typically have higher marginal financing costs and a concomitant decrease in investment.

Subsequent empirical work will distinguish between unionism's direct and indirect effects. The direct union effect on investment is measured by ψ, the coefficient on UN in equation (1), with the rate of return on capital, π_k, included as a control variable. The total union investment effect, comprised of the sum of the direct and indirect effect, can be measured by the coefficient on UN in investment equations with π_k excluded.

Capital investment results. Table 3 presents regression results for capital investment equations, with the log of annual real investment expenditures, ln(INV), as the dependent variable. Results are presented for specifications with and without industry dummies and the profitability measure, π_k. Results on variables other than unionization are briefly examined. The lagged capital stock variable can be considered a scale or output variable, with the coefficient close to unity. The variable ln(L) may also serve as a scale variable, with its positive coefficient indicating a positive relationship between size and investment, ceteris paribus. Investment is significantly lower among older companies. Both company-specific growth and industry sales growth, intended to proxy demand shifts, are positively and significantly related to current capital investment. Capital investment is positively related to the opportunity cost of labor, proxied by I-EARN, measuring the log of average industry compensation in a firm's principal industry. Capital investment is not significantly related to industry concentration but is negatively related to import penetration in the company's principal industry. Following inclusion of industry dummies, industry union density (I-UN) and capital investment are positively related.

TABLE 3

CAPITAL INVESTMENT REGRESSION RESULTS[a]

(absolute value of t-statistics in parentheses)

Variable	(1)	(2)	(3)	(4)
UN-LOW	−0.050	−0.104	−0.092	−0.158
	(2.07)	(4.22)	(3.56)	(6.07)
UN-MED	−0.157	−0.174	−0.236	−0.260
	(6.27)	(6.80)	(8.86)	(9.65)
UN-HIGH	−0.102	−0.101	−0.195	−0.189
	(3.80)	(3.69)	(6.82)	(6.54)
π_k	5.139	4.724	—	—
	(29.72)	(27.31)		
ln(K)(−1)	0.989	0.863	0.965	0.809
	(74.02)	(51.60)	(67.42)	(45.85)
ln(L)	0.063	0.198	0.084	0.252
	(4.19)	(10.80)	(5.23)	(13.06)
AGE/100	−0.239	−0.235	−0.287	−0.292
	(8.65)	(8.43)	(9.69)	(9.88)
GROWTH	0.377	0.381	0.895	0.849
	(7.73)	(7.97)	(18.32)	(17.93)
I-GROWTH	1.162	0.917	1.287	1.018
	(7.32)	(5.60)	(7.55)	(5.85)
I-EARN	0.230	0.319	0.282	0.339
	(4.99)	(4.13)	(5.70)	(4.14)
I-CR	0.094	−0.025	0.178	0.039
	(1.78)	(0.37)	(3.16)	(0.55)
I-IMPORT	−0.539	−0.354	−0.727	−0.419
	(4.35)	(2.58)	(5.48)	(2.87)
I-UN	−0.030	0.206	−0.048	0.285
	(0.47)	(2.19)	(0.70)	(2.86)
IND	No	Yes	No	Yes
YEAR	Yes	Yes	Yes	Yes
R^2	0.909	0.914	0.896	0.903
N	5,841	5,841	5,841	5,841

[a]Low Union (0<UN≤.30); Medium Union (.30≤UN<.60); High Union (UN≥.60). Nonunion (UN=0) is the omitted reference group.

The relationship between union coverage and investment behavior is examined by including in the regression equations three categorical variables corresponding to low, medium, and high levels of union coverage, with nonunion the omitted reference group (UN-LOW = 1 if [0 < UN < .30], UN-MED = 1 if [.30 ≤ UN < .60], and UN-HIGH = 1 if [UN ≥ .60]). The evidence in Table 3 indicates that firm-level union coverage is negatively and significantly related to capital investment. Coefficients on the union variables in column (2) indicate that unionized companies invest from 10 to 16 percent less than do otherwise similar nonunion companies.[17] The magnitude of the union coefficients suggests a nonlinear relationship between the log of capital investment and the extent of union coverage. Companies with medium coverage display the most deleterious effects of unionization on capital investment. Including the union dummies is thus preferable to using the single union coverage variable UN.

The union coefficients in columns (1) and (2) provide estimates of the direct effect of unionization on capital investment resulting from the union tax on quasi-rents that makes up the normal return to investment. Unions also have an indirect effect on investment by decreasing the earnings that provide a source of funds for investment.[18] The total (direct plus indirect) effect of unions on annual capital is shown in columns (3) and (4), where π_k is excluded as a control variable. Based on the results in column (4), the total union investment effect is -14.6, -22.9, and -17.2 percent for the three union categories, respectively. Comparisons of coefficients in columns (2) and (4) indicate that approximately one-third of this total for low and medium union companies is an indirect effect, whereas for high-coverage firms, about half is an indirect effect owing to lower profits in highly unionized companies.[19]

R&D investment results. Union-nonunion differences in R&D investment are examined in a matter largely analogous to the analysis of capital investment.[20] Table 4 presents regression results for the sample of R&D-active firms. The dependent variable is the log of real annual expenditures on R&D; specifications are presented with and without inclusion of industry dummies and π_k. Coefficient estimates on variables other than union coverage can be summarized briefly. R&D investment is positively related to firms' current earnings, measured by the gross rate of return on capital. The lagged R&D stock (net of current investment), physical capital stock, and log of employment variables jointly act to control for scale (output)

---

[17]Letting Φ be the coefficient or logarithmic differential, the percentage difference is approximated by $[\exp(\Phi) - 1]100$. See Giles (1982) for comparison of alternative approximations.

[18]A profitability variable can also be included in an investment equation in order to proxy product demand shifts. The specifications estimated here, however, already include firm and industry sales growth variables intended to capture demand shifts.

[19]Estimates of the total, direct, and indirect effects also can be obtained by calculation of:

$$dlnI/DUN = \partial lnI/\partial UN_{|\pi} + (\partial lnI\partial\pi)_{|UN}(\partial\pi/\partial UN)$$

where the term $(\partial\pi/\partial UN)$ was obtained from estimation of an auxiliary profitability equation and the other terms were obtained from investment equation coefficients. Estimates obtained in this manner are highly similar to those obtained by the simpler method described in the text.

[20]For other empirical evidence on unions and R&D, see Connolly, Hirsch, and Hirschey (1986), Hirsch (1990a, 1990b), and Bronars, Deere, and Tracy (1988); for evidence on other forms of innovative capital, see Hirsch and Link (1987) and Acs and Audretsch (1988).

TABLE 4

R&D Investment Regression Results[a]

(absolute value of t-statistics in parentheses)

Variable	(1)	(2)	(3)	(4)
UN-LOW	−0.291	−0.281	−0.303	−0.292
	(9.34)	(9.10)	(9.67)	(9.42)
UN-MED	−0.301	−0.315	−0.329	−0.340
	(9.43)	(9.78)	(10.25)	(10.56)
UN-HIGH	−0.446	−0.438	−0.477	−0.462
	(12.58)	(12.25)	(13.38)	(12.91)
π_k	2.062	1.692	—	—
	(8.79)	(7.37)		
ln(R&D stock)(−1)	0.629	0.545	0.635	0.550
	(61.45)	(49.56)	(61.67)	(49.78)
ln(K)	0.008	0.171	−0.003	0.153
	(0.47)	(7.13)	(0.18)	(6.40)
ln(L)	0.427	0.361	0.435	0.377
	(19.92)	(14.52)	(20.14)	(15.11)
AGE/100	−0.115	−0.163	−0.139	−0.189
	(3.16)	(4.47)	(3.79)	(5.19)
GROWTH	0.475	0.442	0.703	0.626
	(7.06)	(6.85)	(11.23)	(10.43)
I-GROWTH	0.833	0.277	0.828	0.260
	(4.05)	(1.33)	(3.99)	(1.25)
I-EARN	1.154	0.706	1.170	0.733
	(17.29)	(6.73)	(17.39)	(6.95)
I-CR	−0.334	−0.472	−0.320	−0.479
	(4.77)	(5.40)	(4.53)	(5.44)
I-IMPORT	0.542	0.391	0.451	0.353
	(3.52)	(2.35)	(2.91)	(2.11)
I-UN	−0.595	−0.222	−0.598	−0.186
	(7.28)	(1.70)	(7.25)	(1.42)
IND	No	Yes	No	Yes
YEAR	Yes	Yes	Yes	Yes
$\bar{R}^2$	0.889	0.899	0.886	0.898
N	4,176	4,176	4,176	4,176

[a]Low Union (0<UN≤.30); Medium Union (.30≤UN<.60); High Union (UN≥.60). Nonunion (UN=0) is the omitted reference group.

and firm size. All three have positive and significant coefficients, although that on ln(R&D stock)(−1) is well below unity.[21] Investment in R&D is significantly lower in older firms. R&D investment is positively related to both firm- and industry-specific sales growth, as well as to labor costs as

[21]The sum of the coefficients on the logs of the R&D stock, capital stock, and employment is a little above unity. Coefficients summing to unity would imply that, e.g., 10 percent increases in labor, the R&D stock, and the physical capital stock are associated with a 10 percent increase in current R&D expenditures.

proxied by I-EARN. R&D investment appears to be stimulated by a competitive market structure: It is negatively related to industry concentration and positively related to import competition. Industry union density (I-UN) is negatively related to company R&D investment.

The coefficients on the firm union coverage variables provide support for the thesis that unionization significantly decreases investment in innovative activity. Estimates from column (2) indicate that R&D investments are 25, 27, and 35 percent lower at low, middle, and high coverage firms, respectively, than at similar nonunion companies. These substantial union-nonunion differentials measure only the direct union effect, however. Total union effects are estimated (from coefficients in column 4) to be 25, 29, and 37 percent, indicating that indirect union effects on R&D expenditures are small.[22] These results show that there are large differences in physical capital and R&D investment behavior between union and nonunion companies. These results are investigated further below, first, by considering the possibility that union coefficients capture in part industry effects and, second, by examining the possibility of bias arising from union endogeneity.

Investment behavior varies significantly across industries, independent of union coverage. Regression equations estimated previously included industry dummies at the approximate two-digit level, coupled with relatively detailed firm and industry control variables. As a further check, we include in the investment equations 105 industry dummies defined at the two-, three-, and four-digit level (depending on the specificity of Compustat's designated principal industry code). Inclusion of these detailed dummies, however, has relatively little effect on the union coefficients. The coefficient ($|t|$) on the variable UN-DUM (a dummy variable equal to one if a firm has any union coverage) in the capital investment equation changes from -0.149 (7.08) (see Table 5, column 1), to -0.147 (6.87). In the case of R&D investment, the change is from -0.297 (11.04) (see column 3) to -0.298 (11.27). The relative insensitivity of estimated union effects to inclusion of detailed industry dummies is noteworthy because R&D opportunities and capital investment intensities vary so significantly across industries (on the former, see Levin et al., 1987).

A concern in all econometric analyses of labor unions is the possibility that collective bargaining coverage is not exogenous but, rather, is deter-

---

[22]Similar conclusions are reached when an R&D intensity (R&D/sales) equation is estimated. When the sample is expanded to include non-R&D-active firms, Tobit estimates indicate a somewhat lower union effect on investment. Note also that past unionization has lowered the size of the current R&D stock, which in turn lowers current expenditure.

mined simultaneously with the dependent variable, thus leading to biased coefficients. A standard treatment is to employ simultaneous equation methods and examine the sensitivity of the union coefficient to the use of instrumental variables. Unfortunately, such an approach requires identification and measurement of exogenous variables that are determinants of union coverage but not of investment behavior. There are no obvious candidates in the data set. The system has been overidentified, however, by first estimating a Tobit equation with UN as a function of all exogenous variables in the investment equations, plus the detailed industry dummies at the two-, three-, and four-digit levels as instruments. Predicted UN is then included in two-stage least squares investment equations. Substitution of the predicted for actual UN variable does not support the supposition that our previous findings of negative union effects were simply the result of simultaneity bias.

In a specification of the ln(INV) equation otherwise identical to that shown in Table 3, column (2), the coefficient on UN changes from $-.149$ to $-.757$ following substitution of the UN instrument. This qualitative result is consistent with the expectation that union coverage is more likely in companies with high rates of investment and capital intensity, thus biasing toward zero ordinary least squares estimates of union investment effects. In a ln(R&D) equation similar to that shown in Table 4, column (2), the UN coefficient changes from $-.446$ using UN to $-.422$ with predicted UN. In the absence of richer data and/or theory, however, little confidence can be placed in this set of estimates.

Union Effects on Investment: Estimates by Industry and Year

Union effects on investment behavior are likely to vary considerably across sectors of the economy, just as do union effects on wages and other dimensions of economic performance. Table 5 presents estimates of union effects on both capital and R&D investment, disaggregated for 19 industry groupings at an approximate two-digit level. For ease of presentation, coefficient estimates are given for a single union dummy variable rather than for the three coverage level dummies or for a proportion covered variable. Such a restriction is not unreasonable, given the magnitude of the coefficients reported in the previous section.[23] Separate coefficient estimates are provided for specifications with and without the inclusion of π_k in order to distinguish between direct and total union investment effects.

---

[23]In four industry categories with few nonunion firms—petroleum refining; stone, clay, and glass; primary metals; and aircraft and aerospace—UN-DUM is set equal to one if UN $\geq$ .10 and 0 otherwise.

TABLE 5
Union R&D and Capital Investment Effects by Industry Group, 1972–80[a]

Industry Group	N	Ln(INV) Equations (1) UN-DUM	|t|	(2) UN-DUM	|t|	N	Ln(R&D) Equations (3) UN-DUM	|t|	(4) UN-DUM	|t|
Total	5,841	-0.149	(7.08)	-0.221	(9.97)	4,176	-0.297	(11.04)	-0.316	(11.70)
Food and kindred products	562	-0.144	(1.73)	-0.343	(3.92)	329	0.212	(1.68)	0.216	(1.71)
Textiles and apparel	322	0.011	(0.14)	-0.031	(0.35)	166	-0.009	(0.06)	-0.012	(0.08)
Chemicals, excluding drugs	366	0.093	(0.92)	-0.024	(0.23)	314	-0.338	(2.69)	-0.387	(3.04)
Drugs and medical instruments	316	0.048	(0.81)	0.024	(0.38)	305	-0.511	(8.72)	-0.511	(8.74)
Petroleum refining	246	-0.166	(1.56)	-0.239	(2.27)	151	0.221	(1.49)	0.203	(1.37)
Rubber and misc. plastics	211	-0.245	(2.48)	-0.205	(1.89)	187	0.009	(0.10)	0.010	(0.10)
Stone, clay, and glass	212	-0.332	(2.13)	-0.771	(4.59)	134	[b]		[b]	
Primary metals	354	-0.334	(2.24)	-0.692	(4.57)	132	0.935	(2.70)	0.849	(2.32)
Fabricated metal products	335	0.030	(0.36)	0.001	(0.02)	204	-0.141	(0.95)	-0.085	(0.57)
Engines, farm, and const. equip.	205	-0.138	(0.95)	-0.305	(2.16)	198	-0.105	(0.82)	-0.374	(2.94)
Office, computers, and acct. equip.	174	-0.292	(2.02)	-0.419	(2.79)	168	-0.159	(1.36)	-0.185	(1.62)
Other machinery, not electrical	389	-0.260	(3.60)	-0.352	(5.20)	336	-0.345	(4.98)	-0.422	(6.19)
Electrical equipment and supplies	389	-0.161	(1.92)	-0.174	(2.02)	336	-0.508	(5.93)	-0.513	(5.95)
Communications equipment	226	-0.211	(2.13)	-0.139	(1.33)	199	-0.865	(8.08)	-0.865	(8.09)
Motor vehicle and trans. equip.	338	0.058	(0.57)	0.080	(0.74)	266	-0.149	(1.25)	-0.148	(1.24)
Aircraft and aerospace	97	-0.331	(2.04)	-0.309	(1.93)	83	-0.183	(1.19)	-0.204	(1.32)
Professional and scientific equip.	255	-0.143	(1.87)	-0.206	(2.61)	252	-0.399	(3.71)	-0.422	(3.86)
Lumber, wood, and paper	452	-0.184	(2.28)	-0.394	(4.74)	198	0.154	(0.94)	0.166	(1.05)
Misc. manuf. and conglomerates	392	0.177	(1.63)	0.175	(1.61)	218	0.979	(2.45)	0.925	(2.20)

[a] Columns (1) and (3) include π_K; columns (2) and (4) exclude π_K. All regressions include the control variables ln(L), AGE, GROWTH, I-GROWTH, I-CR, I-IMPORT, and year dummies. The ln(INV) equations include ln(K)(−1), and the ln(R&D) equations include ln(R&D stock) (−1) and ln(K). The all-manufacturing regressions include these controls plus I-UN and industry dummies.

[b] UN-DUM = 1 for all R&D-active firms in the stone, clay, and glass category.

The indirect effect (i.e., the difference in coefficients between the two specifications) will be largest or most negative in industries where there is a large union-nonunion differential in profitability (for evidence on profitability, see Hirsch, 1991b).

The results in Table 5 confirm that union-nonunion differences vary considerably across industries. Union coverage has negative effects on capital investment in most industries, but there is variability in the relative importance of direct and indirect union effects. In no industry is evidence found for a positive and significant relationship between union coverage and capital investment, although some union coefficients are positive and several are close to zero. Union effects on capital investment appear particularly detrimental in food and kindred products; rubber and miscellaneous plastics; stone, clay, and glass; primary metals; office, computers, and accounting equipment; other machinery, not electrical; communications equipment; professional and scientific equipment; aircraft and aerospace; and lumber, wood, and paper.[24]

Estimated union effects on R&D investment also vary considerably across industries. Although union coverage has negative effects on R&D in most industries, several positive union coefficients are obtained.[25] Large negative estimates of union effects on R&D are found in the chemical, drug, nonelectrical machinery, electrical equipment, communications equipment, and professional and scientific equipment industries.

Research providing further evidence of, and explanation for, interindustry differences in union effects on R&D and capital investment is badly needed. There is no evidence on interindustry differences in union effects on R&D investment with which this study's results can be adequately compared. The results in Table 5 do not lend themselves to any simple interpretation. It would be reasonable to expect a similar pattern for capital and R&D investment, since quasi-rents emanating from either source should be appropriable in those industries with effective union rent seeking. In fact, there is a tendency for industries with large union-nonunion differences in capital expenditures to display similar differences in R&D expenditures.[26]

Table 6 provides union dummy coefficients from investment equations

---

[24]Abowd (1989a) relates industry investment to constructed measures of the industry union environment. His results are remarkably consistent with the results presented in Table 5. Abowd finds particularly detrimental union effects in foods, rubber, steel, and communications and finds no detrimental effect in the automobile industry. There appear to be no other studies that examine union investment effects by industry.

[25]Positive coefficients appear more likely where there are few nonunion firms. See note 23.

[26]Primary metals is an exception, but there are no firms with zero coverage in that industry group.

TABLE 6

UNION R&D AND CAPITAL INVESTMENT EFFECTS BY YEAR, 1972–80[a]

Year	N	Ln(INV) Equations (1) UN-DUM	|t|	(2) UN-DUM	|t|	N	Ln(R&D) Equations (3) UN-DUM	|t|	(4) UN-DUM	|t|
1972–80	5,841	−0.149	(7.08)	−0.221	(9.97)	4,176	−0.297	(11.04)	−0.316	(11.70)
1972	628	−0.154	(2.14)	−0.198	(2.76)	447	−0.197	(2.06)	−0.230	(2.39)
1973	648	−0.255	(4.22)	−0.350	(5.36)	473	−0.244	(2.99)	−0.252	(3.07)
1974	675	−0.045	(0.76)	−0.102	(1.59)	497	−0.340	(4.12)	−0.341	(4.13)
1975	690	−0.124	(2.05)	−0.201	(3.17)	500	−0.263	(3.36)	−0.289	(3.69)
1976	706	−0.260	(4.31)	−0.303	(4.82)	510	−0.361	(4.53)	−0.371	(4.63)
1977	684	−0.185	(3.11)	−0.244	(3.93)	485	−0.289	(3.86)	−0.311	(4.14)
1978	654	−0.076	(1.29)	−0.131	(2.07)	458	−0.297	(3.84)	−0.293	(3.81)
1979	590	−0.130	(1.98)	−0.243	(3.45)	414	−0.344	(4.25)	−0.384	(4.73)
1980	566	−0.016	(0.25)	−0.178	(2.50)	392	−0.235	(2.91)	−0.295	(3.63)

[a]Columns (1) and (3) include π_k. Columns (2) and (4) exclude π_k. All regressions include the control variables ln(L), AGE, GROWTH, I-EARN, I-CR, I-IMPORT, I-UN, and industry dummies. The ln(INV) equations include ln(K)(−1), and the ln(R&D) equations include ln(R&D stock) (−1) and ln(K). The pooled 1972–80 regression includes these controls and year dummies.

estimated annually for the years 1972 through 1980, with specifications including and excluding π_k as a right-hand-side variable. Separate annual regressions have the advantage of eliminating serial correlation of within-firm error terms, which biases downward standard errors in the pooled time-series/cross-sectional models previously presented. The results reveal considerable year-to-year variability in point estimates of union effects on capital investment, along with considerable imprecision in estimating these effects (i.e., large standard errors). No discernible secular trend is evident from these results. Table 6 also provides estimates of union coefficients from separate annual R&D investment equations. Estimated union effects are found to exhibit reasonable year-to-year stability and to reinforce the previous conclusion that unionization significantly decreases R&D investment.

Implications for Collective Bargaining Strategy

The evidence presented in this paper demonstrates that unionized companies invested significantly less than did similar nonunion companies in both physical and R&D capital during the 1970s. Even after controlling for firm and industry sales growth rates and other measurable characteristics, as well as including detailed industry dummies, differences in investment behavior were substantial. Unionized companies invested roughly 20 percent less in physical capital than did similar nonunion companies. Approximately half to two-thirds of this impact appears to be a direct union effect (i.e., holding constant current earnings), owing to the union tax on the future earnings stream emanating from the capital stock (firms reduce investment until the after-union rate of return equals marginal financing cost). The remainder is an indirect effect resulting from the lower current earnings and higher financing costs among unionized companies. Union companies also invested significantly less in R&D than did their nonunion counterparts. Unionization was associated with about 30 percent lower R&D investment among R&D-active firms.

What are the implications of these findings? Perhaps the most obvious is that union-nonunion investment differences merit more extensive study. This topic should not continue to be ignored in the empirical literature on capital investment and R&D. The more important implication, however, is that lower investment by unionized companies foreshadows and reflects the continuing decline in the size of the union sector.[27] In the face of a

---

[27]See Freeman (1988c) for a discussion of the decline in private sector unionism. Linneman, Wachter, and Carter (1990) examine sectoral union and nonunion employment changes from 1973 to 1986 and relate these changes to union-nonunion wage differentials. Blanchflower, Millward, and Oswald (1989) examine British evidence and conclude that unionization is associated with slower employment growth.

union tax on future quasi-rents associated with fixed capital, companies decrease their investment in tangible and intangible capital until the post-tax or union rate of return is equivalent to the nonunion rate. Effective union rent seeking at the expense of long-lived specific capital lowers both profits and investment. Subsequently, it decreases employment and output growth as well.

Union strategies. What changes in collective bargaining strategies and outcomes might reduce the negative effects of unionization on investment? Most obvious would be a lower tax on investment returns, as reflected in smaller union-nonunion wage premiums. Despite increased domestic and international competition, most evidence suggests that union premiums were relatively constant or increased during the late 1970s and early 1980s, thus accelerating the shift toward nonunion production (Freeman, 1986c; Linneman, Wachter, and Carter, 1990). Union premiums during 1986–88 were only moderately lower than during 1983–85, and they were above 1979–81 levels (Curme and Macpherson, 1991). The sluggishness with which unions have responded to a more competitive environment lends support to the thesis of "rationally" myopic union behavior. Union bargaining may be dominated by the preferences of senior members who highly discount future employment opportunities. As long as unions remain highly democratic and membership is nontransferable, union rank and file will continue to highly discount the future. Moreover, the decline or slow growth in new employment leads to an older and, perhaps, more myopic rank and file. In response, unionized companies have the incentive to underfund pension plans in order to force current workers to weigh more heavily the future economic viability of the firm (Ippolito, 1985). The effectiveness of this response is somewhat lessened by federally mandated pension guarantees.

A frequently suggested and increasingly common contract provision is to link wage bonuses to firms' profit performance. The major impetus behind the use of profit sharing has been to increase labor productivity, but such arrangements have the potential to affect the time horizon over which rank and file evaluate contract agreements. To the extent that profit-sharing agreements tie worker bonuses to current profits, such arrangements are unlikely to make workers more forward-looking. Indeed, profit sharing is simply a direct tax on the returns from past investments, combined with a redistribution of risk between shareholders and workers. By contrast, tying worker bonuses to changes in the stock market price of the firm (which reflects the present value of current and future company earnings) or the extensive promotion of stock ownership among workers should make workers more forward-looking and, thus, should moderate wage demands. Because of the wide variability in individual stock prices, however, a strategy that ties compensation to a stock price or one that gives employees a relatively large share of wealth in the stock of a single company would be very risky for workers.[28] Few unions have embraced such proposals in the past, and there is no reason to expect that more would do so in the future.

For union bargaining outcomes to have relatively small effects on firm investment behavior, union premiums must not only be modest, but wages (or the union tax) cannot vary directly with the level of quasi-rents. Of course, in the very long run, it is implausible for union gains not to be a tax on quasi-rents. A long-run bargaining protocol that stipulates fixed compensation increases each contract period or that ties wage increases to opportunity cost wage increases outside the firm, however, would be relatively more neutral with respect to company investment policy than are union demands that vary directly with current company earnings. For example, for many years the UAW had a set wage rule of an annual 3 percent increase plus a COLA (Katz, 1987). Operating under protocols in which wage increases are not tied to future earnings will make firms more likely to invest in income-producing tangible and intangible capital. Of course, firms may still retain the incentive to move resources away from union toward lower-cost nonunion plants (see Verma, 1985).

Established protocols, however, require a good labor relations environment, forward-looking behavior by both bargaining parties, the absence of opportunistic (i.e., short-run maximizing) behavior by either of the parties, a prominent role for reputational effects, and, consequently, an environment where long-run promises are credible despite the dependence on short-run repeated bargaining. Equally important, stable protocols require relatively stable product and labor market conditions. Without such stability, even well-established protocols are unlikely to survive. Indeed, the traditional UAW-GM bargaining protocol collapsed under the strain of slow wage growth elsewhere in the private sector during the 1970s, coupled with increased foreign competition and the sharp downturn in automobile sales after 1979 (Katz, 1987).

The level of union representation in an economy is a function of, *inter alia*, past unionization organizing activity and success, the legal and eco-

---

[28]Moreover, because much of this risk is "unsystematic" (i.e., it is uncorrelated with the market return and can be largely eliminated through diversification), it is not compensated in the market by a higher mean return.

nomic environment, and worker and management preferences. Ultimately, union bargaining outcomes that significantly reduce profitability and appropriate firms' quasi-rents will reduce tangible and intangible capital investment, which in turn will lead to declines in union employment. If management resistance to union organizing is to diminish, a necessary (but not sufficient) requirement is that large disparities in economic performance between union and nonunion companies be reduced. Such an outcome would require a moderation in compensation demands on the part of union workforces, coupled with a fuller development of the collective voice and productivity-enhancing aspects of union representation.

Development in these directions will not be easy. Given a tradition of strong management resistance to unions, a highly competitive economy, an unattractive organizing and bargaining environment, and governmental labor policies that increasingly provide to all workers what once was the domain of collective bargaining (e.g., plant closing notification and worker safety regulations), more moderate union policies may hold little appeal for either organized or unorganized workers. If labor unions are to reverse the decline in membership, however, they must help bring about beneficial workplace outcomes that cannot be realized in nonunion work environments, while simultaneously working to lessen the disparities in economic performance between union and nonunion companies.

Data Appendix: Regression Variable Definitions

UN	Proportion of firm's North American workforce covered by a collective bargaining agreement in 1977.
ln(INV)	Log of current investment expenditures, in millions of 1972 dollars, deflated by GNP investment implicit price deflator.
ln(R&D)	Log of R&D expenditures, in millions of 1972 dollars. Deflator shown in Cummins et al. (1985).
π_k	Gross rate of return on capital; gross cash flows (income plus depreciation plus interest income minus inventory and imputed income adjustments), divided by the gross capital stock (plant and inventories) adjusted for inflation (Cummins et al., 1985).

ln(K)	Log of gross inflation-adjusted capital stock, in millions of 1972 dollars, deflated by GNP investment implicit price deflator.
ln(K)(-1)	Log of capital stock net of current investment, in millions of 1972 dollars.
ln(R&D$-$stock)(-1)	Log of R&D stock, net of current expenditures, in millions of 1972 dollars, calculated based on annual R&D expenditures and assumed 15 percent depreciation rate (Body and Jaffe, n.d.). Deflator shown in Cummins et al. (1985).
ln(L)	Log of employment, in thousands.
AGE	Company age, measured by years since incorporation.
GROWTH	Annualized logarithmic growth rate in firm sales between years t and t $-$ 2; sales deflated by industry-specific price indices (Cummins et al., 1985).
I-GROWTH	Annualized logarithmic growth rate in industry shipments between years t and t $-$ 4 in firm's primary reported industry; shipments deflated by industry-specific price indices (Cummins et al., 1985).
I-EARN	Log of average industry earnings, measured by total industry payroll divided by employment, in 1972 dollars, deflated by GNP deflator.
I-CR	Four-firm concentration ratio in firm's primary reported industry, adjusted for regional markets and imports, available for 1972 and 1977. Post-1977 data assigned 1977 values; 1973–76 data assigned values based on linear interpolation.
I-IMPORT	Share of imports in domestic sales in firm's primary reported industry, defined as 100[IMPORTS/(SHIPMENTS+IMPORTS$-$EXPORTS)], available for 1972 and 1977. Post-1977 data assigned 1977 values; 1973–76 data interpolated.
I-UN	Proportion of eligible workers who are union members in firm's primary two- or three-digit industry during 1976–78.

Future Unions

JOSEPH D. REID, JR.*

THE OLD CONCEPTUALIZATIONS of unions as monopolies of labor and as public-spirited champions of all workers, members and nonmembers alike, are changing or being questioned (Freeman and Medoff, 1984). For example, the importance of laws in shaping unionism is now recognized (Ellwood and Fine, 1987; Freeman, 1986b; Reid and Faith, 1987; Reid and Kurth, 1984a, 1984b), and the notion that some groups or classes of employees are naturally unionizable (such as male blue-collar, assembly-line workers) or un-unionizable (such as female clerical workers or governmental professionals) is now disputed (Freeman and Medoff, 1984; Reid and Kurth, 1990).

Declining productivity in the face of significant economic challenges by Asian and European manufacturers is spurring a search for remedies, such as directly strengthening private-sector unionism through legal reforms or indirectly facilitating the growth of unions among public-sector employees (Freeman and Medoff, 1984). An opposite view champions faster retrenchment of labor unions, seeing unionized labor as the cause of the slipping U.S. economy (Heldman, Bennett, and Johnson, 1981).

---

*Department of Economics, George Mason University. This paper benefited from comments and suggestions received from anonymous referees; from James Bennett, Mario Bognanno, Hugh Rockoff, Edward Tower, and Walter Williams; from participants at the meeting of the Public Choice Society in 1990; at seminars at the College of William and Mary, Rutgers University, Columbia University, the University of Chicago, and College of the Holy Cross; and from participants at the Symposium on the Future Roles of Unions, Industry, and Government in Industrial Relations.

Past and Present Unionism in the Private Sector

Those who criticize union monopoly see union powers used to restrict supplies of workers in order to raise members' wages far above opportunity costs (Friedman and Friedman, 1962). Those who favor this monopoly see union power used to countervail large employers' power to employ workers cheaply and inhumanely (Slichter, Healy, and Livernash, 1960). Even though measurements of union monopoly indicate that the toll was small (Hirsch and Addison, 1986),[1] these calculations have been hotly debated, and no reexamination of the applicability or the appropriateness of the monopoly model to unions has been done.

In fact, when applied to unionism, the monopoly model is incomplete. Union members are no unique monopolist. If union members reduce their supply of labor to the monopoly rate, then means must be found to enforce their reduction of labor, such as work sharing or expulsion of workers, and these are not appealing or automatically effective, especially if expelled members can produce substitute outputs for other producers at competitive wages. Nor must employers necessarily buy labor services only from union members. Contracting out, dual union and nonunion firms, and replacement of strikers are now common responses to union wages. In sum, it is not obvious that a union wants to or can monopolize labor, especially when disadvantaged employer-consumers and idled employees have alternatives.

Furthermore, unions may affect members' wages and well-being other than by monopolizing labor. Unions may supply useful information about the consequences and prospects of employment changes and about wages and vacancies elsewhere and may articulate members' questions and responses to their employer. These informing, monitoring, and voicing services require a union model that does not presume the monopoly of labor and that recognizes the separate entities of unions, union members, and employers. Our model begins with the assumption of a competitive (non-monopolizable) labor market, with unions as their members' agents (Faith and Reid, 1987). Even where there is no prospect of labor monopoly, employees will demand a union agent who can raise their wages by an amount greater than his or her cost.

Generally, workers in large, routinized plants will demand—and often share—a union agent, for in large plants the scale economies of shared

---

[1]Reid (1982b) explains why many of these measures (especially those derived from production function regressions) are probably too low and advances indirect empirical evidence of higher rates of employment and market loss by unionized employers that indicate a higher monopoly loss from unions.

work conditions and administered fringes are large. This is reinforced by considering the firm as a Coasian nexus of contracts removed from the market (Coase, 1937; Fama, 1980). As a firm grows and unites more workers in more specialized and interdependent tasks, barriers to the flow of information naturally arise.[2] As the firm grows, it also adds more bureaucratic administration, which reduces face-to-face contact with the managerial hierarchy and the flow and certainty of vertical information (Jacoby, 1985; Nelson, 1975). Furthermore, as the firm's tasks become more specialized and as the firm increases in size, a worker's ability to evaluate probabalistic payoffs (such as, if a suitable opening occurs, the worker will be promoted) diminishes, for actual considerations and consequences become more vertically and horizontally distant.

In sum, while workers at small firms are kept informed through conversations with co-workers and bosses in the course of work, at large plants, segmentation and routinization make such conversations inadequate or impractical. Therefore, workers in large plants have the greatest cost-incentive to accept shared work conditions but the least trust of their employers. Accordingly, workers in large plants will demand a union agent to negotiate and monitor pay and work conditions.

Agents can also keep workers informed of outside conditions, such as trends in demand, technological developments, and the availability of substitutes. Knowledge of new practices and of new places will be valued most by generally skilled workers or craftspeople who can travel from one job to another and have knowledge and tools to protect and keep current. Even in competitive labor markets, generally skilled workers will be most likely to hire a union agent.

Generally skilled craftspeople want their agent to keep them abreast of job conditions. On the other hand, specifically skilled workers, whose skills are valuable only at their immediate employer and were acquired at their own expense, earn higher wages and thus incur higher costs from dismissal (which may return them to the wage for unskilled labor) than do unskilled workers. Thus, specifically skilled workers will be most concerned about job developments at their current employment and less concerned about employment conditions elsewhere or impending supply or technological developments, which they can little affect or respond to independently.

---

[2]Gordon, Edwards, and Reich (1982) argue that firms grew and specialized in order to put up barriers to keep workers disunited. Most modern theorists of the firm argue that scale economies prompt the growth of firms and that barriers to information flow within the firm are the costs rather than the benefits of growth (Reid, 1976; Williamson, 1975).

Unskilled workers have low incomes but a universal market. In a competitive economy, they will get the competitive wage wherever they work. Because of low income and low value of information and confrontation, unskilled workers in a competitive market will have the least demand for a union agent.

In sum, in a competitive labor market the union agent of generally skilled craftspeople will provide services craftwide, standardizing job sites and reporting opportunities elsewhere and in the future. The union agent of specifically or unskilled workers will provide services firmwide, for these are the areas where negotiating, advising, and monitoring can influence their pay.

Although unskilled workers in a competitive labor market will probably consider a union's benefits too little and too costly to justify membership, their employers may find it productive to communicate with workers through a union, which may be a more knowledgeable and credible medium than direct communication and which may save many small individual disruptions that could substantially diminish profitability. Thus, a competitive employer might pay for the union agent of his unskilled workers and share the cost of the union of his specifically skilled workers, but not pay for a union agent of his generally skilled employees, unless its representations were firm-specific.

Thus, unions of craftspeople and of employees at dispersed employments and at large firms practicing mass production may enhance efficiency. Efficiency-enhancing unions could reduce the gap between the complete cost of hiring such labor and its net wage, or the cost of assuaging employment uncertainties, which, historically, unions did. In the past, craftspeople unionized as settlements dispersed along the East Coast and moved westward (Ulman, 1955). Firm-specific company unions, generally subsidized by employers, began to develop around 1900 at a few large firms, whose size and routinization made on-the-job contacts between employees and supervisors an inadequate medium for efficiency-enhancing communication.

Company unions were not numerous, however, and grew much less rapidly than did the number of large, routinized firms, the ones that would most benefit from company unions. This slow growth may support the argument that the gains from union efficiency-enhancing (voice) services are so small that they are not worth the bother—a theoretical curiosity rather than a practical reality. But it was not the small payoffs that slowed the spread of company unions. For one thing, the problem of how to manage labor was attacked in various ways by the managers of mass-production plants, the very plants where the gains to company unions would have been the largest (Reid, 1982a). For another, company unions mushroomed after section 7(a) of the National Industry Recovery Act in 1933 gave workers the right to organize and bargain collectively. Rather, the threat from a union to the returns to quasi-fixed inputs and the resistance of established craft unions combined to retard the growth of company unions.

The threat was that unions that met to discuss job conditions could also discuss how to affect those conditions through control of access to labor. The mass-production employments that would benefit most from union voice were the very employments that most substituted physical capital for human capital. Embodying job design, supervision, and pace in the capital, along with the power to lift and shape, permitted industry to hire masses lacking mechanical skills, education, or strength. The employment solution was fixed in place as huge factories used the threat of their dissolution—and with them the workers' jobs—to protect themselves from disruptions by monopolists of labor.

There were those who thought of labor monopoly as a defense of labor rights. Old-line craftspeople, who resented the downgrading of their value by new technologies, and idealists, who sought to uplift labor or to serve some greater goal by transferring away the earnings of capital or regulating its employments, judged their remedies just. They were joined by those who saw the times as pregnant with opportunity, if not with justice, to halt the growth of quasi-fixed capital in manufacturing employments and in the expansion and rearrangement of voters initiated by the Civil War and continued by immigration and urban patronage (Dickman, 1987; Reid and Kurth, 1988; Tomlins, 1985). There were many experienced and willing people to organize labor: Craft union leaders had long schemed to keep the number of craftspeople low and the prices of crafts high (Montgomery, 1987; Ulman, 1955). In sum, there were motive, means, and opportunity to redistribute to workers or to their unions the returns due other inputs. So where those returns were large, employers fought any opening to unions (Brody, 1960; Gordon, Edwards, and Reich, 1982).

Legal support. This antagonism between employers and unions, arguably efficiency-reducing, was rationale for the National Labor Relations Act (NLRA) of 1935 (Tomlins, 1985), which mandated that wages and working conditions be continuously bargainable and which severely restricted employers' dialogue in union campaigns and employers' involvement in unions. The surge in union membership,[3] especially among mass-production indus-

---

[3]The steady average of 14 percent of the nonagricultural workforce in the first half of the 1930s climbed to 21–27 percent by 1939.

tries, and the subsequent decline in market share and employment of those industries, as new competitors captured sales and associated inputs withdrew, are also testimony to the unions' and employees' taking the opportunity to monopolize given them by the NLRA.[4]

This rise in membership is one example of the impact of regulations and rules on the success of union organizing, as is the positive impact on union security agreements, such as dues checkoff, exclusive representation, and right-to-work legislation. Theoretically, such agreements should have been expected. At no cost to the union, dues checkoff collects fees for what is considered a public good by members and therefore otherwise hard to collect. Exclusive representation hides dissatisfaction with union leadership by letting winner unions claim unanimous support. In contrast, right-to-work legislation makes worker dissatisfaction with union leadership easily and immediately visible in withdrawal from the union. Because disaffiliaters impose an immediate financial penalty and send a signal to rival unions that this is an attractable constituency, union leaders will strive for consensus among right-to-work members in order to keep their support.

Facts support these deductions. Unions organize less rapidly and change members' pay less than equivalent nonmembers' pay in right-to-work states (Reid and Faith, 1987). Unions grow more slowly when they do not enjoy employer support, such as dues checkoff (Reid and Kurth, 1984a, 1984b). Clearly, union accomplishments and membership are sensitive to changes in the regulatory climate.

Laws impact American unionism in other ways as well. Labor law exempts unions from prosecution for collusive acts, such as coordinating pricing (dues), sharing (membership and strike) data, marketing (organizing drive) plans, and participating in restrictive marketing agreements (no-raiding pacts). It also permits particular or federated unions to represent workers of entire industries. Where an industry's production requires workers and where output is proportional to workers, such as the mass-production automobile industry, an across-industry union is a perfect means to monitor and police a cartel to restrain production: Employment data can be shared among federated locals and can proxy for output data, and union job actions can be coordinated and used to control and punish those who produce above the cartel guidelines (Thompson, 1980). Although such employer-union cooperation may seem farfetched, there is evidence of its occurrence (Ulman, 1955; Faith and Lentz, 1983; Weiss, 1966).

---

[4]Hirsch and Addison (1986, Table 3.1) and Ehrenberg and Smith (1987, Table 12.1). In general, there were correlated rising ratios of imports to exports and declining ratios of union members to production workers for selected industries between 1958 and 1974 (Reid, 1982b, Table 1).

The workplace. In the old workplace, before the Civil War, American workers understood the mechanics of how things worked and the arithmetic of what things cost, well enough to do varied and sequential tasks under varied conditions with profit. The workplace of big factories, with workers doing one minutely specialized task repeatedly, originated in antebellum armories and textile mills (Hindle and Lubar, 1986), which utilized their workers' skills and experience to adapt European constructs and raw materials to American prices and resources (Gordon, Edwards, and Reich, 1982; Montgomery, 1987; Porter, 1973). After the war, the exodus of untrained workers displaced from impoverished agriculture in the South and from Southern and Eastern Europe, and the lowered cost and raised speed and dependability of transports, spurred the rise of large factories (Reid, 1982a; Hughes, 1987), organized to minimize the need of operatives who understood or individually decided the production steps. Factory owners' goal was for rigidities and scale economies in the new machine and managerial technologies to fix all work.

Management by the technologies of tasks sufficiently small and simple to be grasped after a barely verbal illustration permitted the efficient hiring of workers without language to understand and without knowledge to help. In the immigrant flood years preceding 1923, such workers were sufficiently replaceable to be uncounted and untraced as well, so factory bosses stopped talking to workers. Management became the drive system and production the immediate goal (Chandler, 1977). This system dissatisfied and drove out knowledgeable workers who did not move up into foreman ranks. Thus, a new class of workers came to staff these factories, workers who were and who could remain mechanically illiterate and unknown (Gordon, Edwards, and Reich, 1982; Montgomery, 1987; Porter, 1973).

Workers' self-interest combined with compulsory education and child labor laws to ensure that few remained verbally illiterate (although the disappearance of farms and wagons meant that general mechanical literacy became scarce in the workplace). Scale economies on assembly lines meant that workers' growing understanding was not needed; only workers' speed was wanted. Ignored as humans and pushed relentlessly, workers began to think of bosses as adversaries rather than as co-workers and to focus on extracting wage demands and work restrictions from an employment system they perceived to be grossly rich and inequitable.

The NLRA empowered and emboldened factory workers, and World War II enhanced and sustained their gains. Labor peace brought war profits and federal investment, which sustained the commitments of other inputs. The destruction of European and Asian factories monopolized postwar demand to American factories, and postwar largesse (such as the Marshall Plan) and subsequent wars (in Korea and Vietnam) kept demand up. By 1970, after 35 years of wanting and getting more in the private sector, unions were secure in their accomplishments and set in their ways, as were factory managers.

Unions were less a voice for factory workers to management than organizers of harassments, such as featherbedding, restrictive work rules and grievance proceedings, and strikes. Although unions contended with management for factory revenues, they joined with management to lobby for subsidies of factory outputs (through voluntary quotas, tariffs, and capital input subsidies). Acclimated to unions, factory managers managed entreaties to the federal government for relief and financial restructurings to take advantage of tax rules and accounting procedures rather than factory labor. Thus, the ingrained relationship between factory managers and factory laborers was adversarial, confrontational, and disrespectful.

Factory work has been the norm of "work," but it was not the only work available. At its peak in 1920, manufacturing and mining and construction employed only 34 percent of the workforce, and not all "manufacturing" took place in huge assembly-line factories (U.S. Bureau of the Census, 1960). Other workers more frequently performed tasks individually framed, paced, and executed—jobs which resembled pre-Civil War jobs more than assembly-line factory jobs. Those other jobs that required more than minimal understanding routinely involved vertical communications in hierarchical employments, which meant that job ideas could be tried (within some range) unilaterally and that queries and complaints could be heard regularly, easily, and individually. Those jobs that required only minimal skills became casual drop-in and drop-out jobs (e.g., department store clerking), which meant that exit was the preferred way to deal with on-the-job dissatisfactions.

In fact, before 1970, militant unionism was nonexistent outside of crafts and factories. No matter the considerable potential payoff from union voice, contemporary unionism arose in the 1930s and grew from the twin roots of craftspeople wanting to control the sale of crafts to consumers and factory workers wanting to control the access of other factory inputs to labor—in order to capture resources from owners of other inputs and from consumers. Unions federated to monopolize the sale of union representation to members and to lobby governments for regulatory reliefs (Faith and Reid, 1987). From long practice, therefore, unions are inexperienced in promoting productivity.

Past and Present Public-Sector Unions

Before 1960, municipal, state, and federal governments encouraged voice articulation through the civil service organizations of their employees, but did not permit militant activities. But during the sixties, union membership and militancy grew rapidly among public-sector employees, by half to over 40 percent of all governmental employees (which approximates the union membership rate of blue-collar manufacturing employees), and work stoppages grew 13-fold to 481 by 1978 (Freeman and Medoff, 1984; Reid and Kurth, 1990, Table 1).

Variants of explanations of union growth among private employers are offered for rapid union growth among public employees: Public wages lagged behind inflation or private wages; public employees felt alienated from a usually hostile and deprecating public and belittling bosses; increased and more inflexible demands since the 1960s seemed to promise more payoff to public unions; new regulatory and legal changes facilitated unionism in the public sector (Edwards, 1989; Freeman, 1986b; Reid and Kurth, 1990). Peculiarly, public-sector explanations are that public employees are able to vote to raise demand for their products (Tullock, 1972); and public employers "cannot break the spirit or letter of the law, as management has done in the private sector" (Freeman, 1986b, p. 49). But it is agreed that much still remains to be learned about unionism among public employees (Reynolds, 1978; Freeman, 1986b).

To explain recent public union growth, the "private-sector-equivalence" explanation is misleading and incomplete. Public-sector unions do better in those states with the most political competition in their legislatures (Reid and Kurth, 1984a, 1984b), but private unions do better where Democrats have greater plurality (Ashenfelter and Pencavel, 1969) and where their employers have market power (Reid, 1982b). In other words, unions do better in the private sector where employers have deeper pockets, and unions win political assistance to contend for employers' profits and rents in the private sector from the political party that can provide the assistance more cheaply (since it doesn't alienate as many alternative contributors to Democrats as to Republicans). But unions win assistance in the public sector only when the help of unions is necessary to keep or win political power.

Nor are the peculiarly public-sector explanations convincing. Both public- and private-sector unions can vote to raise demand for their product, and there is little reason to believe that public-sector union members are more willing to vote their taxes to stimulate demand for other public employees than private-sector union members will for other private employees.

But there is one major difference between public and private unions: Public unions have less legal shelter than private unions. Legislation that permits federal workers to unionize does not permit employees to bargain over wages or to strike, and the legislation proved scant shelter for the striking air traffic controllers, who were summarily fired. Some municipal and state employees have more room to be legally militant over wages and job actions, but politicians have the weight of the electorate's sympathies, the judiciary's subservience, and the police power's immediate direction to support bending of laws in response to militant union activities by public employees. Thus, public managers—more easily than private managers—can "break the spirit or letter of the law." Accordingly, in the public sector, union activities must benefit politicians more than unionists.

Therefore, a different explanation (Reid and Kurth, 1990) for the sudden growth of militant unionism among public employees is needed. Here, a public-choice model of government is more appropriate. Public employees undertake militant job actions (often unknowingly) in support of their politicians' goals, and public employees unionize to gain expert direction in militant job actions. Politicians attract votes with legislative favors to special interests, for example, building a wider highway in their electoral district, thereby winning cash contributions from automotive, asphalt, and engineering special interests, then using these contributions to advertise their road-building accomplishment to other voters in their district or to commission a study of what other legislative accomplishments would be welcomed by voters.

In short, politicians unite to trade political outcomes for minimum winning coalitions of voters. Rival governments are analogous to rival firms embroiled in campaigns and strategies to expand their domains and importance. Just as in private firms, public firms are constrained by law, rivals, shifting technologies, output demands, and input supplies. Analogous to private employees, the controlled organizational form and efforts of public employees enhance the political "profitability" of governmental firms.

In the 1950s, shocks buffeted America's political marketplace, and its political firms responded with changes in their accomplishments and organization. Costs of communication among dispersed voters fell dramatically because of the new technologies, computerization, and media competition. These developments cheapened the costs to reach dispersed minorities and single-interest voters for national issues.

Dispersed special interests used their growing clout to win federal support of goals that were thwarted on the local and state levels. This support was often awarded through revenue sharing that was targeted to and administered in part by the locally ignored minority interest.[5] State and local politicians wanted the federal funds but not the direction. Militancy among public employees through national unions was a way for subordinate politicians to redirect federal funds. National unions were already organized to bring many districts' power to focus at the federal level and were experienced at militant job actions, which plausibly were a way to block undesired spending and to modify that spending back toward local goals.

To reclaim control of spending, then, state and local politicians permitted, perhaps tacitly encouraged, their employees to abandon preexisting employee associations for recognized federated unions in order to substitute militant job actions for meet-and-confer activities. Accordingly, previously meek civil service associations became militant (such as the National Education Association, which repudiated its no-strike clause) or formally unionized (into the American Federation of Teachers, e.g.). Militancy followed federal programs—teachers struck after federal revenues threatened to change local education, police and firemen struck after federal revenues threatened to redirect local practices, etc. The number of public workdays lost in strikes mushroomed from 57,200 in 1960 to 1,496,800 in 1978 (Reid and Kurth, 1990). Militant public employee unions were taking classical union job actions, not against but for their employers. In sum, militant unionism lingered out of place in the private sector and was newly implanted in the public sector.

Future Unionism

In the private sector. Unionism in large factories is predictable. First, large, old-style, assembly-line factories may continue to be profitable, but only if they employ uneducated labor at international wage rates and only if pollution and social regulations do not raise total costs too high.[6] Rising

---

[5]Outside aid as a percentage of local government spending rose from 43 percent to 83 percent between 1960 and 1978. In 1967, 80 percent of federal grant programs providing funds directly to local governments insisted that federal, state, private agencies, or specifically constituted private citizens be involved in co-directing the use of the funds (Advisory Commission on Intergovernmental Relations, 1978, ch. 4).

[6]It could be argued that mass-assembly factories have scant chance in the United States because we will enforce more stringent antipollution ordinances than Third World countries. But aggressive trade policy by First World countries (such as punitive tariffs on offending countries' products) could rapidly bring Third World countries to pollution compliance. The increasingly rapid link between above-world-standard social regulations (minimum wages, safety protections, hours and duties, etc.) and job loss in the super-competitive world economy of the future well may lead to a regeneration of libertarian tolerance of individuals making decisions for themselves about working conditions in the United States.

incomes in the Third World and in the rest of the world will increase the demand for mass-market consumer durables and structural inputs that assembly-line factories do best.

Competitive supplier factories will employ mostly unskilled labor because that's the quality of labor that will be needed (since management and task are built into the assembly line). The products will be crude at first, but the displacement of American by Japanese factories and the imminent displacement of Japanese by Asian factories—with their foreseeable displacement by Southeast Asian factories—are ample evidence that the low costs of unskilled labor make factories profitable anywhere in a competitive world. Therefore, importation of assembly lines will be the way to prosperity for the Third World. Compared with contemporary American norms, the international unskilled wage will be low, because the supply of uneducated labor streaming from the interiors of Third World countries is large and cost-effective locations for combining inputs are many. Thus, assembly-line factories will continue in the United States only if wage legislation and union practices equalize unskilled labor costs with those abroad.

However, U.S. factories that make complex and varied goods in short runs will continue to be profitable because educated workers, quick to grasp production techniques and to suggest steps to reduce costs or raise quality, will be unduplicable in Third World factories. In such factories, workers and bosses must be cooperating co-workers to integrate production and sales and to make sure that misunderstandings and disaffections do not slow production and profits.

Although these factories will be smaller, their intensity and varied difficulties will leave room for unions to articulate voice and to keep members appraised of workforce trends—the education and incomes of these smart factory workers will make them mobile and sufficiently dissimilar that negotiated will replace easily observed wages. International competition among the educated workforces of Europe, North America, and Japan will leave little room for adversarial and monopolizing practices by unions, however. Thus, to sustain a role in American manufacturing, unions must lead current private-sector members into more involved work and become engines of management-worker cooperation, and bosses must become co-managers rather than directors of workers, as is envisioned in worker-manager co-participation schemes (Gyllenhannar, 1977).

Tomorrow's blue-collar workers will be taking up unsupervised and varied jobs similar to those of today's service workers, who will, in turn, be taking jobs as closely regimented and supervised as yesterday's blue-collar factory workers'. Telephone operators are already supervised and paced by computers and evaluated by automatically recorded statistics. As fast as computers can take over reading and filing and filling in routine blanks at other service tasks (such as renting cars, completing loan applications, and preparing legal forms and license applications), these service jobs will be deskilled. The contemporary variety of tasks, control of routine, and incidental communication that keep workers informed and comfortable will diminish. Service workers will want a union to keep them abreast of workplace events, which will become increasingly difficult to grasp and understand. Other services will become more skilled as the incomes and variety of purchasers increase (e.g., more and better day care for toddlers, improved education for youngsters, and nursing care for longer-lived elders). Following the path of skilled industrial workers, these increasingly skilled service workers will want unions to keep them abreast of conditions so that they can concentrate on their jobs.

In sum, the demand for unions will continue in the private sector, growing in services, where many of tomorrow's workers will have externally designed and regimented jobs, and among immigrant and uneducated factory workers at old-style, mass-production jobs. Among these regimented workers, tomorrow's unions will find a market similar to yesterday's market for voice. But not for monopolizing. Competition will be international in assembly-line goods production and domestically pervasive in services, so there will be little ability to charge consumers more than market or to pay associated inputs less, regardless of the production process. Enhancement of low-wage workers' incomes to sustain demand for union services will come, on the job, from aggregating and articulating workers' voices in ways credible to employers and represented workers, and, off the job, in lobbying politicians and passing along scale economies while providing other things wanted by members (e.g., English instruction, general education, and banking services in new neighborhoods).

The forecast is implicit: Low-wage industries will want to subsidize unions in order to minimize the cost of talking with an uneducated and multilingual workforce and to provide shared parts of their pay in kind (after-work classes, day care, etc.). High-wage industries may subsidize their employees' unions—will certainly want to cooperate with them—because employers will have much that is complicated to discuss with workers, and a cooperative union will speed that communication immensely. Employers will not want to use unions' restrictive practices or lobbying powers to effect transfers from government, because large-run factories will have worldwide managerial responsibilities and will depend upon cheap access to capital. This will be unavailable if other inputs get expropriated while in their care, and small-run, high-wage factories will be too numerous to make monopolizing any one task or product valuable.

Thus, to survive in the private sector, unions will take on two distinct specializations and one common feature that will differentiate them from present unions. Unions representing low-wage workers will specialize in getting delivered to their members especially wanted consumptions off the job. Unions representing high-wage service and factory workers will specialize in keeping members advised of marketwide opportunities and challenges and in facilitating sufficient trust between workers and managers for rapid and flexible process experimentation and change. International competition among both old- and new-style plants will mean that unions will not be able to preserve members' jobs with governmental subsidies or to enrich members' earnings with transfers from associated inputs or consumers; the needed subsidies will be too huge for governments to bear, and computerized marketing and distribution will let other inputs and consumers shift rapidly to more favorable suppliers. Consequently, the expertise of private-sector unions at lobbying governments for direct and indirect subsidies will be greatly diminished. The unions' discovery of members' special demands efficiently provided collectively and in cooperation with employers will be prerequisite for continuing union representation of private-sector employees.

To survive, private-sector unions will have to forego monopoly returns in favor of efficiency-enhancing returns or social and political articulation. It may be, however, that existing union leaders are too specialized to change their ways and too entrenched to be replaced by new leaders adept at aggregating and articulating members' voice. Old-style industrial leaders (such as Henry Ford) and political leaders (such as Richard J. Daley of Chicago) who outstayed their time of effectiveness sufficiently to discredit themselves and damage what they championed are not uncommon. The slow and grudging recognition by industrial unions of changed employment conditions after 1970 may be analogous.[7] This paper surely suggests that changes in policy toward labor unions should discourage rather than further encourage adversarial themes; union regulations should be changed to make communication between employers and employees easier rather than more difficult.

---

[7]Unions are rethinking the role of strikes in labor relations, but only because they are winning fewer strikes (Swoboda, 1990b). Recent offers of cut-rate credit cards and health program enrollments to nonmembers in return for reduced or no-dues memberships may be efforts to enroll sufficient users in benefits to enjoy scale economies. But it is also possible that these are efforts to create mailing lists suitable for recruiting members or for impressing politicians, i.e., attempts by unions to regain political hegemony rather than industrial usefulness. The widely reported resistance of both union members and leaders to the few experiments in cooperation with management by the United Auto Workers and to labor-cost renegotiations (Swoboda, 1990a) suggest that it will be difficult to transform industrial unions from adversaries to co-operants of management.

In the public sector. As monopoly unions shrink in the private sector, it is likely that they will grow in the public sector. At the federal level, unions must continue to benefit those who govern, for the government (through liberal interpretation of the Commerce Clause of the Constitution) already has nearly total command of the tax base. So there is nothing that a traditional militant union can do for the federal governors—a union is not needed to monitor or police a cartel nor to lobby superior political levels. Thus, to prosper among federal employees, unions will have to supply voice and organize especially wanted consumptions, similar to what unions in the private sector will do.

Lower levels of government have differing degrees of locational monopoly, and voters will shift to other governments less readily than to purveyors of more private and transportable consumptions, for the cost of moving is too high (Tiebout, 1956). Once started, public-sector unions can look forward to attracting members with transfers of local rents. So once unions are legitimated at state and local levels of government, they need not continue to benefit just governors. At the same time, local and state unions should anticipate that there will be institutional innovations to curtail the transfers to themselves that the unions effect. For instance, aggressive teacher unions will accelerate the spread of tuition vouchers and voluntary transfers among public schools as voters seek restraint of monopoly unions' demands. Because moving costs are so high, legal reforms will facilitate voters' search for ways to restrain monopoly militancy among public employees.

In sum, while labor unions in the private sector will increasingly supply voice to workers, those in the public sector will increasingly lead and orchestrate workers against their adversaries, elected politicians, and the public. The cost of the needed transformation of unions from adversaries to cochampions of productivity could be reduced substantially by legal and regulatory reforms that facilitate union voice but hinder efforts by unions to monopolize labor and efforts by union leaders to monopolize leadership. The future of unionism could be faster and cheaper if competition among unions for members was reinvigorated by labor law and policy.

Enterprise Unions in the United States

SANFORD M. JACOBY and ANIL VERMA*

DURING THE LAST TWENTY YEARS, employee involvement programs (EIPs) have made significant inroads in large American companies. Employers tout EIPs as integrative approaches to employee relations that offer workers new channels for participation in decision making and that encourage cooperation with management in improving productivity. Over one-half of the large firms surveyed by the New York Stock Exchange (1982) said that they had "taken a shift in their basic approach to management" (p. 24) by introducing various participative programs. These run the gamut from quality circles to teams and more complex participation schemes. EIPs initially took hold in the nonunion sector and are now spreading to unionized firms as well. Their basic premise, however, runs counter to that of the traditional adversarial model of collective bargaining. As a result, making EIPs fit into unionized workplaces has not been easy. Critics contend that EIPs sap worker interest in unionism, and for this reason, suspicion of them lingers within the labor movement. Many of the most elaborate and far-reaching EIPs are found today at nonunion companies in high-tech and other industries. Complementing the EIP phi-

*The authors' affiliations are, respectively, Anderson Graduate School of Management, UCLA; and Faculty of Management and Centre for Industrial Relations, University of Toronto. The authors wish to thank Stanley Engerman and Jeffrey Pfeffer for helpful comments and Maury Pearl for research assistance on this project. Funding was provided by the UCLA Institute of Industrial Relations.

137

losophy are a host of personnel policies, such as career development, employment security, and complaint systems (Foulkes, 1980).

Although the new nonunion model is a formidable achievement, it is not without problems. Employee participation occurs chiefly at the job level; more vertical forms of influence are, with a very few exceptions, limited to voice mechanisms that leave hierarchical power relations unchanged. Indeed, EIPs ignore power issues or individualize them. Moreover, employees in new-model nonunion firms lack independent channels for articulating their concerns and must rely on those provided by management. Although managers often try to be fair, employees are unaccustomed to or fearful of expressing their concerns and dissatisfactions. Decisions that are supposed to be made with employee involvement are still made unilaterally. Complaint systems—even in the most progressive nonunion companies—fail to protect against stigmatization and retaliation (Heckscher, 1988; Lewin and Peterson, 1988).

Solving these problems requires some kind of autonomous representation structure to handle individual employee complaints, coordinate EIPs, focus and articulate group concerns, and bring these to management's attention. Obviously, one form this could take is representation by a national union, such as an affiliate of the AFL-CIO. That option should always be readily available to employees, but so far national unions have failed to gain significant support from employees in progressive nonunion firms. Neither industrial solidarity nor the conflictual ethos of national unionism meshes with the communitarian culture and decentralized EIPs found in these firms, and it appears unlikely that national unions will ever gain significant support from employees in these firms. Given the fact that nearly 87 percent of private-sector workers currently lack independent representation, it is time to consider some alternatives.

Industrial relations scholars are beginning to study institutional forms that could remedy defects in the progressive nonunion model. Most of these involve some blend of the integrative and adversarial approaches, hybrids designed to be grafted onto workplaces that make extensive use of EIPs and related policies. Some are entirely new forms of representation, such as Heckscher's (1988) associational unionism, while others are borrowed from abroad, including the works councils and enterprise unions found in Western Europe and Japan (Wever, 1988; McCormick, 1987). The search for new models is laudable and important, but it is also worth looking more closely at domestic alternatives, such as independent local unions (ILUs), which have existed for many years in the United States and whose features overlap those of recently proposed models. ILUs may be a possible remedy for some of the problems that currently exist in American workplaces, even, or especially, the most progressive ones.

Independent Local Unions

Independent local unions (ILUs) are single-employer, unaffiliated unions that usually represent workers at a single plant or facility.[1] ILUs are often associated with employee representation plans started by employers in the 1920s and early 1930s. A majority of the ILUs surveyed in 1967 were organized between 1936 and 1945. Many of these were representation plans that reconstituted themselves because of section 8(2) of the Wagner Act, which made it an unfair labor practice for an employer to dominate, interfere with, or provide financial assistance to a labor organization. Under intense scrutiny from the National Labor Relations Board (NLRB), these former company unions now became financially and otherwise independent of employers and added other features "modeled after trade union organization and procedure" (Saposs, 1936, p. 803; Rosenfarb, 1940). In cases where these unions still received support from an employer or had not established a clean break with an employer-supported predecessor organization, the NLRB ordered their disestablishment and barred them from appearing on election ballots (Rosenfarb, 1940; Crager, 1942). This was a severe remedy, one that the NLRB did not apply to tainted locals of an affiliated union, a "sweetheart" situation. An affiliated union that received illegal employer support could appear on the ballot if it could be proven that the employer had ceased its support.

The rigid application of section 8(2) to unaffiliated unions stemmed from the early NLRB's determination to hasten the demise of company unions, even if it meant stigmatizing those ILUs that were bona fide independent unions supported by their members. The NLRB thought that stringency was necessary in order to protect workers who supported a union out of a "mistaken continued belief that the company-dominated organization affords a genuine agency for collective bargaining" (U.S. Senate, 1947, p. 1912). It rationalized its more lenient treatment of affiliated union locals on the dubious grounds that an affiliated local—as part of a large and powerful national union—could not actually be dominated by the employer. During the 1940s, the NLRB's stance in these cases came under growing criticism from Congress and the courts. As a result, around

---

[1] In 1967, 92 percent of unaffiliated intrastate and single-employer unions had only one local (BLS, 1967).

1944 it began to treat ILUs more leniently (Millis and Brown, 1950). This was not enough to deter including the stipulation in the 1947 Taft-Hartley Act that the NLRB was not to discriminate between affiliated and unaffiliated unions when deciding section 8(2)—now 8(a)(2)—cases.

After passage of the act, the NLRB took a more permissive approach to unaffiliated unions. In section 8(a)(2) cases it now paid no attention to affiliation status. Instead, the distinction applied was that between employer domination—the remedy for which continued to be disestablishment—and lesser forms of illegal employer interference and support, which, if withdrawn by the employer, permitted a union, including an ILU, to appear on the ballot. NLRB chair Paul Herzog supported this approach by noting, "This is 1947, not 1935; in the interim employees have learned much about protecting their own rights and making their own choices with the full facts before them" (Schwab, 1957, p. 356).[2]

One result of this greater leniency was an increase in the formation of ILUs in the late 1940s and 1950s (Troy, 1961). Now, however, ILUs appeared at smaller firms: Those established between 1947 and 1960 accounted for 52 percent of the total number of ILUs surveyed in 1967 but only 26 percent of their total membership (see Table 1). After 1960, however, the pace of ILU formation slackened, then slowed to a trickle during the 1970s and 1980s. ILUs organized in these years are usually the result of a decertification or a local's opting out of a union merger. In 1983, 479,000 workers belonged to some 1,500 ILUs, accounting for about 3 percent of total U.S. union membership. Today, ILUs are found at a few large multiunit companies (Du Pont, Texaco, Exxon, AT&T, Procter & Gamble), several medium-size firms (Dow-Jones, Weirton Steel, Zenith), and numerous small firms in a variety of industries.

Ironically, a spate of studies about ILUs was published in the early 1960s, just when ILUs had begun to lose their organizational momentum (Brandt, 1960; Troy, 1961; Marshall, 1961; Shostak, 1962; Collins, 1964). Their subsequent fading from the industrial relations research agenda was unfortunate because ILUs have the potential to fill the representation gap that exists in large nonunion companies in the United States. As enterprise-oriented

---

[2]The NLRB did not shift entirely to a position of letting employees make these choices on their own. In a 1957 decision, an appeals court overturned the NLRB's disestablishment of a shop committee and then criticized the board by saying that the law "does not make it the duty of the employer, nor a function of the board, to 'baby' along the employees in the direction of choosing an outside union as their bargaining representative" (*Coppus Engineering*, 1957, p. 2321). This issue—whether workers have the experience and sense to judge employer claims and other industrial relations issues—resurfaced in the controversy over the *Law and Reality* study (Getman et al., 1976; Weiler, 1983) and in recent debates over the legality of EIPs.

TABLE 1

PERIOD OF ORGANIZATION OF 1967 ILUs AND ILU MEMBERSHIP IN SELECTED YEARS

	% of Members in 1967	% of ILUs in 1967	Membership (in thousands)
Pre-1930	8	1	
1930–35	4	4	
1936–39	32	17	
1939			163
1940–45	28	19	
1947			469
1946–60	26	52	
1961			452
1961–67	2	7	
1967			475
1983			479

SOURCES: U.S. Bureau of Labor Statistics, "Unaffiliated Intrastate and Single-Employer Unions, 1967," Bulletin No. 1640 (Washington, DC, 1969), pp. 1, 14; Leo Troy, "Local Independent Unions and the American Labor Movement," *Industrial and Labor Relations Review* 14 (April 1961):339; Leo Troy and Neil Sheflin, *U.S. Union Sourcebook* (West Orange, NJ: IRDIS, 1985), pp. 3–7.

organizations, they tend to fit with the insular and communitarian culture found in these companies. At the same time, however, they are unions, with their own officers and funds; unlike EIPs, they are autonomous, possess independent resources, and are capable of providing influence at higher levels than the job or shop floor. Recently, there has been growing interest in new forms of employee representation. In 1989, the AFL-CIO's Committee on the Evolution of Work heard several proposals calling for state or federal legislation that would require employees in almost all companies to elect members of "Worker Representation Committees," which would function like limited ILUs. Oregon and Washington presently have, and the federal government is considering, legislation that establishes joint labor-management health and safety committees in all workplaces, union as well as nonunion. Given these developments, it is appropriate to again take a closer look at ILUs—their rationale, achievements, and limitations.

The earlier literature debated whether ILUs were capable of aggressive bargaining with management. Some argued that ILUs were "holes," sham unions started by employers who wished to keep their labor costs down by giving employees the form but not the substance of unionism (Taft, 1956). Others agreed that management preferred ILUs over national unions because ILUs were more cooperative and struck less often, if at all, but that companies paid for this peace with wages and benefits that matched those negotiated by national unions. This was what national union leaders called the "golden handcuffs" technique: Keep workers satisfied with their ILUs by reducing the incentive for them to join more adversarial, national unions. On the other hand, it was asserted that not all ILUs were passive, that some possessed significant bargaining power, exercised through periodic threats to strike or to affiliate with a national union. A variant of this was Troy's (1960) claim that ILU members eschewed national unions because ILUs preserved skill or geographic wage differentials that a national union might compress and standardize. In short, the debate revolved around alternate hypotheses concerning the ILU wage effect: Did it exist and if so, why?

To test these hypotheses and to revive scholarship in this area, we studied ILUs at TRW Inc., which, before its merger with Ramo-Wooldridge in 1958, was known as Thompson Products, an automotive and aircraft parts company. In the 1940s and 1950s the company was a leading practitioner of independent local unionism. But after 1960 its industrial relations strategy changed, and today TRW is best known as an exemplar of the new nonunion model (Kochan et al., 1986). Its nonunion plants are state-of-the-art workplaces, replete with team system, pay-for-knowledge plans, and employee participation and communication programs, such as attitude surveys and "sensing" sessions (Ziskin, 1986; Oates, 1973).

A case study has obvious limitations, but we feel this approach is warranted by the paucity of current research and aggregate data on ILUs. Moreover, TRW is not just another company, but one of the leading developers of EIPs and other advanced nonunion workplace systems. It also still has some plants that are represented by national unions and others that are represented by ILUs. Therefore, the company provides an unusual opportunity to compare and contrast institutional forms (ILUs, national unions, and the new union model) within the same organizational context. First, we give a history of labor relations at TRW from 1930 to the present. Next, we analyze pay differentials between the company's national union, ILU, and nonunion plants during the period 1979–83. Finally, we discuss these results in light of the earlier debate about ILUs as well as the more recent search for new models of workplace representation.

ILUs at Thompson Products and TRW

Founded in 1901 in Cleveland, Ohio, Thompson Products developed during World War II into a major manufacturer of automotive and aircraft parts. After the war, the company began to diversify through mergers and acquisitions, most of them in the Midwest and Northeast. The process accelerated in the 1960s and 1970s, as the company spread throughout the country and abroad. Today, TRW is a sizable conglomerate, with 75,000 employees worldwide and headquarters in Cleveland.[3]

Prior to the 1930s Thompson Products was a relatively small firm that had not yet adopted modern techniques of personnel management. In 1933 Frederick C. Crawford became Thompson's president and took steps to modernize personnel practices and make the firm impervious to the national unions that had begun to stir in Cleveland. Considering national unions anathema, Crawford pursued dramatic anti-union tactics over the next twenty years (including numerous clashes with the NLRB and the War Labor Board, especially over the free speech issue), which made him a prominent figure among employers and brought him the presidency of the National Association of Manufacturers. Crawford hired Raymond S. Livingstone in 1933 to direct a new corporate personnel department. Livingstone immediately established various employee welfare programs and formalized the company's personnel procedures. In 1934 he started employee representation plans at the company's major plants in Detroit and Cleveland. Until the late 1950s, company unions continued to be established at all of Thompson's new and existing domestic plants. Combined with progressive personnel policies and an aggressive management, these company unions proved resistant to national unions; only two Thompson ILU plants were organized by national unions during those years.

The largest of Thompson's ILUs was the Aircraft Workers Alliance (AWA), which represented workers at the firm's two main Cleveland plants until 1984, when the plants were sold. Although the AWA began in 1934 as a representation plan controlled by management, it gradually became a more aggressive and independent organization. Impelling this evolution were various factors: the NLRB's enforcement of the Wagner Act, competition with national unions (the UAW was a constant presence at the Cleveland plants between 1937 and 1947, during which time it lost six elections), and a management that was willing to give the AWA real power and influence in order to deter "outside" unionism. By 1947, when the appellate courts held that the AWA was lawful and not a dominated or illegally supported organization, it had become far more autonomous and active than it was in the 1930s and continued in this mode through the 1970s. Although it made a point of its strike-free record, the AWA was willing to pressure management during wage negotiations, and a strike

---

[3]This history is based on material at the Harvard Business School and at the Western Reserve Historical Society; see Jacoby (1989) and Shore (1966).

occurred over wage issues in 1979. This is not to say that the AWA came to resemble an affiliated local union in all respects. It was highly loyal to the company and usually took a cooperative, problem-solving approach in its dealings with management. A plant council held monthly meetings to discuss issues and problems, and the AWA regularly participated in a variety of union-management committees.

On the other hand, AWA leaders were susceptible to manipulation by management. The AWA had few contacts with the company's ILUs outside Cleveland and had to rely on a hired attorney for technical expertise. Therefore, it was forced at times to turn to management for information and other assistance, which management willingly provided. This blurred the line between the company and the union, creating what the UAW called "a cozy relationship." But for a variety of reasons, workers preferred the AWA to the UAW. They had good pay and working conditions, which they received for only a fraction of the cost of UAW membership. Also, the AWA offered a less bureaucratic form of representation than a national union. All its officers came from the plant and were known by the members. Elections for union office were contested and publicized. Unlike an affiliated union local, the AWA did not have to answer to a national union or conform to policies it did not choose. Its small size and lack of staff made it less formal and legalistic than a national union.

The AWA's organizational structure and formal mechanisms for dealing with management were reproduced by the company's other ILUs, although the precise mixture of adversarialism and cooperation varied from one ILU to another. Detailed data on industrial relations outcomes during the 1970s are available for three unionized TRW plants (see Table 2). Two were represented by ILUs organized in the 1950s, and one was repre-

TABLE 2

Industrial Relations at Three TRW Plants, 1971–80

	Pennsylvania ILU	Ohio ILU	Connecticut UAW
Plant size[a]	965	878	681
Strikes	0	2	2
Wildcats	0	1	1
Grievance rate[b]			
1971–75	1.3	6.3	10.4
1976–80	1.9	4.2	24.8
Grievances to arbitration	1	80	21

[a]Average number of production workers.
[b]Average number of grievances filed per 100 workers.

sented by the UAW. The plants were similar in some respects. All had blue-collar workforces, were roughly the same size, and were located in small towns. But the similarities stopped there. The Pennsylvania ILU was a relatively quiescent organization that never struck, filed few grievances, and only once in ten years had contested a grievance all the way to arbitration. The Ohio ILU (not the AWA) was more aggressive and in most respects resembled the UAW local in Connecticut. During the 1970s, the Ohio ILU and the UAW local had the same number of strikes and wildcats, and although the UAW local filed more grievances, the Ohio ILU pressed a greater number through to arbitration. We do not know why the Ohio and Pennsylvania ILUs differed, but others have reported similar variations in ILUs: Some are strong and others are weak, both within and across companies (Shostak, 1962).

TRW began to change its industrial relations strategy around 1960. Although ILUs were organized at seven out of the eight plants built or acquired by the company during the 1950s, not a single ILU was organized at any of the 66 plants built or acquired during the 1960s and 1970s.[4] Many of these new plants were located in the South or Southwest, and a majority of them (60% of the plants added in the 1960s and 95% of those from the 1970s) were unorganized.[5] It was in these plants that the company perfected its new nonunion model. The reasons for TRW's shift away from ILUs are not hard to find. First, there was always the danger that an ILU would affiliate with a national union or become as adversarial as an affiliated local (like the Ohio ILU shown in Table 2). Second, collective bargaining and contract administration are time-consuming procedures that limit management's ability to make prompt and unquestioned decisions. Employers were willing to shoulder these burdens when national unions posed a threat, but by the early 1960s that threat had begun to fade, and, at the same time, a new nonunion workplace model became available, one that combined some of the voice features of company unionism with EIPs and other programs for group flexibility and participation (Kochan et al., 1986). Finally, there was the possibility that TRW could cut its labor costs by using nonunion labor if, as some alleged, it paid wage premiums to

---

[4]An ILU organized by the AWA in a warehouse operation in 1962 was more an extension of AWA operations in Cleveland than a fully independent and separate ILU.

[5]If we exclude the acquired plants whose union status was determined prior to acquisition by TRW, only two of 25 plants opened by the company during the period 1960–83 were ever unionized. An Illinois plant was organized in 1967 by the Seafarers' International Union, whose influence at the time extended to areas around the Great Lakes. A second plant producing electronic components in Texas was organized in 1975 by the International Union of Electrical Workers (IUE). The company opposed both these attempts, with the Texas campaign being made a priority by the company. As a result, the union lost the first election, and it took more than one campaign to get certified.

workers represented by ILUs. This was the central issue in the earlier debate on ILUs—whether there was an ILU wage effect.

Analysis of Compensation Costs

For our analysis, we collected data on wage rates and benefits for all 84 of TRW's domestic plants for the period 1979–83 (see Table 3)[6]; of the 84 plants, 56 were nonunion, 9 had independent unions, and the remaining 19 were organized by affiliated unions. The four measures of compensation, according to union status, for the years 1979–83 were: (1) Average Rate: the average of all wage rates paid in the plant weighted by the number of

TABLE 3

Average Compensation and Plant Characteristics

	NU[a]	IU	AU	NU	IU	AU	NU	IU	AU
		(1979)			(1983)			(% change 1979–83)	
Compensation[b]									
Average Rate	6.04	8.26	7.25	8.34	10.94	10.02	38.1	27.0	38.2
Low Rate	4.28	7.77	5.97	5.42	9.77	7.49	26.6	25.7	25.5
High Rate	8.41	9.62	8.81	11.85	12.31	11.63	40.9	28.0	32.0
Total Benefits	2.20	3.82	2.88	3.38	6.35	4.65	53.6	66.2	61.5
No. of production and maintenance workers	250	786	591	197	535	278	−21.2	−31.9	−44.5
Plant Age (yrs.)				17.3	36.2	50.1			
Skill Mix (% skilled)				15.2	13.5	14.3			
Total no. of plants (by region)				56	9	19			
Midwest				16	5	7			
Northeast				6	4	8			
Southwest				17	0	2			
Southeast				17	0	2			
Total no. of plants (by industry)									
Electronics				21	1	6			
Machinery				11	2	8			
Metals				11	1	2			
Transportation				10	4	3			
Other				3	1	0			

[a]NU = 56 nonunion plants; IU = 9 independent unions; AU = 19 affiliated union plants.
[b]Weighted across plants by plant size, expressed in the number of production and maintenance workers per plant.

---

[6]Data for later years are not available as the company launched a major divestment program in 1984, and data from two plants that were sold during the study period are excluded.

employees at each wage rate; (2) Low Rate: the wage rate for the lowest paid occupation in the plant; (3) High Rate: the wage rate for the highest paid occupation in the plant; and (4) Total Benefits: the cost of health and pension benefits, other company benefits, legally required benefits, and pay for time not worked. Benefit costs and wage rates are expressed in dollars per hour, a figure obtained by dividing actual benefits for the year by a standardized work year of 2,080 hours.

In 1979 and 1983, compensation in ILU plants was higher than in either affiliated union or nonunion plants. Perhaps because of their already high levels, Average Rate and High Rate rose more slowly in the ILU plants over the period as compared with the increase in affiliated union plants and in nonunion plants. The increase in Low Rate was roughly the same in all three sectors, while benefits rose most sharply in the ILU plants.

We also examined wage differentials, using multivariate tests, to see if the differences were significant after controlling for other effects. Our wage model (see Table 4) is specified on the basis of factors identified in past studies. Evidence shows that Plant Size, an indicator of employer ability to pay, has a positive impact on wages (Lester, 1967; Masters, 1969; Personick and Barsky, 1982); it is measured by the number of production and maintenance workers. Plant Age is used as a proxy for the age and experience profile of the workforce; older plants are likely to have an older workforce, which is compensated at a higher level. The age coefficient, therefore, is expected to be positive. ILU plants were older than nonunion plants, but younger than affiliated union plants. (Plant Age is measured in 1983 from date of construction for both company-opened and acquired plants.) Following human capital theory, a measure of skill level in the plant is entered as a control—Skill Mix, defined as the percentage of skilled workers in the plant. This was similar across the three sectors; the observed differences are not statistically significant.

Some studies have also shown that union-nonunion wage differentials vary across regions (Personick, 1974), so dummies are included in the specification to control for regional variations in living costs and labor markets; the Northeast is the reference group. The geographic distribution of the ILU plants was similar to the affiliated union plants; both were concentrated in the Northeast and Midwest. Wages also vary across industries (Kochan and Block, 1977), so industry dummies are also included; they are specified with transportation as the reference group. To measure differential union effects, dummy variables are entered separately for Affiliated Union plants and Nonunion plants, with ILU plants as the reference group.

TABLE 4

Weighted Least Squares Regressions on Average Rate
(standard errors in parentheses)

Variable	1979	1980	1981	1982	1983	Pooled[a] 1979–83
Plant Size[b]	0.3017*	0.1909*	0.3358*	0.5622*	0.5857*	0.3722*
	(0.0292)	(0.0317)	(0.0351)	(0.0509)	(0.0598)	(0.0169)
Skill Mix	0.0023	0.0079	0.0157	0.0075	0.0157	0.0218*
	(0.0153)	(0.0131)	(0.0126)	(0.0173)	(0.0186)	(0.0068)
Plant Age	0.0114	0.0079	0.0071	0.0099	0.0110	0.0102*
	(0.0085)	(0.0082)	(0.0082)	(0.0099)	(0.0104)	(0.0041)
Affiliated Union	−0.0599	−0.6227	−0.2824	0.3188	0.5703	0.0888
	(0.5298)	(0.5421)	(0.5375)	(0.6925)	(0.7014)	(0.2712)
Nonunion	−1.1744*	−1.4976*	−1.3630*	−1.3549*	−1.3488*	−1.2888*
	(0.5282)	(0.5016)	(0.4825)	(0.6090)	(0.6352)	(0.2515)
Region						
Southeast	0.2804	0.2900	−0.0926	−0.2302	−0.2406	0.0622
	(0.5823)	(0.5392)	(0.5576)	(0.7126)	(0.7373)	(0.2895)
Southwest	1.5966*	1.6563*	1.7042*	2.5717*	2.6898*	2.0619*
	(0.6505)	(0.6085)	(0.6054)	(0.7454)	(0.7972)	(0.3112)
Midwest	0.6376	0.7512	0.6537	0.7459	0.6070	0.6812*
	(0.4141)	(0.4047)	(0.4231)	(0.4963)	(0.5358)	(0.2091)
Industry						
Metals	0.1592	−0.4521	−0.6907	−0.3253	−0.4716	−0.2091
	(0.4722)	(0.4932)	(0.5157)	(0.6448)	(0.6939)	(0.2589)
Machinery	−0.2403	−0.9225*	−0.7819	0.0837	−0.0796	−0.0559
	(0.3708)	(0.4226)	(0.4479)	(0.5152)	(0.5604)	(0.2108)
Electronics	−2.5897*	−3.2620*	−3.5760*	−3.2537*	−3.5522*	−3.0463*
	(0.4375)	(0.4202)	(0.4435)	(0.5877)	(0.6054)	(0.2330)
Other	−0.2272	−0.6777	−0.2027	−0.0268	−0.7323	0.4737
	(1.0169)	(0.9073)	(0.7611)	(0.9415)	(1.0171)	(0.3925)
Constant	14.9604*	13.4986*	14.1507*	10.3659*	10.3871*	11.3731*
	(1.3403)	(1.0664)	(1.1116)	(0.9682)	(0.9845)	(0.4982)
R^2	0.9508	0.8400	0.8963	0.9571	0.9621	0.9337
N	62	62	65	72	72	333
F-test	78.854*	21.440*	37.434*	107.850*	124.681*	277.447*

*Indicates significance at .05 or lower error level.
[a]Dummy variables were entered to control for year-specific effects; all four dummies were statistically significant.
[b]Number of production and maintenance workers × 100.

The weighted least squares method was used to estimate the effect of union status on wage rates; the results are shown in Table 4 for the Average Rate. Results were also obtained in a cross-sectional regression estimated separately for each year, allowing us to observe the variability in these effects over the five-year period. A separate regression was also estimated with data pooled over the five years. All the regressions were significant, with the R^2 ranging from .84 to .96. The number of observations varied because annual data were not available for all plants.[7] These results clearly establish that Average Rate, a good indicator of compensation costs, was significantly higher in ILU plants than in nonunion plants. There was, however, no significant difference between Affiliated Union and ILU average plant rates. That is, ILU plants were earning roughly the same premiums over nonunion plants as were Affiliated Union plants. This result is consistent across the five years.

Among our other findings, Plant Size had a consistently positive and significant effect on average rate. The coefficient for Skill Mix was positive as expected, but it was significant only in the pooled regression. Such variation can result from varying degrees of wage compression in individual years. Similarly, the coefficient for Plant Age was significant only in the pooled regression and, as expected, had a positive sign. At the regional level, Southeast wages were similar to the reference group, the Northeast. Southwestern plants (including the high-technology sector on the West Coast) had wages that were consistently higher than other regions. The coefficient for the Midwest was occasionally significant, but its sign was consistently positive across the years. A similar pattern is observed for Industry coefficients.

To further explore these findings, we ran the same weighted regressions for High Rate, Low Rate, and Total Benefits. Table 5 shows the nonunion and affiliated union dummy coefficients from weighted ordinary least squares regressions for each dependent variable. The results show that the differences between ILU and nonunion plants were consistently large and significant for Low Rate and Total Benefits and for High Rate in the pooled regression. However, the gap between the ILU and the affiliated union plants was much smaller than the ILU/nonunion gap. In several of the year regressions (Low Rate, Total Benefits) and pooled regressions (High Rate), this gap was insignificant. In short, ILU members are paid as

---

[7]On the basis of the Park-Glejser and Breusch-Pagan tests (Judge et al., 1982), we found that mild heteroscedasticity existed in our data with respect to Plant Size (as measured by employment, PMEMP). We corrected for this by assuming that the correct error variance model was:

$$\text{Ln (var)}_i = a_i + b \, (\text{PMEMP})_i + u_i$$

We estimated this model by regressing on employment the squared residuals from the original ordinary least squares model. From this we derived a weighting variable,

$$[e^{\hat{P}}]^{1/2}$$

where $\hat{P}$ is the predicted value from the preceding regression. This gives us the estimated error variance by which to weight the data. We tried different error variance models from the above, but the results were poor. Our correction for heteroscedasticity improved the significance of several coefficients without changing their magnitudes or signs. Most importantly, there was no change in either the Affiliated Union or Nonunion coefficients.

TABLE 5

Nonunion and Affiliated Union Premiums for High Rate,
Low Rate, and Total Benefits in ILU Plants[a]

| | High Rate | | Low Rate | | Total Benefits | |
Year	NU[b]	AU	NU	AU	NU	AU
1979	−1.1827	−0.7917	−2.1886*	−0.9371*	−1.1390*	−0.8991*
	(0.6662)	(0.7173)	(0.4196)	(0.4638)	(0.4206)	(0.4415)
1980	−1.4232	−1.0871	−2.3511*	−0.9488	−1.5163*	−1.3048*
	(0.7427)	(0.8070)	(0.5026)	(0.5514)	(0.4795)	(0.5246)
1981	−1.0442	−1.2370	−2.4544*	−1.6484*	−1.4401*	−0.9685*
	(0.8538)	(0.9582)	(0.5791)	(0.6507)	(0.4263)	(0.4755)
1982	−0.7891	−0.6781	−2.7642*	−1.5513*	−1.4094*	−0.5766
	(0.8759)	(0.9646)	(0.6653)	(0.7263)	(0.4927)	(0.5433)
1983	−0.9408	−0.4931	−3.4455*	−1.6296*	−1.5550*	−0.6397
	(0.8758)	(0.9587)	(0.5530)	(0.6059)	(0.4969)	(0.5424)
Pooled	−0.9602*	−0.7297	−2.6828*	−1.3553*	−1.3811*	−0.8535*
	(0.3473)	(0.3806)	(0.2327)	(0.2553)	(0.2012)	(0.2207)

*The coefficients are significant at the .05 error level.
[a]Nonunion and affiliated union dummy coefficients are from weighted ordinary least squares regressions on selected dependent variables. Other independent variables entered are Plant Age, Plant Size, Skill Mix, and region and industry dummies.
[b]NU = nonunion plants; AU = affiliated union plants.

well as or slightly better than workers in affiliated union plants and significantly better than those in nonunion plants.

Plant Size, measured by the number of production and maintenance workers, was largest in ILU plants, followed by affiliated union plants and nonunion plants. During the deep recession of the early 1980s, employment decreased in all plants. However, the decline was most pronounced in the affiliated union plants, followed by ILU plants and nonunion plants (see Table 3). These relative employment declines do not fit the pattern of compensation costs observed earlier. Given that ILU compensation was as high as in affiliated union plants and that the industry profile of the two sectors was largely the same, one would expect ILU and affiliated employment declines to be roughly the same. The lesser shrinkage of ILU plants suggests that these plants may have received preferential treatment from management as compared with the affiliated union plants.[8] On the other

---

[8]Data on capital expenditures are available for a sample of six plants for the period 1977–80. Decisions on how to allocate these funds were made at the top corporate level. Previous research with these data found that TRW management followed a strategy of favoring investment in its nonunion plants, although that research did not distinguish between affiliated and independent union plants (Verma, 1985). A reexamination of the data shows that average annual expenditures on plant and

hand, however, relatively high wage rates in the ILU plants may have played a role in the 1984 divestiture plan, which eventually led to the sale of many of the company's ILU plants (Giffiths and Phillips, 1988).[9]

Sensitivity analyses. A number of sensitivity tests were carried out to examine the effect of alternate specifications on the main finding that ILU members received relatively greater compensation. First, since inclusion of Skill Mix reduces our sample size, we estimated the regressions without Skill Mix. The R^2 dropped by approximately .015 on average, but the union dummy coefficients and their statistical significance remained unchanged. Second, as noted earlier, there were no ILU plants in the Southeast or the Southwest. We tested the hypothesis that regional, rather than representational, differences were driving our results by excluding Southeast and Southwest plants from the sample. For Average, Low, and High Rates, a slight decrease in ILU premiums over affiliated union plants was observed, but the coefficients remained insignificant; ILU premiums over nonunion plants increased slightly. Thus, the substance of our findings remains the same; the absence of ILU plants in the Southeast and Southwest is not responsible for the results we observed.

Discussion. The hypothesis that ILUs are a device to pare compensation costs must be rejected, although it is likely that ILUs allow employers to reduce other costs, such as those related to dispute resolution and contract administration. Indeed, during the 1950s managers at Thompson Products and other companies said that they preferred ILUs over national unions because of perceived industrial relations economies. In the oil industry, for example, managers "agreed that [ILUs] had cost their company money, . . . but they quickly added that the additional cost of having an independent union was much less than the cost of a few strikes" (Brandt, 1960, p. 46). These savings, however, were relevant if ILUs were the only

---

machinery per employee was considerably higher in the nonunion plants ($4,685) than the affiliated one ($928), with the ILU plants ($2,034) situated in the middle. Because of the small sample size and categorical variance (one of the nonunion plants received expenditures of only $1,501 per year), it is impossible to say anything more than that the data are consistent with a corporate strategy of favoring ILU over affiliated union plants despite the fact that the average hourly wage rate at the ILU plants in 1979–80 was considerably higher ($8.77) than at the affiliated union plant ($7.79).

[9]We attempted to test the hypothesis that the relative employment declines are significantly different in the three sectors even after effects of plant age, plant size, skill mix, region, and industry are removed. Unfortunately, our results were inconclusive because the regressions showed no statistical significance and explained little of the variance in employment levels. Our sense is that other contributing factors—notably, changes in product markets—account for much of the variance. Thus, even if plant union status was a factor in making employment decisions, that effect was overwhelmed in our data by other influences, such as product market factors, for which no data were available.

perceived alternative to omnipresent national unions. But after 1960, as national unions began to shrink and the new nonunion model took root, TRW and other firms shifted away from ILUs as they discovered that nonunion plants could provide similar advantages at a lower cost.

We must also reject—at least in the case of TRW—Troy's hypothesis that ILU compensation premiums stem from preexisting skill or geographic wage differentials. Troy (1960) had argued that workers in high-wage labor markets or in skilled occupations were drawn to ILUs "in order to maintain differentials that national unions would attempt to eliminate" (p. 489) by policies of geographic standardization and skill compression. As proof, he cited examples drawn from the Bell System—where ILUs were found in high-wage cities such as New York and Chicago, while the Communications Workers (CWA) had its locals in lower-wage cities such as Atlanta, Cleveland, and Philadelphia—and from various industrial unions such as the Transit Workers (TWU) and the Automobile Workers (UAW), which periodically had experienced defections of their skilled trades into ILUs. Troy's argument is a variant of the view that union wage premiums are endogenous, that is, that they exist prior to unionization (Johnson, 1975). While his explanation makes sense in some cases, we do not think it applies to all ILUs, including those at TRW.

Although some ILUs can be found in high-wage regions, others are located in small towns and rural areas that have relatively low wages.[10] Although the data are 30 years old, a BLS (1962) report shows no noticeable difference—at least at the state level—in the geographic distribution of affiliated and unaffiliated unions. At TRW in the 1960s and 1970s, ILU plants were situated in small towns in rural areas and in large cities such as Cleveland. Among large Midwestern industrial cities, however, Cleveland did not pay particularly high wages. Nor did TRW (Thompson) workers in Cleveland receive high pay prior to the formation of the AWA. In the late 1930s and early 1940s, wages at the Cleveland plants were less than prevailing rates for other local automotive and aircraft parts firms (Shore, 1966).

It is also unlikely that TRW workers joined and supported ILUs in order to preserve skill differentials. First, TRW's ILU plants employed roughly the same proportion of skilled workers as its affiliated union plants (see Table 3). Moreover, although the results in Table 5 show that the ILU plants paid more to their highest-paid workers than did the affiliated plants (the coefficients are not statistically significant, however), they also show that the ILU plants paid more to their lowest-paid workers (here the

---

[10]Several federations of ILUs still exist, including the Midwest Independent Union Council in St. Louis and the National Federation of Independent Unions in Philadelphia.

pooled coefficient is significant and larger than in the high-pay regressions). That is, when skill, region, and other variables are controlled for, high-paid and (especially) low-paid ILU members received premiums relative to affiliated union members, a pattern at variance with Troy's examples of ILUs formed to maintain upper-tail skill differentials.

Another possible explanation of these premiums is that they result from higher productivity levels that exist in ILU plants as a result of greater work rule flexibility and more flexible production methods of the sort that have become popular in recent years (Piore and Sabel, 1984). We do not have reliable data on plant productivity levels, but we do know something about work practices, such as the number of job and wage-grade classifications and the use of pay-for-knowledge compensation systems (see Table 6). Although these data are based on a very small subsample of TRW

TABLE 6

WORKPLACE PRACTICES, 1983

	Affiliated Union Plant (N=1)	ILU Plants (N=2)	Old Nonunion Plants (N=2)	New Nonunion Plants (N=3)
Ave. no. of job classifications	125	82	65	6
No. of wage grades	15	13	11	7
Pay-for-knowledge (%)	0	0	0	66
Joint QWL committees (%)	0	100	50	100
Ave. index of employee involve- ment in QWL (1=low, 4=high)	—	2	2	3
Sensing sessions for production workers (%)	0	100	100	66
Employee meetings (%)	0	100	100	100

plants, they show that differences between ILU and affiliated union plants were relatively small in this area as compared with those between older and newer plants. (Some of the nonunion and all of the unionized plants were built before 1960.) Older plants—regardless of union status—had a finer division of labor and a more complex job/wage system than was found in newer plants, which suggests that observed wage premiums had little to do with work rule flexibility. It also suggests that plant age (correlated with capital vintage and state of technology), rather than union status, was the main impediment in TRW's shift to more flexible production and work methods. It simply was easier for the firm to adopt these methods in a "greenfield" setting than in an existing plant.

At the same time, Table 6 shows that various voice and job-level EIPs were equally prevalent in nonunion and ILU plants, but were not found in the affiliated union plant, such things as Quality of Work Life (QWL) committees, sensing sessions for production workers, and periodic employee meetings with management. While the sample is too small for definitive conclusions, the data are consistent with the view that employee relations in ILU plants were favorable to the sort of organizational culture that fosters employee involvement. Therefore, the company's shift away from ILUs after 1960 is all the more striking. It reinforces our claim that management received benefits from ILUs that were similar to those available from the new nonunion model (avoidance of national unions and cooperative employee relations) but that the costs, especially compensation costs, were lower under the new model.

How then can we explain compensation patterns at TRW's ILU plants? One possibility is that the premiums were voluntarily paid by management as a national union avoidance tactic (a bribe), what Troy (1961) called "the employers' desire to maintain differentials that will discourage affiliation." Troy claimed that little evidence "has been adduced to support or contradict this widely held belief" (p. 337), and then presented anecdotal evidence from General Motors that contradicted it. While we also have nothing better to offer than anecdotal evidence, in this case it supports the bribe or "golden handcuffs" explanation of ILU wage premiums. During the 1950s and 1960s, TRW management carefully tracked compensation developments at major automotive and aircraft firms with UAW contracts to ensure that AWA members kept up with or ahead of UAW members. When, for example, it was discovered in 1957 that the GM-UAW COLA formula paid two cents more than the AWA's, an internal management memorandum noted that the company should consider adopting the GM index (Jacoby, 1989). Moreover, our data show a slight decline in the ILU wage premium over affiliated union plants during 1982 and 1983. These were peak concession bargaining years, therefore a time when national unions posed less of an organizational threat to TRW's ILU plants.

It is reasonable to ask why TRW did not pay a similar "bribe" to its nonunion workers. There is a simple answer: The likelihood of affiliation with a national union is far higher for an ILU plant than for a nonunion one. ILU members already are a collectivity familiar with the arcana of unionism: contracts, grievance procedures, officers, elections, and the like. Affiliation with a national union would bring a relatively small change in their work lives as compared with employees in nonunion plants. For that reason, the UAW and other unions regularly made organizing raids at TRW's ILU plants; the CWA and Oil, Chemical, and Atomic Workers (OCAW) did the same with the ILUs in the Bell System and at Exxon.

If the company paid a "bribe" to ILU members to keep them from affiliating with a national union, that would account for the premium that they earned relative to workers in nonunion plants. But what about pay differences between ILU and affiliated union members? It may be that these also were a "bribe." We think that some of that differential (as well as some of the ILU/nonunion differential) resulted from the bargaining power possessed by ILU members. One obvious example of that power is the strike. Aggregate strike data for TRW's ILUs are unavailable, but we do know that some of them (e.g., the AWA and the Ohio ILU shown in Table 2) occasionally did go on strike, not as often as some affiliated union locals but certainly more than unorganized workers.

In addition to strikes, ILUs have other tactics that they can and do use to pressure management. First, even if a strike does not occur, ILU members can threaten to strike. This happened at TRW as well as at Esso, where ILU officers told management during negotiations in 1959 that "[we] have always preferred the peaceful route in negotiations but must confess that our nerves are on edge" (Marshall, 1961, p. 829). Second, ILU members and officers can influence management's perception of the likelihood of a national union takeover and so extract higher pay. Contract rejections, which were a periodic occurrence with the AWA, signal to management (and to national union organizers) that workers are dissatisfied with the negotiated terms. Also, ILU officers at TRW, Esso, and other companies sometimes made thinly veiled threats to management that they would affiliate with a national union if better contract terms were not negotiated (Brandt, 1960; Jacoby, 1989). Finally, because ILUs are relatively democratic and decentralized unions—there is direct ratification, no intermediate bodies, and little hierarchy—they may be especially effective in bargaining, more so than even affiliated union locals. Other research has shown a link between union characteristics and bargaining outcomes (Fiorito and Hendricks, 1987, although not specifically concerned with ILUs).[11]

ILUs and Public Policy

When compared with national unions, ILUs are not without defects, as critics have been pointing out for a long time (Douglas, 1921). First, ILUs

---

[11]The same logic also applies to Japanese enterprise unions. Although often viewed as powerless pawns of management, two recent studies refute that stereotype. Based on attitude surveys, Lincoln and Kalleberg (1985) find "no support for the 'strong corporatist' hypothesis that Japanese enterprise unions function directly to strengthen the bond between the employee and the firm" (p. 753). Freeman and Rebick (1989) find that Japanese enterprise unions have substantial positive effects on women's pay, bonus pay, severance pay, and leisure hours, and that newly organized Japanese unions raise wages in about half the cases studied.

have little influence at the top levels of a corporation because they are typically single-local unions. Therefore, they lack the ability or vision to coordinate policies to affect strategic corporate decisions, an issue of growing importance for today's labor organizations.[12] Second, the logic of company unionism is at variance with the traditional national union objective of taking wages and work standards "out of competition" by standardizing them throughout an industry or occupation. Third, ILUs reinforce, rather than break down, the secretive insularity that pervades many of today's new-model nonunion firms (Heckscher, 1988). Finally, ILUs have the potential—as in the 1920s and early 1930s—to be used by employers as a potent substitute for national unions. Indeed, it was these defects, especially the last, that guided the early NLRB's policy to wipe out unaffiliated single-employer labor organizations, and it nearly succeeded in doing so. As a result, today the United States is unique—as compared with Western Europe and Japan—in lacking this form of representation.

National unions are still necessary, but they are not the solution to all of today's representation problems. Most national unions have not appealed to workers in nonunion firms with EIPs and other progressive personnel policies. Moreover, forces such as deregulation and international competition are making it increasingly difficult for national unions to adhere to the old ideal of wage standardization. Industrywide bargaining is breaking down and giving way to company-oriented wage policies. Mechanisms such as Employee Stock Ownership Plans (ESOPs) and board representation give nonunion employees as much strategic influence as is exercised by some national union members.

In addition, our study raises two other important points. First, some of the purported defects of ILUs—such as their lack of bargaining power or their complacence and inability to be critical of management—are not inherent in this form of organization. Even within a single company like TRW, there was considerable variation among ILUs. Some were aggressive and independent, others less so. Second, what have traditionally been viewed as ILU defects may turn out to be virtues when it comes to representing workers in today's new-model nonunion firms. Not only do ILUs mesh with the EIPs, communications programs, and communitarian culture found inside these firms, but they are also more likely than national unions to appeal to college-educated workers, who are increasingly employed there. These employees have a high degree of corporate loyalty, are able to run organizations without much outside assistance, and may

---

[12]Unlike some of TRW's other ILUs, this was not a problem for the AWA, which was based in Cleveland, the site of company headquarters.

dislike national unions because of their male, blue-collar image, however inaccurate that stereotype may be. Although the most recent data are from 1967, they show that among ILUs, the proportion of white-collar workers was more than twice as high, and the proportion of women nearly twice as high, as it was within national unions (BLS, 1969).

The TRW experience also suggests that new-model nonunion employers are unlikely to welcome or encourage ILUs because labor costs are likely to be higher in ILU facilities than in those lacking collective representation. Even without a significant threat from outside unionism, there still will be some positive ILU/nonunion differential, as at TRW and as in Japan today (Freeman and Rebick, 1989). However, because ILUs have the potential to remedy various voice defects in the new nonunion model, they may raise employee satisfaction and productivity. Whether this would be sufficient to overcome employer preferences for the nonunion model is an open question. Employers who deal with national unions clearly do not give much weight to the productivity offset, whereas ILUs are different from affiliated unions and so employers might be more inclined to value any positive effects. Indeed, some firms practicing the new nonunion model have gone so far as to create EIPs whose representational structures resemble ILUs in many respects (Beer, 1985). Whether these firms are reluctant to go further because of section 8(a)(2) or because they fear creating genuine independent unions is not known.

At this point, public policy may have a role to play. Coordinated market economies such as Japan's and West Germany's exhibit high levels of innovation and an ability to pursue economic restructuring, which some experts attribute to the network of consultative relationships that exist at various levels in these societies, including plant-level works councils and enterprise unions (Wever, 1988; Soskice, 1990). To boost national competitiveness, public policy in the United States could be designed to encourage more industrial participation and consultation (including ILUs) because these would generate positive social externalities. The carrot for employers would come from the recent and growing tendency of courts and legislatures to regulate the workplace—everything from dismissal restrictions to mandated employee benefits. As that process unfolds, employers may prefer ILUs to standardized, top-down legislation and costly dismissal awards, especially if new legislation specifically exempts employers who negotiate private, customized terms with a national or company union.

Before that could happen, however, the law regulating company unions would have to be relaxed. In a piecemeal fashion, the courts have already taken a more permissive approach to the legality of EIPs. Their stance has been criticized by some legal scholars as contrary to the intent of the

Wagner Act (Kohler, 1986) and praised by others for opening up new avenues of choice for employees (Jackson, 1977). Somewhere between these positions are those who argue that the courts are steering the right course but for the wrong reasons: It is argued that all nonunion EIPs (presumably including employer-supported ILUs) should be legalized, not because they offer choices, although they might, but because they do no harm to anyone and pose no greater threat to national unions than benign outcomes such as high wages or good benefits, so long as these are not adopted during the course of a union campaign (Weiler, 1990).

But ILUs would not be appropriate for all workers. National unions still make sense for those sectors where EIPs have not taken hold, where personnel policies are not benign, and where management and workers expect the worst from each other. Yet there is a danger that a revised section 8(a)(2) might make it more difficult to organize or maintain national unions in these sectors. The purpose of any legal reform should be to expand the realm of representation, rather than change its composition. Therefore, a comprehensive revision of section 8(a)(2) might be offered to employers as a quid pro quo for changing those parts of the law that govern organizing campaigns and elections.

Conclusions

These are ambitious proposals to tack on to an empirical analysis of one company's industrial relations experience. We offer them in the hope of stimulating others to pursue more research on this topic. Ironically, American scholars with an interest in industrial relations reform probably know more about European works councils than they do about ILUs in the United States. Future research should occur along several vectors. First, we need to identify factors that cause organizational characteristics of ILUs to vary across and within firms. We know that TRW's ILUs differed from one plant to another, but what caused those variations? How and why do ILUs differ from firm to firm? Second, we need more information on the attitudes of workers, managers, and union leaders toward this kind of unionism, especially more case studies. Finally, we need more research that compares different institutional models for handling industrial relations—both within the United States (e.g., ILUs versus EIPs) and across national boundaries (e.g., EIPs versus works councils)—in terms of their impact on workers, firms, and nations. Policy-oriented research on ILUs holds great promise for those interested in improving workplace relations and economic performance in the United States.

Advance Notice: From Voluntary Exchange to Mandated Benefits

JOHN T. ADDISON and PEDRO PORTUGAL*

WITH THE PASSAGE OF THE Worker Adjustment and Retraining Notification Act (WARN) (Public Law 100–379) in 1988, the United States joined the ranks of the majority of industrialized nations that regulate collective dismissals.[1] The considerable controversy surrounding the U.S. legislation prompts first a review of the cases for and against mandatory notice and then, using three nationally representative displaced worker data sets, an examination of the most obvious potential benefit of notification, namely, its role in facilitating the redeployment of labor. Since our analysis is based on the outcome of a voluntary exchange process, we also investigate the sensitivity of the results to the selection of workers into notification status. Finally, we look at the challenges to government, unions, and employers posed by the new instrument.

The Controversy

The case against mandatory notice. This argument is disarmingly simple. Firms will incur greater liabilities in the event of a business downturn and

---

*The authors' affiliations are, respectively, Department of Economics, University of South Carolina; and Institut für industriewirtschaftliche Forschung, Westfälische Wilhelms Universität Münster and Faculdade de Economia, Universidade do Porto. An earlier version of this paper was presented at the Bundesanstalt für Arbeit, Nürnberg, and the Institut für Quantitative Wirtschaftsforschung, Universität, Hannover. The authors wish to thank seminar participants for their useful comments.

[1]Full details of the legislation and its precursors are given in Addison and Portugal (1991).

159

will cut back on hiring during the expansion phase. The higher costs of doing business resulting from a mandated standard, which may also be viewed as an increase in fixed costs, will discourage new business formation. Market solutions in the form of advance notice can be weighed against other forms of compensation according to workers' preferences and firms' costs, with prenotification part of a "payment bundle" freely negotiated between employers and workers. If workers value prenotification rights, these will enter the package of benefits and will presumably be reflected in a lower wage, ceteris paribus. In some contracts notice will figure; in others it will not. In the former case, the costs to employers will tend to be small relative to the gains to employees, thus providing scope for a beneficial trade. On the other hand, where the costs to employers are relatively large and the benefits to workers relatively small, there will not be notice clauses in individual and collective contracts. Firms that can provide notice most cheaply will attract workers who value prenotification of impending job loss, whereas those for whom notice is more costly will attract workers who value it less. Therefore, in the absence of constraints, a privately optimal incidence (and duration) of notice will result from a purely voluntary exchange process, and there is no scope for political activism.

The case for mandating notice. This argument is equally stark. Workers do not possess sufficient information to make the type of trades envisaged by the market model, with the result that wage differentials do not accurately reflect their differential exposure to unemployment risk. Prenotification improves worker information about the nature of their jobs (so that workers do not continue to make investments in redundant skills), while speeding the reallocation of labor in the event of displacement. By imposing a "tax" on layoffs, it also discourages their use. It is not denied that mandating benefits incurs costs, only that these are likely to be small and the gains relatively large. The market-failure argument is buttressed by the alleged divergence between private and social costs (e.g., community losses do not figure in the private costs of employers and thus are not taken into account in closure and layoff decisions).

The issues. The evidence on these competing claims is mixed. Various studies document compensation for differences in industry cyclicality, for firm-specific and systematic risks of unemployment, for both temporary and permanent layoffs, and for the incidence and/or duration of unemployment (Abowd and Ashenfelter, 1981; Topel, 1984; Adams, 1985; Li, 1986; Hamermesh and Wolfe, 1986). Such differentials are extremely sensitive to unobserved individual heterogeneity (Murphy and Topel, 1987). There is also some evidence that workers are surprised by their displacement to the extent that their investments in firm-specific training do not appear to decline as displacement approaches (Hamermesh, 1987). Yet recent research has questioned the ability of the tenure argument in the conventional wage equation to capture firm-specific training investments (e.g., Addison and Portugal, 1989b). An additional problem is, of course, that worker insurance for unanticipated events can never be complete. Accordingly, unless appropriately qualified, the case for mandatory prenotification based on the provision of insurance for unanticipated events would imply that owners of firms should also be compensated for unanticipated losses of their investments in firm-specific human and physical capital!

Studies of wage differentials and estimates of the human capital losses suffered by ill-informed workers do not provide much guidance on the efficacy of mandated notice. Before turning to more direct evidence, however, are there not other theoretical considerations that might lead us to expect constraints on the ability of workers to trade off wages for an instrument capable of limiting their exposure to market risk? One rather promising line of inquiry focusing on private contracting failure has been suggested by Deere and Wiggins (1988), who argue that efficient contracts may be expected to contain notice provisions in the presence of job-matching costs that create quasi-rent flows in the employment relation. In the case of reliance investments, Deere and Wiggins argue that turnover and investment decisions affect the value of a job match over its life and that a worker who expects to receive notice will evince a lower quit rate than one who does not. Reduced quit behavior influences the expected duration of a job match and therefore the incentives of both sides to invest in productivity-augmenting, job-specific assets. Workers with no notice will exhibit higher quit rates, at least up to the point at which notice is formally communicated to their notified counterparts. Thereafter, notified workers may be expected to quit at rates that are typical for nonnotified workers, but since the notice interval falls below the expected and actual life of the job match, factors that improve the net economic value of the match will dominate and ensure the Pareto optimality of notice. Indeed, in this model, absence of notification emerges as prejudicial to the survival of marginal firms.

But if some positive level of notice is predicted to be a feature of *all* optimal contracts, why is there only a patchwork coverage of notification clauses? Deere and Wiggins (1988) argue that firms' efficient promises to provide notice will not generally be time-consistent: A firm that promises to give notice obtains the benefit of a more stable labor force irrespective of whether or not it actually delivers on its promise. Since the cost of advance notice is a higher turnover rate, the firm has an incentive to renege. In the conventional contracts literature, employer exploitation of information asymmetries is circumscribed by reputation effects.[2] Unfortunately, the reputational effects mechanism presupposes the continued existence of the firm but fails if the firm is going out of business. On the other hand, if the firm is merely shedding a part of its labor force or, if closing, is part of a multiplant entity, the reputation effects mechanism may be sufficient to secure contract enforcement and the credibility of the promise to notify.

Might not contractual remedies exist that also allow the time inconsistency problem to be surmounted? Here, Deere and Wiggins draw a valuable distinction between individual and collective contracts in limiting opportunistic behavior by employers. Although individual contracts may appear optimal by virtue of their flexibility, they are not only costly to reach but also, and more importantly, costly to enforce. In particular, remedial action via the courts has important costs, which may limit the credibility of an individual suit for breach, whereas coordination costs among workers who have not agreed before the event to act in concert may dominate the economies of class-action suits.[3]

In emphasizing the limitations of individual contracts, Deere and Wiggins do not recognize that the price of notice to the individual worker may considerably exceed the costs. Whatever the benefits of notice, the probability of permanent job loss is likely to be small. Moreover, the firm confronts the risk that information supplied to the individual worker will become generalized throughout the labor force, thus raising the price that the individual has to pay for a prenotification clause. Both factors are important in explaining why notice provisions may not be a pervasive feature of individual contracts, and neither possibility is recognized in the authors' model.

Deere and Wiggins do, however, emphasize that the time-inconsistency problem of providing notice is largely surmounted in the presence of unionization. Not only is the process of contract negotiation much simplified, with an attendant reduction in negotiation costs, but also, and much

---

[2]Opportunistic behavior or employer malfeasance will impact on the firm by preempting reliance investments on the part of workers and by raising wage costs.

[3]Individual contracts may contain performance bonds, whereby employer malfeasance activates a tangible monetary penalty. Deere and Wiggins (1988) argue that such "hostages" are unlikely to be effective, either because they are not credible (i.e., they imply too great a departure from employment-at-will) or because they will be subject to duplication. An instrument designed to avoid litigation is thus quickly returned to the courts.

more importantly, the union provides a more effective mechanism for contract enforcement. By definition, unions prevent competitive rent seeking in the pursuit of contractual remedies and provide a more credible threat in those circumstances where few assets are available. (Similarly, unions assist in the negotiating, policing, and disposition of contractual hostages.) Nevertheless, they pose a downside risk: Although facilitating the provision of optimal levels of prenotification, unions may have other effects that reduce the firm's share of the match and therefore reduce capital investment (Addison and Hirsch, 1989). Implicitly, then, advance notice is seen by Deere and Wiggins as offering a substitute for collective action by the workforce.

In sum, the authors provide a number of reasons why one is unlikely to observe comprehensive notice provisions in voluntary trades. The unifying theme is the time inconsistency of promises to give notice. Reputation effects will not constrain firm behavior in the case of single-plant closings, and the substitute mechanism of explicit contracts is unlikely to be effective in the absence of a collective bargaining agreement. Although there is some tension between individual and collective costs and benefits in the authors' underlying model—as a result of which they fail to recognize that the number of employees may be an important determinant of notice in the presence of transaction costs—Deere and Wiggins provide a cogent analysis of why private contractual enforcement systems are costly to use and may fail to provide notice even when it is efficient. Private contracting failure thus provides a basis for mandating notice. The justification of a public rule lies in the enforcement of a promise to give notice; it does not directly address the question of a legislated standard. The strong case for notification rests on plant closings rather than on "mass" layoffs.

A case can also be made for mandating notice even in those situations where reputational effects and contractual remedies are sufficient to generate the privately optimal quantity of advance notice. For example, the presence of unemployment insurance benefits could artificially reduce the costs to employees of not receiving notice, thereby producing too little notification *and* inefficient quits in the system as a whole. Trades that might otherwise be acceptable may not be worthwhile in the presence of an unemployment subsidy. (Here, as earlier, we relax the assumption of Deere and Wiggins' model that all contracts will provide notice, though not the assumption of maximizing behavior, because it is an unnecessary feature of their model that interior solutions will necessarily obtain.) Imperfect experience rating (together with the costs borne by communities in the wake of displacement) may also be expected to produce a divergence between private and social costs, thereby providing a second-best argument for notice. The conventional remedy is to impose a tax on plant closings. Advance notice—to the extent that it raises employment adjustment costs—may be viewed as one such tax. Although it avoids the complexities of other compensation schemes and works in the desired direction of introducing "better decisions" on the part of management, its benefits clearly accrue to workers who may have already been compensated for their greater exposure to unemployment risk.

A final argument is that prenotification allows employers, workers, and the community to see what ways exist to save jobs (Ehrenberg and Jakubson, 1989). Thus, the information asymmetry problem may lead workers to reject proposed wage reductions even if these are legitimate, thereby producing possible allocative inefficiencies (Furubotn and Wiggins, 1984). Advance notice performs the function of concentrating the minds of the parties and assisting in an information exchange process that may prevent closure in those circumstances where viable long-run solutions are possible. The local community may offer tax concessions and various other forms of support, which themselves may carry strings. Minimally, prenotification should enhance the effectiveness of existing manpower instruments if these can be activated prior to, or at least shortly after, the point of layoff. A possible downside risk is that advance notice may trigger lobbying efforts for governmental protection in the manner suggested by the grants-aided economy, that is, to create induced property rights (Hamermesh, 1989).

Thus, a case can be made for the proposition that markets do not necessarily provide either privately or socially optimal levels of notice. Much depends on how labor markets operate *and* the nature of implementation costs. It is one thing to argue that we will observe suboptimal notice provisions in private contracts, quite another to formulate an appropriate public standard. The costs and benefits of providing notice will differ from situation to situation. Although there is some flexibility in the Worker Adjustment and Retraining Act, the 60-day standard remains a thorny issue. A preferred solution—suggested by Deere and Wiggins (1988)—would be to establish some notice interval as a default value and allow the parties to negotiate around this standard. In any event, standards should clearly not reflect supposedly best practice codes set under voluntary agreements, and the inflexibility problem remains a difficult issue for those who support prenotification.

We next investigate the effects of advance notice on one major indicator of dislocation cost, namely, the duration of joblessness following displacement, and examine whether the impact of notice is a chimera produced by sample selection. Our analysis relates primarily to the benefits side, and much more work is required on the cost implications of notice before strong conclusions can be drawn about the efficacy of the U.S. legislation.

Model and Data

If advance notice is to have any beneficial effect on unemployment duration, it must presumably reflect on-the-job search during the notice interval. We do not assume, as have other analysts, that on-the-job search is a preserve of notified workers alone. In our model, we allow for the possibility that both groups search while employed. We anticipate that on-the-job search is more intensive for notified workers during the lead time offered by advance notice than for other workers over a corresponding interval, although this is an empirical question and the focus of our inquiry.

For both groups of workers, observed unemployment will fall short of total search time by the amount of on-the-job search undertaken. For nonnotified workers, the natural logarithm of unemployment duration may be expressed as:

$$LnU_{A_0} = X\beta - OJS_{A_0} + \mu, \tag{1}$$

where the subscript A_0 denotes (non)notification status, X is a vector of search covariates, and OJS denotes on-the-job search.[4] (Expected median unemployment duration is thus $\hat{U} = exp^{X\beta - OJS_{A_0}}$.) Similarly, for notified workers, we may write:

$$LnU_{A_0} = X\beta - OJS_{A_1} + \mu'. \tag{2}$$

Observed unemployment across both groups of workers is:

$$\begin{aligned}
LnU = D_{A_0}(X\beta - OJS_{A_0} + \mu) + D_{A_1}(X\beta - OJS_{A_1} + \mu') \\
= X\beta - OJS_{A_0} + (OJS_{A_0} - OJS_{A_1})D_{A_1} \\
+ \mu + (\mu' - \mu)D_{A_1},
\end{aligned} \tag{3}$$

where D_{A_0} and D_{A_1} are dummy variables identifying the two groups of nonnotified and notified workers. We do not observe on-the-job search and cannot estimate it for either category of worker. The parameter OJS_{A_0} cannot, therefore, be identified from the available data, and the same is

---

[4]Since unemployment duration is a positive random variable, use of a log-linear specification guarantees that predicted values of unemployment will be nonnegative. Moreover, on-the-job search is specified in this model as a proportion of total search time.

true for OJS_{A_1}. As is clear from equation (3), the OJS_{A_0} parameter will be picked up in the intercept term, whereas $(OJS_{A_0} - OJS_{A_1})$ can be estimated directly. In other words, the difference between the unemployment duration of notified and nonnotified workers enables us to capture the differential search intensity of the two groups during the time period corresponding to the notice interval. Moreover, this differential search intensity is scaled in terms of unemployment time.[5] The present model imposes no restrictions on the search intensities of on-the-job search vis-à-vis of-the-job search, merely that the technology of postdisplacement search is the same for equally situated groups.

The model to be estimated is simply:

$$LnU = X\beta' + (OJS_{A_0} - OJS_{A_1})D_{A_1} + \epsilon, \qquad (4)$$

where ϵ represents the composite error term given in equation (3) is assumed to be normally distributed with mean zero and variance σ^2. Experimentation with other distributional assumptions for unemployment duration (and, by implication, the error term) reveal that the lognormal distribution performed either as well or better than the other special cases of the extended generalized gamma distribution.[6] The lognormal distribution implies that the hazard function, depicting the instantaneous escape rate from unemployment, conforms to an inverse U-shape.

Before turning to the specific form of the model, observe that although the model specification guarantees that the dependent variable cannot take negative values, equation (4) cannot be estimated via ordinary least squares methods.[7] This is because of censoring produced by incomplete or otherwise unmeasured spells of joblessness in the data set employed. There are two sources of right censoring in the duration data. Continuous unemployment duration data are supplied for up to 99 weeks of joblessness, at which point the data are top-coded. To those workers who are currently in an ongoing spell of unemployment of shorter duration than the 99-week cutoff, therefore, must be added those groups who may be either employed or unemployed but whose joblessness has exceeded or exceeds 99 weeks by an unknown margin. Using maximum likelihood methods, we

---

[5]Clearly, if the nonnotified do not engage in on-the-job search, as the displacement literature has assumed, then the observed impact of notice will pick up the length of the notice interval (scaled in unemployment time), although some assumption has still to be made as to differential search intensity on and off the job.

[6]For tests of distributional assumption using this data, employing both accelerated failure time and proportional hazards models, see Addison and Portugal (1987a) and Portugal and Addison (1989).

[7]As a practical matter, spells of jobless duration of zero weeks are coded as .25 weeks.

account for both censored and uncensored observations and accommodate the stochastic nature of the point of censoring.[8] The likelihood function is expressed in terms of the parameters of the model:

$$L = \sum_{i=1}^{n} \delta_i \ln [f(\epsilon)/\sigma] + (1 - \delta_i) \ln F(\epsilon), \tag{5}$$

where n is the number of observations, and δ_i is an indicator variable that assumes the value of unity if the observation is not censored and zero if the observation is right censored. Respectively, $f(\epsilon)$ and $F(\epsilon)$ are the density and survivor functions of the error term, and σ is the standard deviation of the error term.

Our basic estimating equation derived from (4) is:

$$\begin{aligned} LnU = {} & \alpha_0 + \alpha_1 ADVNOT + \alpha_2 SCHOOL + \alpha_3 AGE + \alpha_4 \\ & TENURE \\[4pt] & + \alpha_5 \, lnwage1 + \alpha_6 \, MARRIED + \alpha_7 \, WHITE + \alpha_8 \\ & UNSKILLED \\[4pt] & + \alpha_9 \, UNSKILLED \cdot ADVNOT + \alpha_{10} \, CLOSE + \alpha_{11} \\ & ABOLISH \\[4pt] & + \text{year of displacement, city size, industry, and} \\ & \text{regional dummies} \end{aligned} \tag{6}$$

Equation (6) is clearly a reduced form equation in which the variables affect the arrival rate of job offers, the offered wage distribution, and/or search costs. Our focus is, of course, on the role of the advance notification variable (ADVNOT), whose coefficient picks up the differential on-the-job search intensity of notified vis-à-vis nonnotified workers during the time period corresponding to the notice interval, scaled in terms of unemployment time.

Equation (6) is estimated across all three Displaced Worker Surveys, conducted as supplements to the January 1984, 1986, and 1988 Current Population Surveys. This five-year retrospective data set has been well described in Flaim and Seghal (1985), Addison and Portugal (1987b), and Podgursky and Swaim (1987). Briefly, each of the surveys identifies three principal reasons for job loss: plant closings (CLOSE), abolition of shift or

---

[8] Censored observations contribute to the likelihood function through the survival function; in other words, multiple censoring points are accommodated.

position (ABOLISH), and "slack work," which is the reference job-loss category in equation (6).[9] Second, it is important to note that the measure of unemployment in the 1984 and 1986 surveys may include more than one spell of joblessness if the respondent associates these with the initial job loss. It may even include a period of inactivity or nonparticipation. By contrast, the 1988 survey for the first time identifies single spells of jobless-ness in the wake of redundancy, although the reported duration values may still include a spell of nonparticipation. We should thus expect some reduction in reported unemployment duration for the most recent survey, irrespective of favorable macroeconomic developments.

Third, the 1984 and 1986 surveys do not distinguish between written or formally communicated notice; the relevant question in the surveys merely asks, "Did [you] expect a layoff or had [you] received advance notice of a layoff or plant or business closing?" Moreover, no information on the notice duration is provided. The broad notification question is the same in the 1988 survey, but it also asks those responding in the affirmative whether or not they had received formal notice of their impending displace-ment and, if so, the length of notice provided (in intervals of less than one month, more than one month but less than two months, and greater than or equal to two months).[10]

Finally, we restrict our sample to those workers who were displaced from full-time, nonagricultural employment and who were economically active and between 20 and 61 years of age by the end of the survey date. Separate regressions were run for male and female workers by broad occupational status.

Findings

Lognormal distribution estimates of the duration equation are provided in Table 1 for four gender-occupation groups across each of the five-year retrospective surveys. Although the main focus of our inquiry is on the impact of advance notice (ADVNOT) on joblessness, there are other empirical regularities in the data. Common themes across gender and occupation include the significantly negative association between jobless duration and years of schooling (SCHOOL), being white (WHITE), and

---

[9]Other sources of job loss identified in the survey comprise seasonal work cessations, failure of a self-employment business, and the catch-all category "Other," none of which is easily reconciled with dislocation per se.

[10]To ensure consistency among surveys, we do not here distinguish between formal and written notice. However, for an analysis of the differential impact of formal and informal notice, see Addison and Portugal (1989a).

layoff by reason of plant closure (CLOSE). The last reflects the absence of a waiting for recall effect in the case of plant closings, unlike the omitted category of slack work, together with compositional effects attendant upon laying off the entire labor force in the event of plant closure (the two other sources of job loss offering some scope for employer discretion). In addition, there is a positive association between duration and age (AGE), years of tenure on the lost job (TENURE), and, for blue-collar workers, between duration and lower levels of job skill (UNSKILLED). Interestingly, the effects of marital status (MARRIED) are consistently opposite in sign for male and female workers, and the same is true for the natural log of the previous wage (lnWAGE1) in the case of blue-collar versus white-collar workers.

Regarding the impact of advance notification, in all but one of the 12 regressions, negative coefficients were obtained on the notification status dummy. In our model, this reflects much heightened search intensity during the notice interval. Since search is scaled in terms of jobless duration, it follows that prenotification is, in general, associated with heightened search activity during the notice interval and therefore much reduced unemployment in the wake of displacement. Table 2 presents computed median durations of unemployment for our sample on the basis of the coefficients reported in Table 1 and the mean values of the independent variables. In all but one case, the predicted jobless duration of notified workers falls below that for nonnotified workers. The reported percentage savings in unemployment time (last column) are the exponents of the coefficients on ADVNOT − 1 taken from the second row of Table 1.

Although advance notice clearly "works" by stimulating on-the-job search during the notice interval, the instrument has only limited potential for reducing the jobless duration of unskilled blue-collar workers, ceteris paribus. Thus, four out of six of the interaction terms given in Table 1 are both positive and of large magnitude. Apparently, unskilled workers have difficulty in converting the information conveyed by notice into a productive job search. This phenomenon must reflect, at least in part, broader informational deficits, and it may also be true of female versus male workers and blue-collar versus white-collar workers. Another possibility is that notice may be given to those (unskilled) workers most likely to confront reemployment difficulties.[11] Yet another possibility is that, given their information set, the intervals of notice extended to the unskilled are simply too short.

---

[11]This is a problem for the analysis of the jobless duration of female blue-collar workers because the sample is dominated by unskilled workers.

TABLE 1

THE IMPACT OF ADVANCE NOTICE AND OTHER DETERMINANTS OF JOBLESS DURATION BY BROAD OCCUPATIONAL STATUS AND GENDER

(lognormal distribution estimates; asymptotic standard errors in parentheses)

Variable	1984 DWS Blue Collar M	1984 DWS Blue Collar F	1984 DWS White Collar M	1984 DWS White Collar F	1986 DWS Blue Collar M	1986 DWS Blue Collar F	1986 DWS White Collar M	1986 DWS White Collar F	1988 DWS Blue Collar M	1988 DWS Blue Collar F	1988 DWS White Collar M	1988 DWS White Collar F
Constant	3.381*	3.275***	6.841*	5.801*	4.041*	4.559*	5.735*	4.325*	2.354*	.982	3.087*	2.350*
	(.691)	(1.677)	(.800)	(1.024)	(.787)	(1.392)	(.750)	(.952)	(.640)	(1.360)	(.679)	(.768)
ADVNOT	−.254***	−.194	−.461*	−.334**	−.482*	−.590	−.275**	−.087	−.313**	.525	−.344**	−.155
	(.138)	(.437)	(.123)	(.148)	(.154)	(.382)	(.124)	(.144)	(.130)	(.351)	(.118)	(.112)
SCHOOL	−.116*	−.177*	−.103*	−.080**	−.131*	−.164*	−.072*	−.108*	−.022	−.066***	−.041	−.059**
	(.023)	(.045)	(.026)	(.038)	(.026)	(.043)	(.027)	(.036)	(.021)	(.037)	(.266)	(.029)
AGE	.016*	.004	.017**	.016**	.018*	.004	.024*	.022*	.020*	.006	.027*	.018*
	(.006)	(.010)	(.007)	(.008)	(.006)	(.009)	(.008)	(.007)	(.005)	(.009)	(.007)	(.006)
TENURE	.022**	.018	.015	.025	.020**	.017	.014	−.003	.023*	.006	−.010	.004
	(.010)	(.023)	(.012)	(.022)	(.010)	(.017)	(.013)	(.020)	(.008)	(.017)	(.010)	(.014)
lnWAGE1	.138	.711**	−.339**	−.281	.183	.151	−.279**	−.135	.001	.189	−.153	−.025
	(.111)	(.286)	(.148)	(.188)	(.127)	(.227)	(.141)	(.173)	(.105)	(.224)	(.126)	(.146)
MARRIED	−.549*	.083	−.538*	.138	−.298*	−.001	−.558*	.167	−.254**	.377**	−.210	.216***
	(.106)	(.198)	(.140)	(.152)	(.116)	(−.169)	(.136)	(.143)	(.100)	(.166)	(.131)	(.113)
WHITE	−.862*	−1.768*	−1.032*	−1.183*	−1.018*	−.698*	−1.025*	−.893*	−.715*	−.374	−.489**	−.448*
	(.157)	(.286)	(.223)	(.251)	(.170)	(.214)	(.251)	(.217)	(.147)	(.234)	(.194)	(.166)

	(1)	(2)	(3)	(4)	(5)	(6)	(7)	(8)	(9)	(10)	(11)	(12)
UNSKILLED	.117	.224	—	—	.328**	-.239	—	—	.013	.240	—	—
	(.137)	(.374)			(.154)	(.323)			(.138)	(.316)		
UNSKILLED/ ADVNOT	.280	-.080	—	—	.314	.291	—	—	.378**	-.143	—	—
CLOSE	-.499*	-.310	-.623*	-.625*	-.615*	-.289	-.723*	-.560*	-.423*	-.503*	-.273**	-.753*
	(.099)	(.211)	(.139)	(.170)	(.111)	(.193)	(.142)	(.171)	(.096)	(.186)	(.139)	(.140)
ABOLISH	-.262	-.262	-.229	-.2211	-.530*	.091	.192	-.165	-.498*	-.326	-.134	-.257
	(.186)	(.357)	(.178)	(.215)	(.199)	(.356)	(.178)	(.209)	(.174)	(.296)	(.167)	(.174)
YEAR 1	-.218	-.119	-.408***	.381	.300***	-.270	.266	.563**	.157	.464	.180	.721*
	(.171)	(.331)	(.217)	(.269)	(.166)	(.264)	(.207)	(.238)	(.144)	(.288)	(.192)	(.184)
YEAR 2	-.124	-.272	-.509**	-.256	.037	.664**	.347***	.754*	-.199	.486***	-.003	.422*
	(.149)	(.307)	(.203)	(.234)	(.149)	(.270)	(.183)	(.219)	(.142)	(.260)	(.196)	(.176)
YEAR 3	.050	.140	.132	.010	-.117	.113	.064	.538*	.012	.607**	-.165	.441*
	(.135)	(.298)	(.184)	(.214)	(.158)	(.254)	(.190)	(.205)	(.128)	(.243)	(.167)	(.157)
YEAR 4	.383*	.076	.138	.061	-.153	-.164	.007	.178	.201	.506**	.014	.179
	(.126)	(.281)	(.167)	(.196)	(.156)	(.253)	(.172)	(.205)	(.128)	(.243)	(.167)	(.154)
σ	2.004	2.053	1.895	2.022	2.025	1.680	1.892	1.899	1.725	1.466	1.796	1.712
Scale parameter	(.038)	(.082)	(.048)	(.058)	(.042)	(.067)	(.047)	(.054)	(.033)	(.060)	(.042)	(.041)
Log likelihood	-3685.95	-902.03	-1866.06	-1531.57	-3077.41	-766.30	-1874.62	-1452.22	-2970.21	-587.37	-1927.84	-1902.22
N	2,299	598	1,057	876	1,850	509	1,044	808	1,649	363	1,025	1,041

SOURCE: Displaced Worker Surveys, 1984, 1986, 1988.
[a]The equations also included city size, industry, and regional dummies.
*, **, ***denote significance at the .01, .05, and .10 levels, respectively.

TABLE 2

Computed Median Weeks of Jobless Duration by Notification Status, Gender, and Broad Occupational Status

Survey Sample	Nonnotified	Notified	Percentage Reduction
1984 DWS			
BC[a] males	24.829	19.255	−22.450
BC females	38.242	31.509	−17.603
WC[b] males	13.329	8.410	−38.120
WC females	16.549	11.854	−28.370
1986 DWS			
BC males	18.598	11.481	−38.268
BC females	31.354	17.388	−44.543
WC males	9.623	7.308	−24.057
WC females	9.709	8.897	−8.363
1988 DWS			
BC males	7.853	5.742	−26.881
BC females	10.188	17.227	+69.091
WC males	6.818	4.835	−29.085
WC females	6.723	5.756	−14.383

Source: Displaced Worker Surveys, 1984, 1986, 1988.
[a]Blue collar.
[b]White collar.

These results indicate that advance notice is successful in reducing the joblessness of displaced workers, especially for male workers. But it is a very large step to proceed from results such as these to the conclusion that prenotification should be mandated. Opponents of the WARN Act would consider these findings much as expected: Notice is given in precisely those circumstances in which it is beneficial; otherwise, it would not be a feature of the individual or collective contract.

To investigate this issue requires that we at least explore the possible endogeneity of notice and its contribution to the single-equation results. To this end, we ran probit equations in which the independent variables mirror those of the duration equation, but *exclude* the year of displacement and industry dummies and *include* a dummy variable identifying receipt of health insurance benefits on the lost job—a proxy for fringe benefits and possibly union status as well. The probit equations were used to construct two selectivity arguments for inclusion in separate notified worker and nonnotified worker duration equations.

Use of this standard Heckman two-stage approach is precluded in the event of censored duration data. Our unemployment duration data are right-censored. Accordingly, a conscious decision was made to limit the data taken from the Displaced Worker Surveys to the first three years of each, thereby ensuring that two years will have passed since the event of displacement and that the vast majority of employment spells will be completed.

Selection terms from the notified and nonnotified workers duration equations are given in Table 3. With the exception of one coefficient, the inverse Mills' ratio terms are statistically insignificant at conventional levels (and in some cases, the implied correlation coefficients are outside the bounds -1, 1). Every possible combination of signs is encountered: positive and negative selection, negative and positive selection, negative and negative selection, and even positive selection in both the notified and nonnotified worker equations (which is, of course, a theoretical nonsense). Positive and negative selection terms imply a "tortoise-and-hare" effect: Those who would ordinarily suffer greater-than-average unemployment select into the notified worker category, thereby limiting their exposure to displacement costs. Negative and positive selection implies that notified workers are better suited to cope with displacement *and*, in addition, enjoy the benefits of notice. Unlike the previous case, this implies that the single-equation estimates are upwardly biased. Finally, negative selection in both equations suggests that notified and nonnotified workers alike are better off by virtue of their particular notification status: Workers sort themselves into sectors where they have the better possibility of being reemployed.

TABLE 3

SELECTIVITY COEFFICIENTS FROM THE NOTIFIED AND NONNOTIFIED WORKER UNEMPLOYMENT DURATION EQUATIONS

	1984 DWS			1986 DWS			1988 DWS		
	IMR[a]	SD[b]	N	IMR	SD	N	IMR	SD	N
Blue Collar									
Males									
Notified	−2.971	2.829	492	−0.776	2.639	454	−0.796	1.246	471
Nonnotified	0.621	2.539	426	1.835	2.222	434	−0.698	1.284	364
Females									
Notified	9.727	26.519	131	−2.886	3.337	134	0.047	0.973	105
Nonnotified	3.982	10.623	123	1.579	4.414	109	−0.078	0.907	77
White Collar									
Males									
Notified	9.766	13.298	184	−0.686	2.401	190	−0.255	1.541	241
Nonnotified	−3.269	5.544	186	−0.784	1.644	205	−1.064	0.970	266
Females									
Notified	1.142	2.392	148	−1.832	3.830	181	1.974	2.423	263
Nonnotified	1.181	2.455	130	−10.631	3.685	143	3.520	2.179	235

SOURCE: Displaced Worker Surveys, 1984, 1986, 1988.
[a]Inverse Mills' ratio.
[b]Standard deviation.

Had we more faith in the underlying probit equations and a more consistent story to tell, we could use the results to predict the effect of mandating notice. Thus, for example, had we obtained results consistent with a tortoise-and-hare type of explanation, the expected unemployment duration of nonnotified workers computed from the notified worker regression (the product of the coefficients and the mean values of the variables *less* the positive selection term) would imply a gain in terms of reduced unemployment. But if all workers were to be notified, it is also implied that the non-notified-worker gain from being in a nonnotice regime would be lost. The expected duration of nonnotified workers computed from the nonnotified worker regression (which is again the product of the coefficients and the mean values of the corresponding variable but this time *plus* the selection term) would have to be subtracted from the former value. The difference would provide a measure of the effect of mandating notice.

This might appear rather academic, given the insignificance of the inverse Mills' ratio terms, from which one might conclude that notice is exogenous and that the benefits discernible in the single-equation model can be generalized to a regime of mandated notice. Our interpretation of the evidence is that the unemployment-reducing effect of advance notice is not a chimera produced by sample selection. We do not go further because of the failure of the probit equations to provide more precise information on the benefits and costs to employees (that will, in turn, reflect the costs to employers). It is possible that the regressions will be subject to major parameter shifts in the presence of a legislated standard.

Even if our data set had enabled us to identify relevant cost factors, the analytical question remains whether the private costs borne by employers translate into social costs. One's position hinges on one's priors regarding the efficiency of regular markets. Even if such costs are deemed strictly private, a policy of mandated notice may well have to cope with transitory increases in unemployment. Nevertheless, the apparent randomness of notice is clearly a challenge to those who view the incidence and extent of notice as determined by a predictable set of trade-offs, not least because other evidence has pointed to a lack of association between predisplacement wages and notice (Ehrenberg and Jakubson, 1989).

Conclusions

We have seen that advance notice "works" because it produces pronounced reductions in median weeks of postdisplacement joblessness as a result of the heightened search intensity on the part of those notified. This saving in joblessness, if not in search time, is the principal benefit. Although other analyses have suggested that notification does not have a discernible impact on earnings (Podgursky and Swaim, 1987; Ehrenberg and Jakubson, 1989), allowing for the simultaneity between postdisplacement wages and jobless duration produces a strongly negative causal relation running from unemployment to wages. Accordingly, it seems that we can also credit advance notice with a positive *indirect* effect on earnings development (Addison and Portugal, 1989c).

Although advance notice seems to be a powerful determinant of jobless duration, unskilled workers confront greater difficulties than skilled workers in taking advantage of prenotification. The policy implication is that those with skill and informational deficits require more active assistance in job location than the mere provision of notice of impending job loss. But much more work is required on the receptivity of different subgroups to the information imparted by prenotification, including, of course, the possibility that notice is more likely to be given to those facing reemployment difficulties.

There is also some indication that white-collar workers have a bigger payoff from prenotification than blue-collar workers, although this result is not observed across all three surveys (Addison and Portugal, 1989c). This presumably reflects the better information networks possessed by white-collar workers and the fact that they appear to enjoy longer notification intervals *and* more comprehensive reemployment assistance, although our data do not allow us to address these issues.

Although in the case of female workers the coefficients on the advance notice dummy are both sizable and negative, they fail to achieve significance. These results should not be interpreted as implying that notice does not "work" for such groups because the alternatives available to females are imperfectly captured in our estimating equations. More work is required on modeling the differential supply responsiveness of females in an environment of notice.

Other intriguing issues that remain to be addressed concern the role of macroeconomic and local labor market variables in mediating the impact of notice, whether notice has longer-term benefits via its effects on the quality of the subsequent job match, and the precise mechanism by which the instrument achieves its apparent impact. New issues raised by the 1988 Displaced Worker Survey concern the length of the notice interval and the distinction between written and informal notice.

There are a number of difficulties when considering the implications of an analysis based on voluntary notice for a regime of mandated notice. Although we have outlined a procedure that in principle allows one to calculate the effects of mandated notice, its efficacy hinges on the performance of the underlying probit equation used to predict notification status. We are reluctant to place much weight on the probit equations, not least because of their failure systematically to incorporate the costs and benefits of notice to each side. In fact, the selection coefficients differ markedly in both magnitude and sign across surveys. Their insignificance suggests that notice is exogenous.

However, all this result really establishes is that the *benefits* of notice obtained in our single-equation model are not a chimera produced by sample selection. Failure adequately to model the different cost conditions and the implicit trade-offs confronting the diversity of employers in a voluntary notice regime means that our equations will be subject to parameter shifts following the introduction of mandatory notice. Therefore, we must be wary of arguing that the benefits carry over to a regime of mandated notice. Predictable employer responses to increases in employment adjustment/fixed costs point to reductions in the quantity of labor demanded. This will lead to an increase in duration, ceteris paribus. At issue is the precise scale of these *social* costs vis-à-vis the benefits.

Employers have perhaps exaggerated the cost implications of the Worker Adjustment and Retraining Notification Act. Moreover, there is an emerging body of evidence suggesting that firms do not lose their most qualified manpower during the notice interval or confront shirking behavior and other sources of productivity loss at this time. This analytical and case study material, however, falls short of an analysis of the costs of notice and how these may be expected to vary from firm to firm.

Given the exceptions contained in the legislation, the limitations on private contracting in regular labor markets, and the sheer scale of the private benefits recorded (which themselves imply major savings to the public purse), the legislation could produce substantial benefits on net. We are, of course, aware of the arbitrary nature of a 60-day standard and have outlined what we consider a better alternative.

The challenges to government, employers, and unions. The federal government needs to recognize the essentially experimental nature of the WARN Act and to monitor its consequences carefully. If the costs are more substantial than we surmise, there is a case for reducing the standard or for making it more flexible. Or the government could fund a share of the unemployment benefits received by notified workers and/or reduce firms' income tax rates. We are aware of no substantive analysis that suggests that the legislation should be strengthened or otherwise augmented on the lines envisaged in the plant-closing legislation of the 1970s.

Finally, our duration analysis points to a reduced emphasis on categorical manpower programs in favor of more selective instruments that meet the needs of those confronting special reemployment difficulties. Such groups include the unskilled, those with educational deficits, and blacks, none of whom has conspicuously benefited from past programs.

Employer resistance to the WARN Act, noted earlier, has less to do with the content of the legislation than with a fear that it is the thin end of an intrusive legislative wedge (McKenzie, 1989). Otherwise, there is no sense in the comparisons being drawn by employer groups between the WARN Act and the panoply of European job security legislation or to the over-simplistic parallels between comparative growth rates in employment across two very different market regimes. Judging the WARN Act as a single piece of legislation, however naive this might appear to some, the case for the new initiative still stands and, as our theoretical discussion has indicated, may even be associated with efficient contract formation. Given the problems of a uniform standard, however, employers should press for modifications in the legislation if their flexibility is impaired.

The position of unions has been to press for legislation at the state and federal levels (see, e.g., McKenzie and Yandle, 1982). In part, this activism has reflected developments in labor law wherein decision bargaining has not been construed as falling within the ambit of mandatory bargaining or the cost-effectiveness of the legislative route vis-à-vis the alternative of direct bargaining in which wages are traded for a measure of job security. And yet, if our analysis is correct, the extension of prenotification rights to all workers could weaken their incentive to join unions, and not only in declining sectors. Unions may have embarked on a legislative program that will have the effect of weakening their power. Now it is conceivable that union support for legislation is motivated by a concern for all workers. This is the position taken by Ehrenberg (1986), who, writing on union support for state laws limiting the common law at-will doctrine in a similar context of declining membership, notes: "This is not the first time that econometric evidence on the effects of labor legislation on union growth has had little effect on the position unions take with respect to the legislation" (p. 297). We do not think it a cynical view, however, to argue that unions, any less than other partisan groups, lobby for self-interest legislation. Judged in the narrowest of terms, prenotification might be expected to raise the demand for union labor by increasing the cost of nonunion labor, among which groups the incidence of notice is lower. Equally, one should not be surprised that the outcome of legislation has unintended consequences, especially in those circumstances where the basic legislation is much modified during the course of the legislative process. This very process of modification allows elected representatives to serve several constituencies simultaneously.

The challenge of the new legislation for unions is to develop more constructive policies with respect to the process of job destruction, specifically contractual measures that facilitate the redeployment of labor. Arguably, the Worker Adjustment and Retraining Notification Act could clear the way to a more cooperative attitude by both sides to the increasingly politicized issue of job security.

Incentive and Redistributive Effects of Private-Sector Union Pension Plans in Canada

JAMES E. PESANDO, MORLEY GUNDERSON,
and PAULINE SHUM*

WHILE PENSION COVERAGE IS higher in private-sector union firms than in private-sector nonunion firms in both Canada and the United States,[1] the type of pension plan is typically quite different in union firms than in nonunion firms. In the former, the majority of workers belong to flat benefit plans,[2] in which the pension benefit is equal to a fixed dollar amount for each year of service. By contrast, in the nonunion sector, the vast majority of members are in plans in which the pension benefit is linked by formula to the member's earnings in the years just prior to retirement. Analyzing the work incentive created by flat benefit plans in

*Director, Institute for Policy Analysis; director, Centre for Industrial Relations; and Ph.D. candidate, Department of Economics—all at the University of Toronto. We are indebted to David Fujimagari for programming assistance and to the Social Sciences and Humanities Research Council of Canada for financial support. Useful comments at the symposium were provided by our discussants Charles Davis, James Vaupel, and Paula Voos.

[1]In Canada, in 1984, nearly 77 percent of workers who were union members were covered by pension plans, compared with only 47 percent for the nonunion labor force (Statistics Canada, 1986). In the United States, in 1979, 76.4 percent of private-sector employees who were union members were covered by pension plans, compared with only 35.0 percent of nonunion employees (Kotlikoff and Smith, 1983).

[2]In Canada, in 1984, 83 percent of members of plans restricted to union members belonged to flat benefit plans; in the United States, in 1977, it was 59.3 percent compared with only 19.8 percent in the nonunion sector (Kotlikoff and Smith, 1983).

union firms, Mitchell and Fields (1985) and Kotlikoff and Wise (1987) recognized the importance of periodic enrichments to the benefit formula, but neither study examined the explicit enrichments that actually occur in union-negotiated plans.

This paper has four objectives: (1) to document the key provisions of flat benefit plans in Canada and their evolution over the period 1974–84, with particular attention to the periodic enrichment of flat benefit formulas; (2) to identify the work incentives created by flat benefit plans, with particular attention to early retirement provisions[3]; (3) to demonstrate how the retroactive enrichment of flat benefit formulas redistributes wealth across different age and service cohorts within union membership[4]; and (4) to explore the importance of anticipated enrichments to the benefit formula on the timing of early retirement decisions.

Flat Benefit Plans in Canada

The two key provisions of representative flat benefit plans in Canada are (1) a formula that defines the pension due at the normal retirement age set by the plan, and (2) the conditions under which a male member can retire with a pension before the plan's normal retirement age.

Normal retirement pensions. The typical flat benefit formula specifies that the pension due at the normal retirement age is equal to a fixed monthly amount for each year of service.[5] For example, if a plan member aged 55 has 20 years of service and if the current benefit formula is $20.00 per month, then the member is entitled on the basis of service now completed to a pension equal to $400.00 per month, beginning at the normal retirement age set by the plan, usually age 65.[6]

Because flat benefit formulas specify a fixed monthly payment for each

---

[3]According to Allen and Clark (1986), plan members tend to retire earlier under collectively bargained plans. In both Canada and the United States, participation rates for older males continued to fall. In Canada, at the beginning of 1986, the participation rate for males aged 55 to 64 stood at 69.4 percent, down sharply from 85.9 percent in 1961.

[4]Freeman (1985) hypothesizes that older workers exert a disproportionate impact on collectively bargained outcomes.

[5]We are using a database of 132 flat benefit plans, all under the jurisdiction of the Province of Ontario; these plans had 200 or more members in 1984.

[6]In 1984, e.g., 95.2 percent of members of flat benefit plans in Ontario were in plans with a normal retirement age of 65. This figure is based on a special run on the databank maintained by Statistics Canada for the publication *Pension Plans in Canada* because Statistics Canada does not publish data on normal retirement age in flat benefit plans. We found that considerably more than 50 percent of the members of flat benefit plans in Canada belong to plans registered in Ontario. Of the 132 flat benefit plans in our database, 120 had a normal retirement age of 65.

year of service, they are periodically updated through the collective bargaining process (and are usually made retroactive) during periods of inflation, as unions seek to maintain or increase the ratio of pension benefits to preretirement earnings. For example, during the time period of our study, 1974–84, the nominal benefit received by the median member of a flat benefit plan rose from $7.50 to $15.00 (Statistics Canada, 1986); however, the real benefit (i.e., the nominal benefit adjusted for inflation) received by the median plan member actually fell slightly, by 13.7 percent.

To appreciate the variation in both the magnitude and frequency of updating these formulas, the time paths in individual plans need to be examined. Table 1 presents the annual values of the flat benefit formulas

TABLE 1

BENEFIT FORMULAS FOR REPRESENTATIVE FLAT BENEFIT PLANS IN ONTARIO, 1974–84

Plan	1974	1976	1978	1980	1982	1984	Enrichment Ratio 1984/1974
1	5.00	5.00	8.00	8.00	10.00	10.00	2.00
2	7.00	7.00	10.00	10.00	10.00	12.50	1.67
3	6.25	7.25	8.50	9.00	10.00	12.00	1.92
4	7.25	9.75	13.50	13.50	13.50	13.50	1.86
5	4.35	7.00	8.00	9.50	10.50	11.00	2.53
6	5.00	7.00	8.50	8.50	8.50	8.50	1.70
7	7.50	9.50	9.50	11.00	16.00	16.00	2.13
8	6.00	8.00	8.00	10.50	10.50	15.00	2.50
9	4.50	4.50	6.50	9.00	9.00	11.50	2.56
10	8.00	10.00	12.00	12.00	15.00	17.00	2.13
11	6.00	6.00	8.00	12.00	12.00	13.00	2.17
12	6.25	8.75	10.00	11.00	13.00	13.50	2.16
13	4.25	6.50	8.00	8.00	8.00	12.00	2.82
14	6.50	6.50	7.50	9.25	11.00	12.50	1.92
15	4.50	6.00	6.00	8.00	10.00	11.00	2.44
16	5.00	6.00	6.00	7.50	10.00	10.00	2.00
17	7.25	9.25	9.25	11.75	14.25	15.00	2.07
18	7.00	7.00	10.00	12.00	12.00	17.00	2.43
19	13.00	17.90	17.90	17.90	17.90	17.90	1.38
20	11.00	11.00	11.00	18.45	18.45	18.45	1.67
21	6.50	8.00	9.00	10.50	11.00	12.50	1.92
22	5.75	5.75	7.50	11.00	13.30	18.45	3.21
23	5.75	5.75	9.50	9.50	17.00	17.00	2.96
24	7.50	11.00	12.00	12.00	15.00	16.00	2.13
25	8.00	8.00	8.00	8.00	10.00	14.00	1.75
Mean	6.61	7.94	9.28	10.71	12.23	13.81	2.09
Median	6.25	7.00	8.50	10.50	12.00	13.50	2.16

SOURCE: Pension Commission of Ontario.

for several representative plans in Ontario for selected years between 1974 and 1984. The experience of the median *plan* (12) in this sample is quite similar to that of the median plan *member* for the entire universe of flat benefit plans noted above. The benefit rose from $6.25 in 1974 to $13.50 in 1984.

Flat benefit formulas are often fixed for a succession of years and then increase sharply. Benefit enrichments of 30 to 40 percent in a single year are not uncommon. On the other hand, benefit formulas may increase every year, though the maximum is generally low. To the extent that workers can anticipate the timing of an enrichment, and especially if the enrichment is large, retirements may be deferred until an imminent increase in the benefit formula actually takes place.[7] This incentive effect is essential when considering the timing and magnitude of benefit enrichments.

Early retirement provisions. If a plan member qualifies for "early retirement," the member can retire at any time and draw an immediate, but *reduced*, annual pension benefit. The reduction in the annual pension benefit may be subsidized or unsubsidized (an actuarially fair reduction). If a plan member also qualifies for "special retirement," the member can retire and draw an immediate and unreduced annual pension benefit. Early retirees may also receive a "bridging supplement," a series of special payments designed to bridge the gap between early (or special) retirement and age 65, when the member is eligible to receive a public pension (Canada/Quebec Pension Plan) as well as Old Age Security.

Early retirement provisions are virtually universal in Canada and the United States. In our sample of 132 flat benefit plans in Ontario, 128, or 97.0 percent, contain early retirement provisions. There are two prevalent requirements for early retirement: the attainment of a minimum age, usually age 55, or the attainment of a minimum age *and* the completion of a minimum number of years of service. In our sample, the most prevalent requirement (in 33 plans) for early retirement was the attainment of age 55 and the completion of 10 years of service.

Early retirement plans require a reduction in the annual pension benefit that is either actuarially fair (so that no subsidy is involved) or a smaller reduction that involves a subsidy. The actuarially fair adjustment exactly compensates for the fact that the pension is payable immediately *and* over

---

[7]For a discussion of the impact of anticipated versus unanticipated increases in pension wealth on retirement behavior, see Anderson, Burkhauser, and Quinn (1986). An unanticipated enrichment in the benefit formula would represent an unanticipated increase in pension wealth, and hence an incentive to consume more leisure time, i.e., to retire.

a longer life expectancy. There is no change in the cost incurred by the employer, and there is no subsidy. For example, if a male plan member retires at age 55 with 20 years of service and if the interest rate is 8 percent (1974–84 time period), the actuarially fair early retirement pension would be $126.76 per month, instead of $400 per month, the pension due at normal retirement age (following the benefit formula of $20.00 per month for each year of service).

In contrast, a benefit reduction formula will typically provide a subsidy. This would be the case, for example, if the 55-year-old male qualifies for early retirement subject to a reduction of 5 percent for each year by which early retirement precedes the normal retirement age of 65. For a 55-year-old male who elects to retire, the early retirement pension will thus equal 50 percent of the pension due at the normal retirement age of 65, or $200 per month. This exceeds the actuarially fair pension by 58.8 percent. In our sample of 128 plans with early retirement provisions, subsidized early retirement is twice as prevalent as actuarially fair early retirement.

"Special retirement" provisions have more stringent eligibility conditions than those for early retirement. The early retiree receives *unreduced* annual pension benefits, which are payable immediately, last for a longer period, and involve a large subsidy.

Special retirement is generally directed toward the older, long-service worker. Typically, it requires either a higher age or a larger number of years of service, or both. In our sample, 43 percent of the 132 plans (57 plans) had special retirement provisions; 31 of the plans had no special retirement provisions *and* no subsidized early retirement. In these 31 plans (23% of the sample), there is no incentive to retire before age 65.

Because special retirement provisions provide particularly strong incentives, it is important to note that the incidence of special retirement has increased sharply over time. Of the 57 plans, 27 introduced the provision between 1974 and 1984. By contrast, of the 128 plans with early retirement, only five had introduced the provision during the same period. "Bridging supplements" in flat benefit plans bridge the period from early retirement to age 65 (and the subsequent receipt of public pension benefits). Like the flat benefit formula, they are expressed as a fixed monthly amount for each year of service, often to a maximum of 25 or 30 years. Bridging supplements can be large relative to the size of the normal retirement benefit. For example, in the master pension plan recently negotiated by the Canadian Auto Workers, the normal retirement benefit is $22.05 per month, while the bridging supplement is $18.00 per month, 81.6 percent of the basic benefit. About 50 percent of the flat benefit plans on file at the Pension Commission of Ontario provide bridging supplements, which range in value from 50 to 85 percent of the normal retirement benefit. Like the flat benefit formulas, bridging supplements tend to be negotiated upward over time.

The Time Path of Benefit Accruals

By calculating the time path of benefit accruals (expressed as a fraction of wages) for members of representative flat benefit plans, we can demonstrate the interaction, over a plan member's expected work life, of early, special, and normal retirement provisions, together with the periodic enrichment of the flat benefit formula. This interaction helps to identify the work incentives created by flat benefit plans.

Table 2 lists the pension benefits accrued by a hypothetical worker for two different pension plans. The worker began employment and plan membership at age 25, with an annual salary of $26,000. In the "stripped-down" plan, with actuarially reduced early retirement, no special retirement, and no bridging supplement, there is no subsidy for retirement before the normal retirement age of 65. The subsidized plan allows for early retirement at age 55 with 10 years of service, special retirement at age 58 with 30 years of service, and a bridging supplement equal to 70 percent of the normal retirement benefit. In both plans, pension benefits vest (i.e., the member becomes entitled to a nonforfeitable pension) after the member has completed 10 years of service.

The time paths of benefit accruals are calculated for an inflation rate of 5 percent, and the flat benefit formula is assumed to be enriched every third year by an amount equal to the cumulative inflation rate since the previous enrichment. The flat benefit formulas thus keep pace with inflation, with a lag, but do not increase in real terms. The interest rate used to value the annuities (pensions) due under the terms of the plan is set equal to the nominal interest rate of 8.15 percent.[8]

In the "stripped-down" plan, one observes the standard "backloading" of pension accruals,[9] which rose from less than 1 percent of wages when

---

[8]If retirees receive ad hoc cost-of-living adjustments, a lower interest rate would be appropriate. We reran these simulations with the interest rate set equal to 5.5 percent to reflect the case of partial inflation protection. This increases the value of the pension accruals but leaves their time paths essentially unchanged.

[9]Let PW(a) equal the member's pension wealth at age a. This equals the present value, discounted by interest and mortality, of the pension payments due the worker if the worker quits the plan at age a. The pension accrual at age (a+1) equals PW(a+1) − (1+r)*PW(a), and is scaled by the worker's wage at (a+1). The purpose of multiplying PW(a) by the interest factor is to recognize that if the worker left the plan at age a, the worker's pension wealth would increase by the interest factor. (One could imagine, e.g., pension wealth being transferred to the worker's own defined contribution or money

TABLE 2
The Time Path of Benefit Accruals

Benefit Formula	Age	Years of Service	Benefit Accrual/Wage "Stripped-Down" Plan	Subsidized Plan
15.00	25	0	0.0000	0.0000
15.00	26	1	0.0000	0.0000
15.00	27	2	0.0000	0.0000
17.36	28	3	0.0000	0.0000
17.36	29	4	0.0000	0.0000
17.36	30	5	0.0000	0.0000
20.10	31	6	0.0000	0.0000
20.10	32	7	0.0000	0.0000
20.10	33	8	0.0000	0.0000
23.26	34	9	0.0000	0.0000
23.26	35	10	0.0403	0.0403
23.26	36	11	0.0042	0.0042
26.93	37	12	0.0121	0.0121
26.93	38	13	0.0050	0.0050
26.93	39	14	0.0051	0.0051
31.17	40	15	0.0172	0.0172
31.17	41	16	0.0062	0.0062
31.17	42	17	0.0063	0.0063
36.09	43	18	0.0240	0.0240
36.09	44	19	0.0077	0.0077
36.09	45	20	0.0079	0.0079
41.77	46	21	0.0330	0.0330
41.77	47	22	0.0097	0.0097
41.77	48	23	0.0100	0.0100
48.36	49	24	0.0454	0.0454
48.36	50	25	0.0124	0.0124
48.36	51	26	0.0129	0.0129
55.98	52	27	0.0620	0.0620
55.98	53	28	0.0163	0.0163
55.98	54	29	0.0171	0.0171
64.80	55	30	0.0849	1.3680
64.80	56	31	0.0220	−0.0719
64.80	57	32	0.0233	−0.0786
75.01	58	33	0.1169	0.4823
75.01	59	34	0.0306	−0.1999
75.01	60	35	0.0327	−0.1963
86.83	61	36	0.1624	0.0726
86.83	62	37	0.0440	−0.2188
86.83	63	38	0.0478	−0.2146
100.52	64	39	0.2291	0.0074
100.52	65	40	0.0662	−0.2396

the worker was age 36 to almost 7 percent of wages at age 65. In years in which there is a discrete jump in accruals in response to a retroactive benefit enrichment, the results were far more dramatic. Accruals rose from about 1 percent of wages at age 37 to 23 percent at age 64.

In subsidized plans, there is a sharp spike in pension accruals at age 55, to 136 percent of wages. This is the age at which the worker qualifies for both subsidized early retirement *and* for the bridging supplement. Clearly, there is a strong incentive to defer retirement, at least until age 55. Pension accruals are negative at all subsequent ages, except in years in which the benefit formula is retroactively enriched. After the worker has qualified for special retirement at age 58, these negative accruals are substantial, averaging about 20 percent of wages.

Because flat benefit plans vary in the extent to which they subsidize retirement before age 65, one cannot associate the existence of a union pension plan with a universal incentive to retire before age 65. Such an incentive is likely to exist when there are provisions for subsidized early retirement *and* a bridging supplement *or* for special retirement. Such retirement provisions may serve as a partial substitute for mandatory retirement (Burkhauser and Quinn, 1983; Lazear, 1983), and the increased prevalence of special retirement provisions (in particular) may be contributing to the observed trend among males toward earlier retirement.[10] However, such retirement-inducing features of union pension plans are far from universal. Therefore, we caution against the conclusion that pension plans, in general, can serve as a substitute for mandatory retirement.[11]

Redistributive Effects of Enrichments

When unions negotiate increases in fringe benefits, the cost of these increases is presumably offset by wages or other concessions by the employee group as a whole. If a class of employees receives a disproportionately large increase in its fringe benefits, those employees are the recipients of an internal redistribution of wealth at that point in time. In

---

purchase plan at the date of termination.) For this reason, it is not appropriate to include the interest factor in the calculation of the pension benefit accrued during the year. Note that PW $(a+1) = (1+r)*$ PW(a), which implies a pension accrual equal to zero, also implies that the employer experiences no increase in costs, assuming the pension fund earns interest at the rate r during the year.

[10]Allen and Clark (1986) note that members of collectively bargained plans in the United States are more likely to retire early. In Canada, special or unreduced early retirement is far more prevalent in union than in nonunion plans. In 1984, e.g., 53.8 percent of flat benefit plans in Ontario could qualify for special retirement, compared with 30.0 percent of members of nonunion plans.

[11]Pesando and Gunderson (1988) draw a similar conclusion in their analysis of the earnings-based pension plans that predominate in the nonunion sector in Canada.

this sense, the periodic enrichment of flat benefit formulas serves to redistribute wealth to older, long-service employees. The greater the number of years of service credits that are enriched and the closer the commencement date of the pension, the larger will be the value of the enhancement to the pension benefit. Historical simulations that quantify these effects support two hypotheses: (1) that older workers exert a disproportionate impact on collectively bargained outcomes (Freeman, 1985), and (2) that the underfunding of flat benefit plans is designed to provide union members with a stake in the long-run viability of their employer (Ippolito, 1985).

In Table 3, the simulations illustrate the benefits accrued by three hypothetical workers for the selected years between 1974 and 1984 under the terms of four actual plans. The "young" worker is age 35 with 10 years of service; the "middle-age" worker is age 45 with 20 years of service; and the "older" worker is age 55 with 30 years of service. The pension accrual in each year is expressed as a fraction of the average industrial wage in that year. The plans vary considerably in the timing and magnitude of the enrichments to their benefit formulas, as well as in their early and special retirement provisions. Plans 1 and 2 have subsidized early retirement, special retirement, and a bridging supplement. Plan 3 provides no subsidy for retirement before age 65. Plan 4 introduced subsidized early and special retirement in 1978 and 1979, respectively, and thus provides an opportunity to assess the impact of the retroactive introduction of such provisions. Plans 1 and 4 provide inflation adjustments for retired workers, with these adjustments averaging about 40 percent of the inflation rate.[12]

These historical simulations highlight the importance of retroactive enrichments to flat benefit formulas, as well as to the retroactive introduction of subsidized early and special retirement. Four points merit emphasis.

1. Older workers gain disproportionately from the periodic enrichments to flat benefit formulas. For example, the increase in the benefit formula in plan 1 from $12.00 to $17.00 per month in 1983 yields a pension accrual equal to 58.7 percent of wages for the "older" worker, but only 5.3 percent for the "younger" worker.

2. The demographics of the four plans suggest that, in a representative year in the early 1980s, from 43 to 69 percent of plan members received *no* pension benefits. This is due to the 10-year vesting rule in the four plans,

---

[12]These inflation updates are reflected in the choice of an annuity rate of 7 percent, not the assumed nominal interest rate of 10 percent. During 1974–84, the inflation rate averaged about 8 percent. Forty percent of this figure is about 3 percent, which is then subtracted from the nominal interest rate of 10 percent.

TABLE 3
REDISTRIBUTIVE EFFECTS OF ENRICHMENT TO FLAT BENEFIT FORMULAS

Year	Age	Service	Plan 1[a] Formula	Plan 1[a] Benefit Accrual/ Wage	Plan 2 Formula	Plan 2 Benefit Accrual/ Wage	Plan 3 Formula	Plan 3 Benefit Accrual/ Wage	Plan 4 Formula	Plan 4 Benefit Accrual/ Wage
Young Worker										
1975	36	11	7.00	0.003	6.50	0.011	4.50	.002	6.50	.003
1978	39	14	10.00	0.005	8.00	0.011	6.50	.008	7.50	.007
1981	42	17	12.00	0.006	8.00	0.003	9.00	.004	9.25	.005
1983	44	19	17.00	0.053	8.00	0.003	9.00	.004	11.75	.013
1984	45	20	17.00	0.009	12.00	0.038	11.50	.026	12.50	.014
Middle-Age Worker										
1975	46	21	7.00	0.009	6.50	0.051	4.50	0.005	6.50	0.008
1978	49	24	10.00	0.014	8.00	0.045	6.50	0.031	7.50	0.025
1981	52	27	12.00	0.018	8.00	0.010	9.00	0.011	9.25	0.014
1983	54	29	17.00	0.217	8.00	0.011	9.00	0.013	11.75	0.048
1984	55	30	17.00	2.232	12.00	1.446	11.50	0.103	12.50	1.548
Older Worker										
1975	56	31	7.00	-0.130	6.50	0.644	4.50	0.016	6.50	0.028
1978	59	34	10.00	-0.447	8.00	0.290	6.50	0.123	7.50	1.392
1981	62	37	12.00	-0.441	8.00	-0.158	9.00	0.045	9.25	-0.216
1983	64	39	17.00	0.587	8.00	-0.232	9.00	0.055	11.75	-0.223
1984	65	40	17.00	-0.563	12.00	0.348	11.50	0.424	12.50	-0.258

[a]Plan	Early Retirement	Reduction Formula	Special Retirement	Bridging Supplement	Cost-of-Living Adjustment
1	55/10	0.5% per month to age 62	62/10 or 58/30	70% of basic benefit	Annuity rate = 7%
2	60/10 or 55 *and* age + service = 85	0.5 per month to age 62	62/10	70% of basic benefit	Annuity rate = Nominal Interest rate = 10%
3	55/10	Actuarial	None	None	Annuity rate = Nominal Interest rate = 10%
4	Age 60 (to 1977); 55/10 (from 1978)	Actuarial (to 1977); 0.4% to age 65	None (to 1978); 62/30 (from 1979)	70% of basic benefit	Annuity rate = 7%

which implies that workers with less than 10 years of service receive no current pension accruals.[13]

3. Older workers who have already qualified for special retirement typically earn negative pension accruals, unless an enrichment occurs. If an anticipated enrichment is imminent, these workers may rationally elect to defer retirement until that time.

4. For "younger," "middle-age," and "older" workers, there is substantial variation in pension accruals across plans, much of which is associated with the differential timing and magnitude of benefit enrichments.

These results provide a useful perspective on the well-known pension "puzzle" of the tendency for pension plans to be less than fully funded. Flat benefit plans tend to be less well funded than earnings-based plans in both Canada (Ezra, 1983) and the United States (Ippolito, 1985). Ippolito argues that the underfunding of these plans provides unions with an important stake in the long-run viability of the firm and thus preempts "holdups" by the union. The redistributive effects suggest an additional perspective, consistent with the proposition that collectively bargained outcomes disproportionately reflect the interest of older workers (Freeman, 1985). When a flat benefit formula is enriched, the previously accrued pensions of still-active workers rise in value. This serves to create a new unfunded liability, which must be amortized by a series of special payments over a period of not more than 15 years. The succession of such enrichments creates a succession of unfunded liabilities. This explains—in an institutional sense—the tendency for flat benefit plans to be less than fully funded. Both unions and management recognize that flat benefit formulas will be renegotiated upward over time, but they prefer not to anticipate such enrichments in their funding targets. From a management perspective, the desire not to prefund these future enrichments may represent a means of ensuring that the enrichments appear as an explicit cost component at each round of collective bargaining.

From a union perspective, the enrichment of the pension formula represents a highly visible benefit improvement, and explicit prefunding of the enrichment is likely to reduce the "credit" accorded the union leadership by the rank and file. In addition, prefunding would presumably make it

---

[13]The fraction of workers aged 29 or younger ranged from 25.6 percent (plan 3) to 53.9 percent (plan 4). These workers had an average of 3.10 (plan 4) to 4.99 (plan 1) years of service. The fraction of workers aged 30 to 39 ranged from 30 to 35 percent, with an average of 8 to 10 years of service. We assume that all of the workers aged 29 or less, and one-half of the workers aged 30 to 39, had not yet vested.

Pension legislation introduced by the federal government and most provinces in 1986 and 1987 now requires that pension benefits vest after two years of service. As emphasized by Lazear and Moore (1988), younger workers do benefit from the pension option associated with working one additional year, and thus becoming one year closer to qualifying for a pension benefit.

more difficult for unions to negotiate large enrichments, since such enrichments would have a more immediate impact on the cash flows of their employers. For both unions and management, underfunding may also reduce the uncertainty and potential conflict over the proprietary right to any surplus assets in the pension plan, an issue that has created considerable controversy and litigation in both Canada and the United States.[14]

The Timing of Early Retirement

Flat benefit formulas are periodically and retroactively enriched. These enrichments, especially for older and long-service workers, significantly increase pension wealth. Workers who are eligible to retire early and who anticipate an enrichment to the benefit formula have a strong incentive to postpone retirement until the enrichment takes effect.

Table 4 shows monthly data on early retirees from a major union pension plan in Ontario for the period 1980–87. The early retirees are for the age cohort 60 to 64 on December 31 of the preceding year. The union negotiated its contract every third year, and any enrichments to the pension plan typically came into force on August 1.

TABLE 4

Numbers Retiring (by Month), Ages 60 to 64, on December 31 of Preceding Year[a]

Year	Jan	Feb	Mar	Apr	May	Jun	Jul	Aug	Sep	Oct	Nov	Dec	No. Active, Ages 60–64 on Dec. 31 Year	No. Active, Ages 60–64 on Dec. 31 Number
1980	21	19	13	12	7	6	7	7	4	2	0	1	1979	641
1981	7	4	6	1	4	1	1	1	0	4	0	1	1980	793
1982	22*	7	6	20	40	24	19	9	9	2	4	1	1981	1,013
1983	62	23	28	23	13	33	14	7	3	4	0	0	1982	1,044
1984	53	8	13	6	6	2	8	114	27	23	129	0	1983	921
1985	14	7	13	5	4	3	5	13	12	5	2	5	1984	676
1986	25	24	127	3	0	0	2	0	0	0	1	0	1985	795
1987	4	3	0	2	2	0	0	43**	5	4	2	0	1986	745

*Increase from $13.00 to $17.00 per month goes into effect.
**Increase from $17.00 to $28.00 per month goes into effect.
[a]Retirements at age 65 and any retirements on disability pensions are not included.

[14]Ippolito (1987) has written persuasively about implicit pension contracts between workers and firms. The analysis of the retroactive enrichment of flat benefit formulas focuses attention on another potential set of implicit contracts—those that involve different generations of union workers. It seems likely, e.g., that younger union members agree to generous retroactive enrichments, in part, in anticipation that early retirement will be accelerated, and hence that their job security will be enhanced.

During this time period, there were two enrichments to the flat benefit formula: from $13.00 to $17.00 per month per year of service, effective January 1982,[15] and from $17.00 to $28.00, effective August 1987. In addition, a special retirement window of four months duration was introduced in August 1984. Under the terms of this window, the reduction formula was waived for members who had attained age 60, and a special bridging supplement was introduced.

One would predict that early retirements would fall prior to the two enrichments as eligible plan members waited for the benefit improvement. In 1984, when no enrichment occurred (and none was apparently anticipated), workers under age 60 had no incentive to defer retirement. By contrast, workers aged 60 presumably anticipated the introduction of the special retirement window and adjusted the timing of their retirements accordingly.

The timing of the early retirements accords with expectations. The strategic behavior of these workers is perhaps most evident in the sharp reduction in early retirements during the full year prior to the enrichment from $17.00 to $28.00, which occurred in August 1987. Apparently, the combination of large enrichments recently won by other unions, together with the extended period (six years) in which the benefit formula was fixed, produced a widespread belief that the flat benefit would be increased sharply. Similarly, there is a sharp reduction in early retirements prior to the increase from $13.00 to $17.00 in January 1982, and there is a sharp decline in early retirements prior to the introduction of the special retirement window in August 1984. This result is expected and provides additional evidence of how the timing of early retirement is linked to anticipated changes in the value of the early retirement benefit.

Conclusion

To analyze the work incentive and redistributive effects of flat benefit plans, one must first acquire considerable institutional detail about their operation. Of particular importance are the periodic enrichments, which are part of flat benefit formulas, especially in an inflationary climate. During 1974–84, enrichments to flat benefit formulas in Canada were large but typically fell short of the inflation rate. More importantly, the magnitude and the timing of these enrichments varied sharply across plans.

---

[15]By August 1981, it was known that the enrichment would be at least $17.00 per month. Because all but one of the union's locals were on strike until December, the enrichment for the vast majority of members did not go into effect until January 1982.

Workers who anticipate an increase in the flat benefit formula are likely to postpone retirement until a new contract is negotiated. Therefore, retirement probability models that ignore this "bunching" effect are likely to prove deficient.

All flat benefit plans tend to "backload" pension accruals, providing a strong incentive for members to remain at the firm at least until the member qualifies for subsidized early retirement, if provided by the plan. If the plan provides for a special, unreduced early retirement pension, then the qualifying member is likely to experience a strong incentive to retire from the current job. This incentive is strengthened by the bridging supplements in plans that contain the special retirement provision. This incentive effect is attenuated if the member can anticipate future enrichments to the benefit formula.

Less than one-half of the members of flat benefit plans usually qualify for special retirement, and therefore one cannot assert that these plans provide a strong incentive to retire before the normal retirement age of 65. But plans are increasingly providing this incentive, which has contributed to the current trend toward early retirement.

Freeman (1985) has argued that collectively bargained outcomes are likely to favor older workers (the "median" union voter) rather than the interests of the marginal worker, who is likely to be younger and more mobile.[16] These internal redistributive effects[17] may also help explain why flat benefit plans tend to be underfunded. Because of their retroactivity, periodic enrichments create periodic unfunded liabilities, which are typically amortized over the full 15 years allowed by Canadian law. The underfunding of union pension plans may not be the objective, but only the by-product, of this internal redistribution of wealth.

These issues are relevant to several topical policy issues in both Canada and the United States: (1) the continuing trend toward early retirement and the possibility of future labor shortages; (2) the risks posed by the existence of underfunded pension plans, including the risks borne by third-party insurer of pension benefits (the Pension Benefit Guarantee Corporation [PBGC] in the United States and the Guarantee Fund in the Province

---

[16]There is also substantial backloading of pension accruals in final earnings plans (Pesando and Gunderson, 1988). However, the ability of union leaders to negotiate enrichments to flat benefit formulas provides them with direct control over the backloading of pension accruals. In final earnings plans, by contrast, the backloading of pension accruals is tied to the wage increases granted by employers in (typically) nonunion establishments.

[17]In reviewing alternative rationales for union-nonunion differences in pension plan characteristics, Gustman and Steinmeier (1986) note the potential importance of the union pension plan as a vehicle for transferring rents across different generations of union workers.

of Ontario); and (3) the possibility that the backloading of pension benefits constitutes systemic discrimination since females—who have higher turnover rates—are less likely to qualify for benefits targeted to long-service workers.

Since flat benefit plans frequently contain provisions that heavily subsidize early retirement, they penalize members who continue to work after qualifying for early retirement. For this reason, subsidized early retirement provisions have contributed to the documented trend toward earlier retirement. If policymakers wish to reverse this trend, legislation could be passed to limit the implicit tax on continued work contained in subsidized early retirement pensions and bridging supplements.[18] Stock and Wise (1988) documented the potential of such plan provisions to affect retirement behavior. However, to limit the size of extant subsidies to early retirement would conflict with the current preferences of union workers. For at least some younger workers, a legislative initiative to limit the subsidy to early retirement would lead to reduced job security, since the pace of early retirements by older workers with long seniority would be reduced.

Flat benefit plans tend to be less well funded than earnings-based plans, primarily as a result of retroactive enrichments to flat benefit formulas. These plans thus represent a greater potential claim on the third-party insurer of pension benefits. If new legislation required that retroactive enrichments to flat benefit formulas be funded more rapidly, the degree of underfunding would fall. However, the size of retroactive benefit enrichments would likely decrease as well, since employers could less readily defer the costs of such enrichments. If Ippolito (1985) is correct and underfunding serves to create important incentive effects, efficiency would be reduced. If the primary purpose of these retroactive enrichments is to redistribute wealth across age and service cohorts, there is no such loss in efficiency. However, union members might seek alternative means to ensure that older, long-service workers receive a premium in total compensation.[19]

These results highlight the substantial backloading of pension benefits in flat benefit plans, at least until the date that the member qualifies for an unreduced early retirement pension. Backloading imposes significant penalties on those employee subgroups with above-average turnover. Since the cost of pension benefits is internalized at the level of the union workforce as

---

[18]This could be accomplished, e.g., by imposing a minimum age (such as 60) before which workers could qualify for unreduced retirement pensions.

[19]Clearly, seniority-based protection in the event of layoffs and the backloading of pension compensation with age and service serve to create a time path of total compensation in union establishments that rises with age and years of service, even if cash wages do not.

a whole, employee subgroups with above-average turnover subsidize their co-workers. For covered (as well as uncovered) workers, females have higher turnover rates than their male counterparts. This fact suggests that backloading arising from the combination of early retirement provisions and retroactive enrichments to flat benefit formulas may constitute systemic discrimination, since females as a group are likely to be at a disadvantage. This concern, of course, applies as well to earnings-based plans, which also contain substantial backloading and which—in Canada—cover a much larger fraction of female workers (Pesando, Gunderson, and McLaren, 1990).

Comparable Worth and Factor Point Pay Analysis in State Government

PETER F. ORAZEM, J. PETER MATTILA,
and SHERRY K. WEIKUM*

ONE OF THE BASIC FUNCTIONS of public-sector personnel management is the setting of relative pay for different jobs in the pay system. However, there is no consensus as to the process by which relative pay should be set. One widely used option is to set pay for each job on the basis of information for similar jobs in other firms or organizations in the local labor market. This procedure may break down for jobs that are unique to the public sector (e.g., parole officer and firefighter). It may also lead to significant pay disparities within groups of similarly skilled employees. The lack of relevant market information on pay for all jobs and the desire to promote internal pay equity are two commonly cited justifications for setting pay on the basis of job content. Such systems establish a hierarchy of jobs on the basis of measured levels of several different job attributes and skill requirements. Relative pay may then be set in accordance with the derived hierarchy of jobs.

A commonly used method of job content analysis is the factor point-

---
*Department of Economics, Iowa State University. We wish to thank the many personnel analysts in the various states who supplied data in response to our survey questionnaire and also Dorothy Sally, Darryl Stark, and Tom Hunsberger for their assistance in compiling the data. Thanks also to Karl Egge, Jonathan Leonard, Barbara Nelson, Ross Azevedo, and two anonymous reviewers for their suggestions.

count method, which assigns scores on several job factors, usually measures of skill, effort, responsibility, and working conditions. These factors are assigned weights on the basis of their value or importance to the organization. The sum of the weighted factor scores yields an overall point total for the job. Jobs with the highest point totals receive the highest pay whereas jobs with equal or near equal totals receive equal pay.

Although such systems date back to the 1920s, factor point systems have become common only recently in state governments. The oldest factor point system was New Hampshire's, implemented in 1950. None was introduced until 1970, and 16 of the 23 systems studied here have been initiated only since 1979 (see Table 1). This increased use of factor point systems by state governments is due partly to the increase in computer technology, which made implementation of these systems affordable, and to the surge in public interest in comparable worth (Treiman and Hartmann, 1981;

TABLE 1

STATE FACTOR POINT-COUNT SYSTEM

State	Date of Implementation[a]	Hay System	Comparable Worth
Connecticut	1981		X
Delaware	1973	X	
Idaho	1977	X	
Illinois[b]	1983	X	
Iowa	1984		X
Kentucky	1982		
Louisiana[b]	1988		
Maine	1976	X	
Massachusetts[b]	1979	X	
Michigan	1972		X
Minnesota	1979	X	X
New Hampshire	1950		
New Jersey[b]	1970	X	
New Mexico	1987		
New York[b]	1985		X
North Dakota[b]	1982	X	
Ohio[b]	1989		
Oklahoma	1980	X	
Oregon	1985	X	X
South Dakota[b]	1985	X	
Tennessee[b]	1987		
Washington	1974		X
Wisconsin	1986		X

[a]Based on telephone conversations with state personnel administrators and on documentation provided by state governments.
[b]Not used in this study because data were unavailable.

Hartmann, 1985; Ehrenberg and Smith, 1987; Ehrenberg, 1989; Michael and Hartmann, 1989). Comparable worth proponents presume that the labor market undervalues jobs held predominantly by women and argue that basing pay on market wages will ensure that market discrimination is reflected in the state pay structure. Because factor point pay systems need not incorporate market information, they are commonly used in comparable worth pay plans. In fact, of the eight states that have implemented comparable worth plans (Connecticut, Iowa, Michigan, Minnesota, New York, Oregon, Washington, and Wisconsin), all used some form of factor point pay analysis.

Despite the interest, little is known about how these systems affect the pay structure, how the plans affect jobs that are disproportionately female or minority or commonly covered by collective bargaining agreements, and the extent to which the plans reflect relative market pay. Furthermore, the treatment of these groups and the importance of market forces in shaping the pay system is likely to change if it is explicitly designed to be a comparable worth system. These effects may also differ if unions can participate in the process of evaluating jobs, setting factor weights, and negotiating over the implementation of the pay system.

Comparable Worth

In comparable worth states, the justification for switching to a factor point system is couched in terms of treating predominantly female jobs more equitably. For this reason, one would expect that comparable worth plans would tend to benefit jobs with a higher proportion of female incumbents. Less clear is whether comparable worth analyses differ from factor point analyses that are not mandated to be comparable worth. For example, the Hay System, commonly used in both state government and the private sector, was used for comparable worth plans in Minnesota and Oregon and for plans not designated as comparable worth in Delaware, Idaho, Illinois, Maine, Massachusetts, New Jersey, North Dakota, Oklahoma, and South Dakota.[1] To the extent that similar or identical Hay procedures are used in all such states, the relative job points may not differ greatly with the comparable worth orientation of the state. However, there may be more obvious differences among states in terms of implemented

---

[1]The Hay System is used by over 5,000 employers around the world, including 150 of the 500 largest corporations in the United States. Its proponents consider it a factor comparison system, not a factor point system. For our purposes, the distinction blurs since both Hay plans and other plans generate a hierarchy of jobs based on a total point score (Milkovich and Newman, 1984).

pay plans based on factor points. Comparable worth states try to avoid making explicit market pay comparisons whereas other states presumably have no such compulsion. However, if the impact of comparable worth plans is not distinguishable from those of factor point systems in general, concerns over comparable worth are either overblown or apply to all factor point systems.

Another area of concern is the impact on minorities. If a policy is oriented toward raising relative pay for one group, relative pay for other groups will fall. Because minorities are disproportionately represented in blue-collar occupations, they may lose from a policy that raises pay for, say, clerical and health jobs. There is evidence supporting this conjecture for Iowa (Orazem and Mattila, 1990), where minorities lost about 1 percent in relative pay, and mixed evidence in Minnesota (Killingsworth, 1990). However, both sets of results must be interpreted cautiously because of the small numbers of minorities in Iowa and Minnesota. All other studies of which we are aware have dealt exclusively with the impacts on women. This study is the first to examine the treatment of minorities across several states.

A third area of concern is the impact of comparable worth plans on the relationship between public- and private-sector pay. The presumption is that these plans reduce the importance of market factors, which is confirmed in the Iowa case. However, the role of market factors can still be large because market wages are likely to shape analysts' perceptions of relative job worth, even if the wage information is not used explicitly in setting job points. Also, large deviations from market pay rates are likely motivation for adjusting points, both to raise proposed pay for jobs that are undervalued relative to the market and, perhaps less likely, to lower proposed pay for jobs that are paid large premiums relative to market. Thus, although in Iowa the ultimate impact of the comparable worth plan was to reduce the influence of market pay, the impact of market pay remained large and significant. In fact, the impact varied over time as appeals and compromises altered the original proposed pay plan (Orazem and Mattila, 1990).

Effect on Unions

On the surface, the move to a factor point pay structure seems risky to a public-sector union. The outcome is likely to raise the relative wages of some members and lower them for others. It also has the potential of raising the pay of supervisory or other nonunion positions relative to union members. Furthermore, these pay systems could limit union latitude to bargain for pay increases since the cost of implementing the system may limit the state's ability to afford future across-the-board raises. Despite these potential adverse impacts, public-sector unions have been among the strongest supporters of comparable worth in states where it has been implemented.

There are several reasons why unions support factor point pay systems. First, they remove variation in pay among similarly skilled workers. A commonly held goal of unions in the private sector is to reduce pay dispersion among workers, which both institutional and empirical evidence supports (Freeman, 1980a, 1982; Hirsch, 1982; Hirsch and Addison, 1986). If the results of factor point analyses are consistent across different state systems, the move to such systems could reduce the variance in relative pay across states as well. On the other hand, if factor point pay systems differ greatly in their relative evaluations of the same job, the dispersion of earnings for public-sector occupational labor markets could increase. Of the few studies that have examined the consistency of outcomes from different pay systems, Schwab (1985) concluded that no consensus could be found since some studies found high degrees of consistency and others did not.

Second, unions could influence the outcome of the factor point pay analysis by influencing which job factors are included in the analysis, by participating in the measurement of factor levels by job and in establishing the relative factor weights, and, finally, by negotiating over how the points are used in establishing pay once the job hierarchy based on total points is established.[2] In essence, these systems may serve to expand union influence on pay structure relative to traditional collective bargaining. Virtually every job's pay could become negotiable if the union has a sufficiently large role in the factor point pay analysis and implementation. This study will shed some light on whether unions can affect the variance of pay in public-sector pay systems and whether they can alter the outcome of factor point analysis.

Empirical Specification

The Hay System is the most commonly used factor point system in the private sector. Of the 23 states with factor point systems, 11 use the Hay System. The question is, does it differ from other systems in its treatment

---

[2]Unions have had an important role in several of the state pay analyses. In Iowa, Connecticut, New York, and Oregon, implementation of the pay structure was subject to collective bargaining. Union lawsuits have influenced the outcome and/or pace of implementation in Illinois, Michigan, and Washington. In several states with public-sector unions, unions served on steering committees or on committees evaluating jobs.

of women, minorities, and workers covered by collective bargaining agreements?

State pay structure may be altered by means of two methods: collective bargaining between a union and the state and conducting a factor point pay analysis. Comparable worth plans and Hay plans are two variations of factor pay analyses, and four factors may influence pay in different states, depending upon the method used to establish the pay structure. These four include the proportion of female incumbents on the job (F), the proportion of minority incumbents on the job (M), the proportion of workers on the job covered by collective bargaining (U), and the market opportunity wage for the job (W_M). The two dependent variables are the total points for each job in each state (P) and the entry-level pay for each job in each state (SW), each of which is converted to ratio form (relative to a base level).

The estimating equation is:

$$P = \delta_0 + \delta_F + \delta_M + \delta_U + \delta_{WM}$$
$$+ \delta_{CF}\, C^*F + \delta_{CM}\, C^*M + \delta_{CU}\, C^*U + \delta_{CW}\, C^*W_M$$
$$+ \delta_{HF}\, H^*F + \delta_{HM}\, H^*M + \delta_{HU}\, H^*U + \delta_{HW}\, H^*W_M$$
$$+ \delta_{UF}\, U^*F + \delta_{UM}\, U^*M + \delta_{UW}\, U^*W_M \qquad (1)$$

where C is a dummy variable, taking the value of 1 if the state is a comparable worth state, and H is a dummy variable, taking the value of 1 if the state uses a Hay plan. The interaction terms reflect changes in the influence of market wages and predominantly female, minority, and union jobs on the pay structure in comparable worth, Hay, and union collective bargaining settings. The noninteracted terms measure the average influences of demographic composition, market wage, and union status in the absence of comparable worth, Hay, and union pay-setting plans. Individual state dummy variables are also included to help control for differences in the type of pay analysis system used and for any systematic variation across states in cost-of-living or public-sector labor demand.

There is no necessity for a state to adopt a proposed pay plan in whole or in part. Once the plan is announced and winners and losers become known, political and economic interest groups may go to work to protect their interests. In particular, the actual pay becomes a subject of negotiations in states where unions are recognized bargaining agents. Some states used direct transformations from points to pay, but others modified their plans on implementation. Two states—New Mexico and Wisconsin—

discarded the initial plan and started over. New York rejected two plans and implemented a hybrid variant of the two original proposals. Many states allowed for adjusting individual job pay to market conditions if their proposed pay was not competitive. Most states did not implement proposed pay cuts, two partial exceptions being Washington and New York. In Iowa, proposed pay cuts were canceled and proposed pay increases were reduced as a result of a negotiated compromise with the union. Because implemented pay plans can significantly differ from the proposed pay structure, equation (1) was also estimated with state entry-level pay (SW) as the dependent variable.

A comparison of the coefficients in the two regressions highlights the expected outcome of moving completely to a factor point system without modification. Alternatively, the comparison indicates how factor point systems may be modified in order to build a consensus for implementation. To make this comparison easier, the following was also estimated:

$$P - SW = \Sigma \gamma_i X_i \tag{2}$$

where $\gamma_i = \delta_i - \omega_i$ is the difference in estimated influence of variable i between the factor point system and the state wage system, δ_i is the coefficient on a variable X_i in equation (1), and ω_i is the associated coefficient from the corresponding regression of equation (1) substituting state job pay, SW, as the dependent variable. A positive coefficient implies that the variable raises points more than pay; a negative coefficient implies that the variable has the larger impact on pay. The dependent variables are normalized to ensure that P and SW are measured in the same units.

Also examined are the determinants of the deviation in points and pay across state pay systems. Equations are estimated as:

$$\sigma_P = \alpha_0 + \alpha_W \sigma_W + \alpha_F F + \alpha_M M + \alpha_U U \tag{3}$$

where σ_P is the variance in factor points across states for a job and σ_W is the variance in private-sector wages for the occupation. The same specification is used for estimating wage variance regressions, substituting σ_{SW} as the dependent variable. Since unions lower the standard deviation of pay in the private sector, the coefficient on proportion unionized is expected to be negative, implying that more highly unionized jobs have more standardization of wages across states. The coefficient on σ_W is expected to be positive, implying that jobs with higher variance in market pay would have greater variation in factor points and pay across states. It is not clear what would be expected about the signs of the other coefficients, nor about the relative size of the impacts of these variables on total points versus pay.

Data

The basic data set was obtained by contacting the 23 states, based on information provided by the General Accounting Office and supplemented by Ehrenberg and Smith (1987) and our own research on comparable worth pay plans. After obtaining a listing of job titles from each state, a list of 78 job titles was compiled that were common to most states. Each state was mailed the list of specific jobs, with the request to supply for each job the total factor points, actual pay, proportion female and minority, and union contract coverage. Jobs were selected to span a wide variety of skill levels and a range of female- and male-dominated and mixed positions (see Table 2). In addition, jobs were selected that were easily recognizable, relying on respondents to match the titles to their positions and to leave blank those titles for which they had no close match.

Several states did not have job points or declined to supply them. Two

TABLE 2

THE 78 JOB TITLES USED IN SURVEY

Accountant[c]	Electrician[d]	Physical Therapist
Administrative Assistant	Engineering Technician	Physician
Airplane Pilot[d]	Equipment Operator[a,d]	Plumber[d]
Attorney	Food Service Worker	Postal Clerk[c]
Audiologist	Forest Ranger	Probation & Parole Officer
Auditor[c]	Grounds Keeper	Programmer
Auto Mechanic[d]	Highway Patrol Officer	Psychologist
Baker	Interviewer[c]	Psychologist Assistant[c]
Barber	Lab Assistant	Purchasing Agent[c]
Beautician	Laboratory Technician[a]	Receptionist[b]
Budget Analyst	Laborer	Registered Nurse
Business Manager	Laundry Worker[a]	Safety Officer
Carpenter	Librarian[a]	Seamstress
Cashier	Library Assistant[a]	Secretary[a,b]
Chaplain[d]	Locksmith[d]	Security Guard
Chemist[c]	Licensed Practical Nurse[a]	Social Worker[a]
Clerk[a,b]	Maintenance Mechanic[d]	Speech Therapist
Computer Operator[a,c]	Mason	Statistical Analyst[c]
Cook[a,c]	Medical Lab Technician	Switchboard Operator[b]
Correctional Officer	Microbiologist	Tax Auditor[a,c]
Custodial Worker	Nursing Aide	Typist[b]
Data Entry Operator[b]	Occupational Therapist[a]	Veterinarian[d]
Dental Assistant[a,b]	Painter[d]	Vocational-Rehab Counselor
Dental Hygienist[b]	Personnel Assistant[b]	Welder[d]
Dentist	Personnel Officer	Word Processor Operator[b]
Dietitian[b]	Pharmacist	X-Ray Technician

[a]The 14 jobs for which points and pay were received from all states.
[b]The 11 most female-dominated jobs (more than 85% female).
[c]The 11 mixed jobs (43 to 57% female).
[d]The 11 most male-dominated jobs (less than 10% female).

states were deleted because their pay varied among divisions of state government or because of insufficient staff to provide the data. The final result was a data set for 14 states, which supplied an average of 67 jobs per state, a total of 940 observations.[3] This sample is well distributed geographically, with four in the Northeast (Connecticut, Delaware, Maine, New Hampshire), four in the Midwest (Iowa, Michigan, Minnesota, Wisconsin), two in the South (Kentucky, Oklahoma), and four in the West (Idaho, New Mexico, Oregon, Washington).

The states also span a wide variety of pay-setting plans. Six of the states used the Hay consulting firm in evaluating jobs and determining factor points. The rest used a variety of other consulting firms or in-house systems. Seven of the states conducted their factor point-count analysis as part of a comparable worth process, while the other seven did not.[4]

Points in one state are not likely to be comparable with points in other states because different systems used different scales. For this reason, two alternative normalizations were used to eliminate this problem. The first normalization was choosing a common base job in all states and recomputing points for each job relative to this base. The job of cook was selected as the base because it was available in each state and had the lowest coefficient of variation in points. The measure becomes, for job i and state j

$$\hat{P}_{i,j} = \frac{P_{i,j}}{P_{cook,j}} \tag{4}$$

The same transformation was applied to actual pay to create measures for each job in each state relative to the pay for cooks in the state. Use of relative pay removes variation across states caused by cost-of-living differences. It also removes any biases caused by differences in standard work hours, fringe benefits, vacation time, or other compensating differentials that may not be captured by pay levels. Finally, because relative points and relative pay are measured in the same units, it is easy to compare the relative impacts of a variable on point structure or pay structure by looking at the relative size of the coefficients across the point and pay regressions.[5]

---

[3]All data supplied by the states were reviewed for inconsistencies and improbable magnitudes. A few jobs were discarded when they were not easily recognized by respondents in the sample.

[4]Connecticut and Washington relied in part on Willis Associates, Iowa employed Arthur Young, and the other four states relied heavily on internal methodology. States using consultants often made their own modifications, and states using in-house systems often consulted with outside professionals.

[5]Using a single base, cooks will have the same relative points and relative pay in all states. A specification was tried that computed average points and pay for each state over a sample of 14 jobs common to all states. This measure was used in the denominator of equation (4), which has the advantage of not forcing cooks to be treated identically in all states. The results did not differ greatly between these two measures, so only results using ratios relative to cooks are reported.

It was also necessary to control for variation among jobs in the levels of human capital required and for minimum pay necessary to fill those positions. Annual earnings of year-round, full-time workers by job and state as computed from the 1980 census were used.[6] In addition, the proportion female in three states (and selected jobs in a few other states) that couldn't provide such data was estimated using 1980 census employment statistics.[7] These proxy measures for proportion female are present only in the largest data set of 940 observations and were not used in the smaller data set of 583 observations. Our major conclusions are not sensitive to the size of data set or to the use of this proxy.

Each state was asked to indicate whether each job was covered by a collective bargaining contract. Four of the states (Kentucky, Idaho, Oklahoma, and Washington) do not engage in collective bargaining at all. In most other states, jobs were assigned a value of 1 if covered or zero if not covered by union contracts. In a few cases, the state assigned fractional values if union coverage of a job differed among divisions. We determined whether states were comparable worth (CW) and Hay System states by using state-supplied information. The dummy variables CW and Hay were assigned values of 1 for all jobs in comparable worth states and by Hay states, respectively (see Table 3).

Results

Table 4 provides an overview of relative pay ratios averaged over various state and job groupings. The ratios are larger in the 10 states that use no form of factor point-count analysis. It may be that those states pay less to cooks and other less skilled jobs. The change in the ratios from female-dominated to mixed jobs and to male-dominated jobs may be more meaningful. It is clear that the mixed jobs (nearly 50% female) gain the most

---

[6]In most cases (e.g., carpenters), a weighted average of male and female earnings, as computed directly from the census data, was used. However, 34 of the 78 jobs were not available directly from the census by state. In these cases, job earnings were estimated by multiplying national ratios for the job to the next highest occupational group (e.g., psychologists as a ratio of social scientists) from the 1984 Current Population Survey by the 1980 census state earnings of the next highest occupational group (e.g., social scientists). CPS data were used because many states did not conduct market wage surveys or were not able to provide such data. Most of the job classes were matched to their private-sector equivalents. However, some relate to local government equivalents (e.g., Highway Patrol relates to police and detectives).

[7]Idaho, Kentucky, and New Mexico supplied no data on proportion female. Oklahoma supplied data for broad occupational groups by agency, from which reasonably good estimates were made for specific jobs. Proportion female was not supplied for 40 jobs in all other states.

TABLE 3

SUMMARY STATISTICS

Variables	940 Observations		583 Observations	
	Mean	S.D.	Mean	S.D.
Dependent Variables				
Point Ratio	1.652	.843	1.716	.903
Wage Ratio	1.332	.417	1.298	.405
Point-Wage Ratios	.320	.558	.418	.605
Explanatory Variables				
Market Wage Ratio	1.870	.874	1.814	.892
Female	.4994	.3568	.5110	.3536
Minority	—	—	.1215	.1619
Union	.6160	.4823	.6712	.4637
CW	.4979	.5003	.5180	.5001
CW × Female	.2513	.3535	.2651	.3541
CW × Minority	—	—	.0668	.1229
CW × Union	.3851	.4869	.3842	.4868
Hay	.4394	.4966	.4631	.4990
Hay × Female	.2180	.3421	.2319	.3494
Hay × Minority	—	—	.0527	.1276
Hay × Union	.2398	.4227	.2655	.4356
Union × Female	.3192	.3851	.3570	.3944
Union × Minority	—	—	.0713	.1418
CW × Market Wage Ratio	.9128	1.0785	.9396	1.0835
Hay × Market Wage Ratio	.8310	1.1125	.8748	1.1511
Union × Market Wage Ratio	1.0499	.9884	1.1051	.9435

relative to female jobs in nonfactor point states and gain the least in comparable worth states. It is not clear why this occurs, although it may be that comparable worth states emphasized raising pay for only a few heavily female jobs, bringing up female-dominated jobs relative to mixed jobs. Oddly enough, male-dominated jobs do best relative to female-dominated jobs in comparable worth states. The gap may have been even larger in those states before comparable worth (indeed, a large gap may have provided the impetus for the comparable worth plan), or comparable worth may not have been very effective in raising pay in female-dominated jobs.

In order to investigate some of these issues in more depth, regression estimates are provided for the states in our sample in Table 5. The regressions in columns (1) through (3) exclude the Minority variable whereas those in columns (4) through (6) include it. Because several interacted terms were used, also computed were derivatives of the dependent variables with respect to Market Wage, the proportion Female, Minority, and

TABLE 4

Pay Ratios (Relative to Cooks) by Job and State Groupings

	Female-Dominated (N=11)		Mixed (N=11)		Male-Dominated (N=11)
States (10) not using factor point-count methods[a]	1.138	(+27%)[b]	1.450	(+32%)[c]	1.507
States (7) using factor point-count methods (noncomparable worth)[d]	1.109	(+23%)[b]	1.364	(+32%)[c]	1.463
States (7) using comparable worth factor point-count method[d]	1.067	(+16%)[b]	1.243	(+40%)[c]	1.490

[a]Alabama, Arkansas, Colorado, Florida, Hawaii, Nebraska, Nevada, Rhode Island, Virginia, and West Virginia. Data for these states were not available when this study was originally conducted; they are not included in Tables 3 and 5–7.
[b]The percentage increase in the average pay ratio from the Female-Dominated jobs (85% plus female) to the Mixed jobs (43 to 57% female).
[c]The percentage increase in the average pay ratio from the Female-Dominated jobs to the Male-Dominated jobs (less than 10% female) (jobs are identified in Table 2).
[d]See Table 1.

Union (i.e., covered by collective bargaining), and the Comparable Worth and Hay dummy variables (see Table 6).

The results were not very sensitive to the use of the alternative dependent variable (ratios relative to a 14-job average). They are also robust to changing the specification by using the logarithm of the pay ratio as the dependent variable. Overall, the regressions in Table 4 explain more than one-half of the variation in relative points and almost two-thirds of the variation in relative pay.

The market wage is positively and significantly associated with relative points and relative pay. Computing partial derivatives and elasticities with respect to the market wage, sizable elasticities of .76 and .79 were found for points and .54 and .52 for pay (see Table 6). Clearly, market wages are an important determinant of both points and pay in these states. Even though market wages may not be an explicit job factor, factor point pay analyses appear implicitly to take market forces into account. It is interesting to note that the elasticity on points is larger than on pay. If, as is likely, factor point systems tend to deemphasize the role of market wages (as compared with a system that relies totally on wage surveys), these results suggest that actual pay implementation further deemphasizes the role of the market in these states.

Thus, setting relative pay strictly on the basis of factor points results in a pay structure that more closely reflects relative market pay than do the actual implemented systems. Therefore, the implementation process, and not the factor point study itself, may be the means by which groups gain or lose. This speculation is supported by the comparable worth interaction terms. Apparently, comparable worth pay analyses differ little from other factor point pay analyses. The estimated derivative of points on comparable worth in Table 6 is insignificant, and the null hypothesis that the comparable worth interaction terms are jointly zero cannot be rejected. The interaction term, CW Female, is positive (predominantly female jobs are rated higher) but not significant. There is evidence that comparable worth pay analyses rank predominantly minority jobs lower relative to other factor point pay analyses. In the larger sample, union-covered jobs are also ranked lower, but significance drops in the smaller sample.

While comparable worth analysis does not differ substantially from others in its impact on relative points, the outcomes of the implementation do differ. The joint test of significance and the estimated derivative are highly significant in both samples. Implemented comparable worth plans lower the importance of relative market wages. However, these plans do not raise relative pay for predominantly female jobs more than do the traditional factor point pay systems.[8] The interaction term, CW Female, is negative in both samples and marginally significant in the large sample.[9] There is also evidence that comparable worth plans lower relative pay for union jobs and jobs held by minorities, implying that traditional factor point systems, as implemented, have tended to treat more heavily minority (and perhaps female) jobs better than have the comparable worth plans.

One can speculate as to why women have fared no better under comparable worth plans than under other factor point plans. One possibility is that when a plan is preordained as a system to raise the pay of a certain group, other interest groups will resist implementing the plan. Then, the process of building a consensus for implementation will require that some of the

---

[8]Women may gain absolutely along with men if comparable worth states raise the size of the total payroll, as in Iowa (Orazem and Mattila, 1990). The present study looks only at relative gains for women, not absolute gains.

[9]This finding does not mean that women lose in relative pay because of comparable worth implementation. The sample is restricted to states with factor point systems, and these results imply that comparable worth states are no more successful in raising pay for predominantly female jobs than are other factor point systems. Ehrenberg's (1989) survey shows that implementation of comparable worth uniformly raises relative pay for women. Our results lead to the hypothesis that similar analysis performed on noncomparable worth factor point implementation would raise relative pay for women by similar magnitudes.

TABLE 5

Regressions on Point Ratios and Wage Ratios
(t-ratios in parentheses)

Variable	Point Ratio (1)	Wage Ratio (2)	Point Ratio – Wage Ratio (3)	Point Ratio (4)	Wage Ratio (5)	Point Ratio – Wage Ratio (6)
Intercept	1.342***	.959***	.383**	.949***	.697***	.252
	(6.36)	(10.49)	(2.42)	(3.30)	(6.32)	(1.13)
Market Wage	.419***	.377***	.042	.609***	.488***	.122
	(7.40)	(15.39)	(.98)	(6.16)	(12.83)	(1.58)
Female	-.023	.101*	-.124	-.282	-.017	-.265
	(.17)	(1.76)	(1.25)	(1.26)	(.19)	(1.52)
Minority				.632	.149	.483
				(.93)	(.57)	(.91)
Union	-.392*	-.208**	-.184	-.445	-.093	.351
	(1.70)	(2.08)	(1.07)	(1.43)	(.78)	(1.45)
CW × Female	.079	-.107*	.187**	.231	-.017	.249*
	(.62)	(1.95)	(1.96)	(1.36)	(.27)	(1.88)
CW × Minority				-.960*	-.476**	-.484
				(1.70)	(2.19)	(1.10)
CW × Union	-.314*	-.264***	-.050	-.017	-.109	.092
	(1.71)	(3.31)	(.36)	(.07)	(1.14)	(.47)
Hay × Female	-.025	-.124**	.099	.040	-.044	.084
	(.20)	(2.37)	(1.10)	(.23)	(.66)	(.62)

Hay × Minority	-.268			-.80	-.406*	-.394
	(1.49)			(1.30)	(1.72)	(.83)
Hay × Union		.046	-.314**	.029	.029	-.001
		(.59)	(2.33)	(.12)	(.30)	(.001)
Union × Female	.238*	.074	.163	.369*	.129*	.24
	(1.77)	(1.28)	(1.63)	(1.88)	(1.71)	(1.57)
Union × Minority				-.111	.158	-.269
				(.22)	(.83)	(.70)
CW × Market Wage	.003	-.078***	.081*	-.045	-.116***	.071
	(.05)	(3.10)	(1.87)	(.51)	(3.43)	(1.04)
Hay × Market Wage	.325***	-.025	.350***	.175*	-.132***	.306***
	(5.58)	(.98)	(8.02)	(1.88)	(3.69)	(4.24)
Union × Market Wage	.176***	.090***	.086**	.120*	.014	.106**
	(3.29)	(3.89)	(2.14)	(1.66)	(.49)	(1.90)
State Dummies	13	13	13	8	8	8
R^2	.562	.663	.439	.580	.692	.433
N	940	940	940	583	583	583

*Significant at 10% level; **significant at 5% level; ***significant at 1% level.

TABLE 6
ELASTICITIES[a] COMPUTED FROM TABLE 5
(t-ratios in parentheses; F-test statistics in brackets)[b]

Variable	Excluding Minority			Including Minority		
	Point Ratio (1)	Wage Ratio (2)	Point Ratio – Wage Ratio (3)	Point Ratio (4)	Wage Ratio (5)	Point Ratio – Wage Ratio (6)
Market Wage	.761	.538	1.691	.790	.525	1.613
	(25.27)***	(33.25)***	(14.52)***	(20.86)***	(27.31)***	(13.34)***
	[189.9]***	[316.7]***	[76.6]***	[135.2]***	[234.6]***	[59.6]***
Female	.046	.015	.176	.031	.016	.078
	(2.63)***	(1.56)	(2.60)***	(1.32)	(1.33)	(1.03)
	[3.43]***	[3.14]**	[4.25]***	[2.55]**	[1.98]*	[2.27]*
Minority				-.022	-.017	-.038
				(1.57)	(2.36)**	(.85)
				[1.06]	[2.38]*	[.55]
Union	-.081	-.052	-.203	-.018	-.014	-.033
	(2.81)***	(3.35)***	(1.82)*	(.44)	(.65)	(.25)
	[4.32]***	[9.36]***	[2.90]**	[.83]	[1.24]	[.93]
Comparable Worth	-.045	-.136	.334	-.027	-.139	.320
	(.71)	(4.01)***	(1.37)	(.29)	(2.89)***	(1.06)
	[1.21]	[5.47]***	[2.02]	[1.61]	[4.45]***	[1.35]
Hay	.115	-.026	.703	.070	-.104	.610
	(2.10)**	(.90)	(3.33)***	(.81)	(2.36)**	(2.20)**
	[17.2]***	[2.10]*	[32.5]***	[1.49]	[5.25]***	[5.80]***

*Significant at 10% level; **significant at 5% level; ***significant at 1% level.
[a]Elasticities computed at means of variables.
[b]T-ratios computed for derivatives of equations in Table 5 with respect to each respective variable; F-test statistics test the joint hypothesis that the variable has zero effects across all level and interaction terms for that respective variable.

relative gains originally scheduled to go to women's jobs are dissipated while relative pay for other groups increases. The findings for the Iowa implementation process (Orazem and Mattila, 1990) were that initial gains for women based on the consultants' plan would have increased relative pay by 8.8 percent. Ultimately, the implemented plan raised women's relative pay by less than 2 percent as compromises and modifications occurred.

No prior expectations existed concerning the signs of the Hay System interaction variables, other than the presumption that a system used widely in the private sector might emphasize market factors more than other methods. Table 5 indicates that the Hay System does indeed place more weight on market wages (or its correlates such as education, training, and experience) in the points regressions. The other interaction terms are all insignificant, implying that Hay analysis is neutral toward female, minority, and union jobs. However, this neutrality disappears under implemented Hay plans. One must be cautious in interpreting the Hay coefficients in the actual pay regressions. As with comparable worth, many other modifications and political interests may intervene between determination of the points and actual pay. The Hay System may have relatively little direct impact on actual pay. Subject to this qualification, the interaction term between Hay and proportion female and Hay and proportion minority are each significantly negative in one regression. In addition, the strong positive relationship between Hay points and relative market pay disappears upon implementation.

Two additional interaction terms involving unions are available in Table 5. First, the results are consistent with Freeman's (1986b) conclusion that unions generate larger pay gains for women than for men in the public sector. The coefficients on Union Female are positive, although only marginally significant. In fact, there is a slight tendency for unions to assist heavily female jobs more in setting points than in setting pay. These results also indicate that more emphasis is placed on market wages in determining points and pay in union than in nonunion jobs. This is consistent with a union strategy of using pay comparability studies and principles as a mechanism for raising pay for workers in the public sector. Public-sector unions attempt to transfer private-sector union wage gains to corresponding jobs in government.

What has been the overall impact of unions on points and pay? The partial derivatives with respect to Union were computed at the means of the other control variables. These derivatives were negative, although significant only in the larger sample. Apparently, factor point systems tend to lower relative pay for heavily unionized jobs.

Elasticities at variable means for the Female variable were also computed. As seen in Table 6, these elasticities are positive, although only significant for the points regression excluding minority control variables. Factor point plans may give more points to predominantly female jobs, but there is no evidence that these jobs receive higher relative pay. Nevertheless, the joint hypothesis that the terms that interacted with Female were equal to zero was rejected across all regressions, so the proportion of female incumbents in the job helps to explain variation in points and pay.

The CW Minority interaction variable is negative and significant for both points and pay in Table 5, consistent with the hypothesis that any gains to females via a comparable worth process may come at the expense, in part, of minorities, corroborating previous findings for Iowa but strengthening the inclusion of observations from states with much larger minority populations. Clearly, minority workers stand to lose from comparable worth plans relative to factor point plans in general.

The other minority coefficients tend to be statistically insignificant. Hay plans may lower pay slightly in minority jobs, but the coefficient is insignificant in the factor point regression. The overall elasticity of Minority on the pay ratio is negative and significant (see Table 6), implying that, as implemented, factor point plans tend to lower relative pay for jobs with large proportions of minority incumbents.

Also examined was how the variance in points and pay by occupation was related to market variance in pay and to demographic and union composition of the job. Sample standard deviations of the dependent variables and sample means of the independent variables for each of 78 jobs across the sample of state pay systems were computed. Market standard deviation in pay, σ_{mkt}, was computed using unpublished tabulations on national wage distributions (see Table 7).

The variance in market pay is positively correlated with the variation in occupational pay in state governments, and factor points are more sensitive to market variation than are entry-level wages. A common criticism of market wages is that they do not follow the "law of one price" (Dunlop, 1957). Apparently, a move toward institutional establishment of wages through factor point analysis would not greatly diminish variance in pay. The elasticities imply that a 10 percent increase in the standard deviation of market pay would cause an 8 percent increase in the variance of job factor points. Taken literally, these results suggest that setting relative pay equal to relative points would reduce somewhat the variance in pay across states, but this is a weak conclusion. Because the measure of market wage variation allows for variation caused by human capital and cost-of-living differences, it overstates the dispersion of pay for workers of equal skill. This measurement error can bias the estimated elasticities. A better test

TABLE 7

REGRESSIONS OF THE STANDARD DEVIATION OF OCCUPATIONAL POINTS
AND WAGES ACROSS STATE GOVERNMENTS
(t-statistics in parentheses; elasticities in brackets)

Variable	Standard Deviation of Occupational	
	Point Ratio	Wage Ratio
Intercept	.778***	.279***
	(3.06)	(3.16)
$\sigma_{mkt}{}^{a}$	.0024***	.007***
	[.76]	[.61]
	(4.16)	(3.31)
Female	.126	−.080**
	[.12]	[−.20]
	(1.19)	(2.18)
Minority	.023	−.191
	[.00]	[−.11]
	(.048)	(1.17)
Union	−1.19***	−.224**
	[−1.34]	[−.69]
	(4.78	(2.60)
R^2	.64	.54
N	78	78

*Significant at 10% level; **significant at 5% level; ***significant at 1% level.
aThe standard deviation of weekly wages in the national occupational labor market,
 computed from unpublished 1984 Current Population Survey data on the distribution of
 weekly wages by occupation. The sample average for σ_{mkt} is 168.6.

would use a quality-constant measure of wage dispersion in the private
sector, but no such measure was available for this study.

The other consistent finding from Table 7 is that jobs with higher levels
of union representation have lower deviations in both points and pay,
implying that unions reduce wage inequality in both the public and private
sectors. Interestingly, the impact is stronger in points, signaling future
reductions in the variance in pay in highly unionized jobs if the move
toward implementing factor point systems continues in state government.

One other noteworthy finding is that jobs with higher proportions of
female incumbents have lower standard deviations in pay but not in points,
implying that implementing factor point systems literally (e.g., setting
relative pay proportional to relative points) would increase the variance in
pay of predominantly female jobs.[10] Unlike female incumbency, the pro-

---

[10]No other study has examined the dispersion of female earnings under factor point pay analysis.
However, in a related study, Smith (1988) presented evidence that partial coverage of employees under
comparable worth laws would increase the variance in pay. Our results indicate that full coverage could
also increase the variance in pay in predominantly female jobs due to inconsistencies across pay
analyses in the allocation of points to predominantly female occupations.

portion of incumbents who are members of minority groups had no significant impact on the dispersion of job pay or points.

Conclusions

Factor point-count systems are being used more frequently as methods of setting pay in the public sector. This paper has attempted to examine the impact of such systems on state government. Among the findings:

1. Factor point pay analysis is greatly influenced by market forces despite the desire of some to divorce pay from the market. In fact, there is a stronger relationship between points and market wages than between pay and market wages. Apparently, the implementation process reduces some of the influence of market forces that show up in the setting of factor points.

2. Comparable worth pay implementation yields significantly different results versus traditional factor point pay systems, although they do not significantly alter factor points. These plans tend to harm minority jobs and are less sensitive to market forces than traditional factor point systems. They do not seem to raise pay for predominantly female jobs relative to other factor point plans.

3. The Hay plans are more sensitive to market forces than are non-Hay plans. This effect disappears upon implementation of the plans.

4. Factor point systems don't benefit heavily unionized jobs, especially comparable worth systems. These negative effects are moderated somewhat in implemented relative pay plans, presumably because unions can negotiate over how the point system is translated into pay.

5. The observed reduction in pay dispersion, which has been reported for private-sector pay due to unions, appears to carry over to the public sector. This is true for both actual pay and for estimated job points.

6. Factor point systems do not cause equality in pay. However, they may slightly reduce pay dispersion across states for the same job relative to systems that match the market.

7. State-level, public-sector unions increase the influence of market wages on job points. There is also evidence that unions raise factor points and pay for predominantly female jobs.

Some qualifications should be noted. The sample is limited to 14 states. It would be desirable to expand the set of factor point states and, indeed, compare them to pay in states that use no point-count policy. The analysis is also limited by nonresponse from several states, which did not have data on the proportion female or minority by job classification.

We were also limited in our ability to control for market wages by state.

Although our proxy performed well, census data have several inherent limitations. Perhaps most serious, they relate to average earnings of workers rather than entry-level earnings, which may be distorted by differences in the distribution of work experience or education among occupations. In addition, weeks and hours per week of work may differ among occupations, even within the set of year-round (50–52 weeks) and full-time (35 or more hours) workers that were studied. Unfortunately, there is no dominating source of data, although it would be interesting to update this study with 1990 census earnings data.

In some of the states, the factor point analysis plan was abandoned and new analyses are in process. For these states, the relationship between points and actual pay has less meaning than in states in which the point analysis was in fact implemented, even if modified. It will be useful to reevaluate these results once the new factor point plans have been completed and implemented. Despite these caveats, our preliminary findings would appear to justify further research into the impacts of factor point analysis on pay structure.

References

Abowd, John M. 1989a. "The Effects of Differential Unionization Environments on the Pattern of Interindustry Investment." Mimeographed paper. Cornell University.

———. 1989b. "The Effect of Wage Bargains on the Stock Market Value of the Firm." *American Economic Review* 79 (September):774–800.

Abowd, John M., and Orley Ashenfelter. 1981. "Anticipated Unemployment, Temporary Layoffs, and Compensating Wage Differentials." In *Studies in Labor Markets*, edited by Sherwin Rosen, pp. 141–70. Chicago: University of Chicago Press for National Bureau of Economic Research.

Acs, Zoltan J., and David B. Audretsch. 1988. "Innovation in Large and Small Firms: An Empirical Analysis." *American Economic Review* 78 (September):678–90.

Adams, James D. 1985. "Permanent Differences in Unemployment and Permanent Wage Differentials." *Quarterly Journal of Economics* 100 (February):29–56.

Addison, John T., and Barry T. Hirsch. 1989. "Union Effects on Productivity, Profits, and Growth: Has the Long Run Arrived?" *Journal of Labor Economics* 7 (January):72–105.

Addison, John T., and Pedro Portugal. 1991. "Advance Notice." In *Job Displacement: Consequences and Implications for Policy*, edited by John T. Addison. Detroit, MI: Wayne State University Press.

———. 1989a. "Advance Notice and Unemployment: New Evidence from the 1988 Displaced Worker Survey." Mimeographed paper. University of South Carolina. Forthcoming in *ILRR*.

———. 1989b. "On the Costs of Worker Displacement: The Case of Dissipated Firm-Specific Training Investments." *Southern Economic Journal* 55 (July):166–82.

———. 1989c. "Job Displacement, Relative Wage Changes, and Duration of Unemployment." *Journal of Labor Economics* 7 (July):281–302.

———. 1987a. "On The Distributional Shape of Unemployment Duration." *Review of Economics and Statistics* 68 (August):520–26.

———. 1987b. "The Effect of Plant Closings on Unemployment." *Industrial and Labor Relations Review* 41 (October):3–16.

Advisory Commission on Intergovernmental Relations. 1978. *Categorical Grants: Their Role and Design*. Washington, DC.

Allen, S. 1988. "Human Resource Policies and Union-Nonunion Productivity Differences." Working Paper No. 2744. Cambridge, MA: National Bureau of Economic Research.

Allen, Steven G., and Robert L. Clark. 1986. "Unions, Pension Wealth, and Age-Compensation Profiles." *Industrial and Labor Relations Review* 39 (July):502–517.

Anderson, Kathryn H., Richard V. Burkhauser, and Joseph F. Quinn. 1986. "Do Retirement Dreams Come True? The Effect of Unanticipated Events on Retirement Plans." *Industrial and Labor Relations Review* 39 (July):518–25.

Aschauer, David Alan. 1989a. "Is Public Expenditure Productive?" *Journal of Monetary Economics* 23:177–200.

———. 1989b. "Public Investment and Productivity Growth in Seven Countries." *Economic Perspective* (Federal Reserve Bank of Chicago) (September-October):17–25.

———. 1988. "Rx for Productivity: Build Infrastructure." *Chicago Fed Letter* (September).

Ashenfelter, Orley, and James Heckman. 1976. "Measuring the Effect of an Anti-Discrimination Program." In *Evaluating the Labor Market Effects of Social Programs*, edited by Orley Ashenfelter and James Blum, pp. 46–84. Princeton: Princeton University, Industrial Relations Section.

Ashenfelter, Orley, and John Pencavel. 1969. "American Trade Union Growth, 1900–1960." *Quarterly Journal of Economics* 83 (August):434–48.

Baldwin, Carliss Y. 1983. "Productivity and Labor Unions: An Application of the Theory of Self-Enforcing Contracts." *Journal of Business* 56 (April):155–85.

Bean, R. 1989. *International Labour Statistics*. London: Routledge.

Becker, Brian E., and Craig A. Olson. 1987. "Labor Relations and Firm Performance." In *Human Resources and the Performance of the Firm*, edited by Morris M. Kleiner, Richard Block, Myron Roomkin, and Sidney Salsburg, pp. 43–85. Madison, WI: Industrial Relations Research Association.

Beer, Michael. 1985. "Sedalia Engine Plant." In *Human Resource Management: A General Managers' Perspective*, edited by Michael Beer et al., pp. 607–40. New York: Free Press.

Belman, D. 1989. "Unions, the Quality of Labor Relations and Firm Performance." Mimeographed paper. Washington, DC: Economic Policy Institute.

Betcherman, G. 1988. "Technological Change and Its Impacts: Do Unions Make a Difference?" *Proceedings*. 1987 annual meeting of the Canadian Industrial Relations Association.

Blanchflower, David G. 1991. "Fear, Unemployment, and Pay Flexibility." *Economic Journal* 101(406) (May):483–96.

———. 1984. "Union Relative Wage Effects: A Cross-Section Analysis Using Establishment Data." *British Journal of Industrial Relations* 22:311–32.

Blanchflower, David G., Neil Millward, and Andrew J. Oswald. 1991. "Unionism and Employment Behaviour." *Economic Journal* 101(407) (July):815–34.

Blanchflower, David G., and Andrew J. Oswald. 1989. "International Patterns of Work." In *British Social Attitudes: Special International Report*, edited by Roger Jowell, Sharon Witherspoon, and Lindsay Brook. Aldershot, England: Gower.

———. 1988a. "Internal and External Influences upon Pay Settlements." *British Journal of Industrial Relations* 26(3) (November):363–70.

———. 1988b. "Profit-Related Pay: Prose Discovered?" *Economic Journal* 98 (September):720–30.

———. 1988c. "The Economic Effects of Britain's Trade Unions." Paper No. 324. London School of Economics, Centre for Labour Economics.

Blasi, J. 1988. *Employee Ownership. Revolution or Ripoff?* Cambridge, MA: Ballinger.

Blinder, Alan. 1989–90. "Pay, Participation, and Productivity." *Brookings Review* (Winter):33–38.

Blinder, Alan, ed. 1990. *Paying for Productivity: A Look at the Evidence*. Washington, DC: Brookings Institution.

Blyth, C. 1979. "Level of National Bargaining." In *Collective Government and National Policies*. Paris: Organization for Economic Cooperation and Development.

Boal, March. 1984. "Unionism and Productivity in West Virginia Coal Mining." Unpublished paper. Stanford University.

Body, David, and Adam Jaffe. n.d. "Documentation for Data Set SPV." Mimeographed paper. Cambridge, MA: National Bureau of Economic Research.

Bound, John, Clint Cummins, Zvi Griliches, Bronwyn H. Hall, and Adam Jaffe. 1984. "Who Does R&D and Who Patents?" In *R&D, Patents, and Productivity*, edited by Zvi Griliches, pp. 21–54. Chicago: University of Chicago Press.

Brandt, Floyd S. 1960. "Independent and National Unionism in the Oil Refining Industry." Ph.D. dissertation, Harvard Business School.

Brody, David. 1960. *Steelworkers in America: The Nonunion Era*. New York: Harper & Row.

Bronars, Stephen G., and Donald R. Deere. 1988. "Union Membership Rights, Rent Sharing, and Firm Behavior." Mimeographed paper. University of California, Santa Barbara, and Texas A&M.

Bronars, Stephen G., Donald R. Deere, and Joseph Tracy. 1988. "Estimating the Influence of Unionization on Firm Behavior Using Firm-Specific Unionization Rates." Mimeographed paper. University of California at Santa Barbara, Texas A&M, and Yale University.

Brown, Charles, and James L. Medoff. 1978. "Trade Unions in the Production Process." *Journal of Political Economy* 86 (June):355–78.

Brown, James N., and Orley Ashenfelter. 1986. "Testing the Efficiency of Employment Contracts." *Journal of Political Economy* 94 (June, supplement):S40–87.

Bruno, M., and J. Sachs. 1985. *Economics of World Stagflation*. Cambridge, MA: Harvard University Press.

Burkhauser, Richard V., and Joseph F. Quinn. 1983. "The Effect of Pension Plans on the Pattern of Life Cycle Compensation." In *The Measurement of Labor Cost*, edited by Jack E. Triplett. Chicago: University of Chicago Press for the National Bureau of Economic Research.

California Department of Industrial Relations. Various years. *Union Labor in California*. Sacramento.

Callaghan, W. 1989. "Trade Unions, Pay, Productivity and Jobs." Mimeographed paper. London: Trades Union Congress.

Calmfors, L., and J. Driffil. 1988. "Bargaining Structure, Corporatism and Macroeconomic Performance." *Economic Policy* 6:13–62.

Carnevale, Anthony. 1983. *Human Capital: A High-Yield Corporate Investment*. Washington, DC: American Society for Training and Development.

Chandler, Alfred D., Jr. 1977. *The Visible Hand*. Cambridge, MA: Harvard University Press.

Clark, Kim B. 1984. "Unionization and Firm Performance: The Impact on Profits, Growth, and Productivity." *American Economic Review* 74 (December):893–919.

———. 1980a. "Unionization and Productivity: Micro-Econometric Evidence." *Quarterly Journal of Economics* 95 (December):613–40.

———. 1980b. "The Impact of Unionization on Productivity: A Case Study." *Industrial and Labor Relations Review* 33 (July):451–69.

Coase, Ronald H. 1937. "The Nature of the Firm." *Economica* 4 (November):386–405.

Collins, John J. 1964. *Never Off Pay: The Story of the Independent Tanker Union, 1937–1962*. New York: Fordham University Press.

Commission on Skills of the American Workforce. 1990. *America's Choice: High Skills or Low Wages!* Rochester, NY: Center on Education and the Economy.

Connerton, Marshall, R. B. Freeman, and James L. Medoff. 1983. "Industrial Relations and Productivity: A Study of the U.S. Bituminous Coal Industry." Unpublished paper. Harvard University.

Connolly, Robert A., Barry T. Hirsch, and Mark Hirschey. 1986. "Union Rent Seeking, Intangible Capital, and Market Value of the Firm." *Review of Economics and Statistics* 68 (November): 567–77.

Cooke, William. 1990. *Labor-Management Cooperation: New Partnerships Are Going in Circles?* Kalamazoo, MI: W.E. Upjohn Institute for Employment Research.

Coppus Engineering Corp. v. *NLRB*. 1957. 39 LRRM 2315 (1 CCA).

Council on Competitiveness. 1990. *Competitive Index*. Washington, DC.

Crager, Burton. 1942. "Company Unions Under the National Labor Relations Act." *Michigan Law Review* 40 (April):831–55.

Crawford, Vincent. 1988. "Long-Term Relationships Governed by Short-Term Contracts." *American Economic Review* 78 (December):485–99.

Crouch, Colin. 1985. "Conditions for Trade Union Wage Restraint." In *The Politics of Inflation and Economic Stagnation*, edited by Leon N. Lindberg and Charles S. Maier, pp. 105–39. Washington, DC: Brookings Institution.

Cummins, Clint, Bronwyn H. Hall, Elizabeth S. Laderman, and Joy Mundy. 1985. "The R&D Master File: Documentation." Mimeographed paper. Cambridge, MA: National Bureau of Economic Research.

Curme, Michael A., Barry T. Hirsch, and David A. Macpherson. 1990. "Union Membership and Contract Coverage in the United States, 1983–1988." *Industrial and Labor Relations Review* 44(1) (October):5–11.

Curme, Michael A., and David A. Macpherson. 1991. "Union Wage Differentials and the Effects of Industry and Local Union Density." *Journal of Labor Research* 12 (Fall):425–33.

Daniel, W. W. 1987. *Workplace Industrial Relations and Technical Change*. London: Frances Pinter.

Deere, Donald R., and Steven W. Wiggins. 1988. "Plant Closing, Advance Notice, and Private Contractual Failure." Working Paper 88–39. College Station: Texas A&M University.

Dertouzes, Michael L., Richard K. Lester, and Robert M. Solow. 1989. *Made in America*. Cambridge, MA: MIT Press.

Dertouzos, James N., and John H. Pencavel. 1981. "Wage and Employment Determination Under Trade Unionism: The International Typographical Union." *Journal of Political Economy* 89 (December):1162–81.

Dickens, William T., and Jonathan S. Leonard. 1985. "Accounting for the Decline in Union Membership, 1950–1980." *Industrial and Labor Relations Review* 38(3) (April):323–34.

Dickman, Howard. 1987. *Industrial Democracy in America*. La Salle, IL: Open Court.

Doeringer, Peter. 1990. *Turbulence in the American Work Place*. New York: Oxford University Press.

Douglas, Paul H. 1921. "Shop Committees: Substitute or Supplement to Trade Unions." *Journal of Political Economy* 29 (February):89–107.

Dunlop, John T. 1989. "Maintaining Dynamism in Service Through Public/Private Interaction." In *Management Challenges for the 1990s*, pp. 17–21. New York: World Management Congress, September 21–23.

———. 1987. "The Legal Framework of Industrial Relations and the Economic Future of the United States." In *American Labor Policy: A Critical Appraisal of the National Labor Relations Act*, edited by Charles J. Morris, pp. 1–15. Washington, DC: Bureau of National Affairs.

———. 1958. *Industrial Relations Systems*. New York: Henry Holt and Company.

———. 1957. "The Task of Contemporary Wage Theory." In *New Concepts in Wage Determination*, edited by George W. Taylor and Frank C. Pierson, pp. 128–39. New York: McGraw-Hill.

———. 1944. *Wage Determination Under Trade Unions*. New York: Macmillan.

Dunn, Timothy, Mark J. Roberts, and Larry Samuelson. 1989. "The Growth and Failure of U.S. Manufacturing Plants." Unpublished ms. Pennsylvania State University.

Eaton, A. E., and P. B. Voos. 1989. "Unions and Contemporary Innovations in Work Organisation, Compensation, and Employee Participation." Mimeographed paper. Washington, DC: Economic Policy Institute.

Economic Policy Council of the United Nations Association. *The Common Interests of Employees and Employers in the 1990s*. New York.

Edwards, Linda N. 1989. "Whither Unions?" *American Economic Review* 79 (May):161–65.

Ehrenberg, Ronald G. 1989. "Empirical Consequences of Comparable Worth." In *Comparable Worth: Analyses and Evidence*, edited by M. Ann Hill and Mark R. Killingsworth, pp. 90–106. Ithaca, NY: ILR Press.

———. 1986. "Workers' Rights: Rethinking Protective Labor Legislation." *Research in Labor Economics* 8 (Part B):285–317.

Ehrenberg, Ronald, G., and George H. Jakubson. 1989. *Advance Notice Provisions in Plant Closing Legislation*. Kalamazoo, MI: W.E. Upjohn Institute for Employment Research.

Ehrenberg, Ronald G., and Robert S. Smith. 1987. "Comparable Worth in the Public Sector." In *Public Sector Payrolls*, edited by David Wise, pp. 243–88. Chicago: University of Chicago Press.

Elias, P., and David G. Blanchflower. 1989. *Occupations, Earnings, and Work Histories of Young Adults: Who Gets the Good Jobs?* Paper No. 68. London: Department of Employment Research.

Ellwood, David, and Glenn Fine. 1987. "The Impact of Right-to-Work Laws on Union Organizing." *Journal of Political Economy* 95 (April):250–73.

Evans, David S. 1987. "Tests of Alternative Theories of Firm Growth." *Journal of Political Economy* 95(4) (August):657–74.

Ezra, D. Don. 1983. *The Struggle for Pension Fund Wealth*. Toronto: Pagurian Press Ltd.

Faith, Roger L., and Bernard Lentz. 1983. "The Intertemporal Impact of Strikes on Profits." Mimeographed paper. Virginia Polytechnic Institute and State University.

Faith, Roger L., and Joseph D. Reid, Jr. 1987. "An Agency Theory of Unionism." *Journal of Economic Behavior and Organization* 8 (March):39–60.

———. 1983. "The Labor Union as Its Members' Agent." *Research in Labor Economics* (Supplement 2):3–25.

Fama, Eugene F. 1980. "Agency Problems and the Theory of the Firm." *Journal of Political Economy* 88 (April):288–307.

Farber, Henry S. 1978. "Individual Preferences and Union Wage Determination: The Case of the United Mine Workers." *Journal of Political Economy* 86 (October):923–42.

——. 1986. "The Analysis of Union Behavior." In *Handbook of Labor Economics*, edited by Orley Ashenfelter and Richard Layard, pp. 1039–89. Amsterdam: North-Holland.

——. 1978. "Individual Preferences and Union Wage Determination: The Case of the United Mine Workers." *Journal of Political Economy* 86 (October):923–42.

Fiorito, Jack, and Wallace E. Hendricks. 1987. "Union Characteristics and Bargaining Outcomes." *Industrial and Labor Relations Review* 40 (July):569–84.

Flaim, Paul, and Ellen Seghal. 1985. "Displaced Workers of 1979–83: How Well Have They Fared?" *Monthly Labor Review* 108 (June):3–16.

Foulkes, Fred K. 1980. *Personnel Policies in Large Nonunion Companies*. Englewood Cliffs, NJ: Prentice Hall.

Freeman, Richard B. 1990. "De-Unionization of the United States: Good, Bad, or Irrelevant?" Mimeographed paper. Washington, DC: Economic Policy Institute.

——. 1989. "On the Divergence in Unionism Among Developed Countries." Discussion Paper No. 2817. Cambridge, MA: National Bureau of Economic Research.

——, ed. 1988a. *Immigration, Trade, and the Labor Market*. Summary Report. Cambridge, MA: National Bureau of Economic Research.

——. 1988b. "Labor Market Institutions and Economic Performance." *Economic Policy* 6 (April): 64–80.

——. 1988c. "Contraction and Expansion: The Divergence of Private-Sector and Public-Sector Unionism in the United States." *Journal of Economic Perspectives* 2 (Spring):63–88.

——. 1986a. "The Effect of the Union Wage Differential on Management Opposition and Organizing Success." *American Economic Review* 76 (May):92–96.

——. 1986b. "Unionism Comes to the Public Sector." *Journal of Economic Literature* 24 (March): 41–86.

——. 1986c. "In Search of Union Wage Concessions in Standard Data Sets." *Industrial Relations* 25 (Spring):131–45.

——. 1985. "Unions, Pensions, and Union Pension Funds." In *Pensions, Labor and Individual Choice*, edited by David E. Wise, pp. 89–122. Chicago: University of Chicago Press for the National Bureau of Economic Research.

——. 1983. "Unionism, Price-Cost Margins, and the Return to Capital." Working Paper No. 1164. Cambridge, MA: National Bureau of Economic Research.

——. 1982. "Union Wage Practices and Wage Dispersion Within Establishments." *Industrial and Labor Relations Review* 36(1) (October):3–21.

——. 1980a. "Unionism and the Dispersion of Wages." *Industrial and Labor Relations Review* 34(1) (October):3–23.

——. 1980b. "The Exit-Voice Tradeoff in the Labor Market: Unionism, Job Tenure, Quits, and Separations." *Quarterly Journal of Economics* 94 (June):643–73.

Freeman, Richard B., and Casey Ichniowski, eds. 1989. *When Public-Sector Workers Unionize*. Chicago: University of Chicago Press.

Freeman, Richard B., and Morris M. Kleiner. 1990a. "The Impact of New Unionization on Wages and Working Conditions." *Journal of Labor Economics* 8(1) (pt. 2) (January):S8–25.

——. 1990b. "Employer Behavior in the Face of Union Organizing Drives." *Industrial and Labor Relations Review* 43(4) (April):351–65.

Freeman, Richard B., and James L. Medoff. 1984. *What Do Unions Do?* New York: Basic Books.

——. 1982. "Substitution Between Production Labor and Other Inputs in Union and Nonunion Manufacturing." *Review of Economics and Statistics* 64:220–33.

——. 1981. "The Impact of Collective Bargaining: Illusion or Reality?" In *U.S. Industrial Relations, 1950–1980: A Critical Assessment*, edited by Jack Stieber, Robert B. McKersie, and D. Quinn Mills. Madison, WI: Industrial Relations Research Association.

——. 1979. "New Estimates of Private-Sector Unionism." *Industrial and Labor Relations Review* 32(2) (January):143–74.

Freeman, Richard B., and Jeffrey Pelletier. 1990. "The Impact of Industrial Relations Legislation on British Union Density." *British Journal of Industrial Relations* 28(2) (April):141–64.

Freeman, Richard B., and Mark Rebick. 1989. "Crumbling Pillar? Declining Union Density in Japan." Paper presented at the Conference on Labor Relations and the Firm, Tokyo Center of Economic Research.

Friedman, Milton, and Rose Friedman. 1962. *Capitalism and Freedom*. Chicago: University of Chicago Press.

Furubotn, Eirik G., and Steven N. Wiggins. 1984. "Plant Closings, Worker Reallocation Costs, and Efficiency Gains to Labor Representation on Boards of Directors." *Zeitschrift für die gesamte Staatswissenschaft* 140 (March):176–92.

Getman, Julius, Stephen Goldberg, and Jeanne Herman. 1976. *Union Representation Elections: Law and Reality*. New York: Russell Sage.

Giffiths, Dave, and Stephen Phillips. 1988. "The Legal Eagle Who Will Rule the Roost at TRW." *Business Week*, March 21, pp. 100–104.

Giles, David E. A. 1982. "The Interpretation of Dummy Variables in Semilogarithmic Equations: Unbiased Estimation." *Economics Letters* 10:77–79.

Gordon, David M., Richard Edwards, and Michael Reich. 1982. *Segmented Work, Divided Workers*. New York: Cambridge University Press.

Green, F., G. Hadjimatheou, and R. Smail. 1985. "Fringe Benefit Distribution in Britain." *British Journal of Industrial Relations* 23:261–80.

Grout, Paul A. 1984. "Investment and Wages in the Absence of Binding Contracts: A Nash Bargaining Approach." *Econometrica* 52 (March):449–60.

Grubb, D., R. Jackman, and R. Layard. 1983. "Wage Rigidity and Unemployment in OECD Countries." *European Economic Review* 21(1):11–50.

Gunderson, Morley. 1982. "Union Impact on Wages, Fringe Benefits, and Productivity." In *Union-Management Relations in Canada*, edited by John Anderson and Morley Gunderson. Menlo Park, CA: Addison-Wesley.

Gustman, Alan L., and Thomas L. Steinmeier. 1986. "Pensions, Unions, and Implicit Contracts." Mimeographed paper.

Gyllenhannar, T. T. 1977. *People at Work*. Reading, MA: Addison-Wesley.

Hamermesh, Daniel S. 1989. "The Demand for Workers and Hours and the Effects of Job Security Policies: Theory and Evidence." In *Employment, Unemployment, and Labor Utilization*, edited by Robert H. Hart, pp. 9–32. London and Boston: Unwin Hyman.

———. 1987. "The Costs of Worker Displacement." *Quarterly Journal of Economics* 102 (February): 51–75.

Hamermesh, Daniel S., and John R. Wolfe. 1986. "Compensating Differentials and the Duration of Wage Loss." Mimeographed paper. East Lansing: Michigan State University.

Harbison, Frederick H., and Robert Dubin. 1947. *Patterns of Union-Management Relations*. Industrial Relations Center, University of Chicago.

Hartmann, Heidi I., ed. 1985. *Comparable Worth: New Directions for Research*. Washington, DC: National Academy Press.

Heckscher, Charles C. 1988. *The New Unionism: Employee Involvement in the Changing Corporation*. New York: Basic Books.

Heldman, Dan C., James T. Bennett, and Manuel H. Johnson. 1981. *Deregulating Labor Relations*. Dallas, TX: Fisher Institute.

Hindle, Brooke, and Steven Lubar. 1986. *Engines of Change: The American Industrial Revolution, 1790–1860*. Washington, DC: Smithsonian Institution.

Hirsch, Barry T. 1991a. *Labor Unions and the Economic Performance of Firms*. Kalamazoo, MI: W.E. Upjohn Institute for Employment Research.

———. 1991b. "Union Coverage and Profitability Among U.S. Firms." *Review of Economics and Statistics* 73 (February):69–77.

———. 1990a. "Innovative Activity, Productivity Growth, and Firm Performance: Are Labor Unions a Spur or a Deterrent?" *Advances in Applied Microeconomics* 5:69–104. Greenwich, CT: JAI Press.

———. 1990b. "Market Structure, Union Rent Seeking, and Firm Profitability." *Economics Letters* 32:75–79.

———. 1982. "The Interindustry Structure of Unionism, Earnings, and Earnings Dispersion." *Industrial and Labor Relations Review* 36 (October):22–39.

Hirsch, Barry T., and John T. Addison. 1986. *The Economic Analysis of Unions: New Approaches and Evidence*. Boston: Allen & Unwin.

Hirsch, Barry T., and Albert N. Link. 1987. "Labor Union Effects on Innovative Activity." *Journal of Labor Research* 8 (Fall):323–32.

Hughes, Jonathan. 1987. *American Economic History*. 2d ed. Glenview, IL: Scott, Foresman and Company.

Ippolito, Richard A. 1987. "The Implicit Pension Contract: Developments and New Directions." *Journal of Human Resources* 22 (Summer):441–67.

———. 1985. "The Economic Function of Underfunded Pension Plans." *Journal of Law and Economics* 28 (October):611–51.

Jackson, Charles. 1977. "An Alternative to Unionization and the Wholly Unorganized Shop: A Legal Basis for Sanctioning Joint Employer-Employee Committees and Increasing Employee Free Choice." *Syracuse Law Review* 28 (Fall):809–45.

Jacoby, Sanford M. 1989. "Reckoning with Company Unions: The Case of Thompson Products, 1934–1964." *Industrial and Labor Relations Review* 43 (October):19–40.

———. 1985. *Employing Bureaucracy: Managers, Unions, and the Transformation of Work in American Industry, 1900–1945*. New York: Columbia University Press.

Jensen, Vernon H. 1964. *Hiring of Dock Workers and Employment Practices in the Ports of New York: Liverpool, London, Rotterdam, and Marseilles*. Cambridge, MA: Harvard University Press.

Johnson, G. 1981. "Changes Over Time in the Union/Nonunion Differential in the United States." Mimeographed paper. University of Michigan.

Johnson, George E. 1975. "Economic Analysis of Trade Unionism." *American Economic Review* 65 (May):23–28.

Jowell, Roger, Sharon Witherspoon, and Lindsay Brook, eds. 1989. *British Social Attitudes: Special International Report*. Aldershot, England: Gower.

Judge, George, et al. 1982. *Introduction to the Theory and Practice of Econometrics*. New York: Wiley.

Katz, Harry C. 1987. "Automobiles." In *Collective Bargaining in American Industry: Contemporary Perspectives and Future Directions,*, edited by David B. Lipsky and Clifford B. Donn. Lexington, MA: Lexington Books.

Keefe, J. 1989. "Do Unions Hinder Technological Change?" Mimeographed paper. Washington, DC: Economic Policy Institute.

Kerr, Clark, John T. Dunlop, Frederick H. Harbison, and Cecil H. Meyers. 1964. *Industrialism and Industrial Man: The Problems of Labor and Management in Economic Growth*. 2d ed. New York: Oxford University Press.

Killingsworth, Mark R. 1990. *The Economics of Comparable Worth*. Kalamazoo, MI: W.E. Upjohn Institute for Employment Research.

Klein, Benjamin, Robert G. Crawford, and Armen A. Alchian. 1978. "Vertical Integration, Appropriable Rents, and the Competitive Contracting Process." *Journal of Law and Economics* 21 (October):297–326.

Kleiner, Morris. 1984. "Unionism and Employer Discrimination: Analysis of 8(a)(3) Violations." *Industrial Relations* 23 (Spring):234–43.

Kleiner, Morris, M., Richard Block, Myron Roomkin, and Sidney Salsburg, eds. 1987. *Human Resources and the Performance of the Firm*. Madison, WI: Industrial Relations Research Association.

Kochan, Thomas A., and Richard N. Block. 1977. "An Interindustry Analysis of Bargaining Outcomes." *Quarterly Journal of Economics* 91 (August):431–52.

Kochan, Thomas A., Harry Katz, and Robert McKersie. 1986. *The Transformation of American Industrial Relations*. New York: Basic Books.

Kohler, Thomas C. 1986. "Models of Worker Participation: The Uncertain Significance of Section 8(a)(2)." *Boston College Law Review* 27 (May):499–551.

Kokkelenberg, Edward C., and Donna R. Sockell. 1985. "Union Membership in the United States, 1973–1981." *Industrial and Labor Relations Review* 38 (July):497–543.

Kornfeld, Robert. 1990. "Effects of Unions on Young Workers in Australia." Mimeographed paper. Harvard University.

Kotlikoff, Lawrence J., and Daniel E. Smith. 1987. *Pensions in the American Economy*. Chicago: University of Chicago Press for the National Bureau of Economic Research.

Kotlikoff, Lawrence J., and David Wise. 1987. "The Incentive Effects of Private Pension Plans." In *Issues in Pension Economics*, edited by Zvi Bodie, John B. Shoven, and David A. Wise. Chicago: University of Chicago Press for the National Bureau of Economic Research.

Krafcik, John. 1989. "Triumph of the Lear Production System." *Sloan Management Review* (Fall):41–52.

Kumar, Pradeep, M. Coates, and D. Arrowsmith. 1988. *The Current Industrial Relations Scene in Canada*. Industrial Relations Section, Queen's University, Ontario.

Kupferschmidt, M., and R. Swidinsky. 1989. "Longitudinal Estimates of the Union Effect on Wages, Wage Dispersion, and Pension Fringe Benefits." University of Guelph, Ontario.

Lach, Saul, and Mark Schankerman. 1989. "Dynamics of R&D and Investment in the Scientific Sector." *Journal of Political Economy* 97 (August):880–904.

Lawrence, Colin, and Robert Z. Lawrence. 1985. "Manufacturing Wage Dispersion: An End Game Interpretation." *Brookings Papers on Economic Activity* 1:47–106.

Lazear, Edward P. 1983a. "Pensions as Severance Pay." In *Financial Aspects of the United States Pension System*, edited by Zvi Bodie and John B. Shoven. Chicago: University of Chicago Press for the National Bureau of Economic Research.

———. 1983b. "A Competitive Theory of Monopoly Unionism." *American Economic Review* 73(4) (September):631–43.

Lazear, Edward P., and Robert L. Moore. 1988. "Pensions and Turnover." In *Pensions in the U.S. Economy*, edited by Zvi Bodie, John B. Shoven, and David A. Wise. Chicago: University of Chicago Press for the National Bureau of Economic Research.

Leonard, Jonathan. 1986. "Employment Variability and Wage Rigidity: A Comparison of Union and Nonunion Plants." Mimeographed paper. University of California at Berkeley.

Lester, Richard. 1967. "Pay Differentials by Size of Establishment." *Industrial Relations* 7 (October): 57–67.

Levin, Richard C., Alvin K. Klevorick, Richard R. Nelson, and Sidney G. Winter. 1987. "Appropriating the Returns from Industrial Research and Development." *Brookings Papers on Economic Activity* 3:783–820.

Lewin, David, and Richard B. Peterson. 1988. *The Modern Grievance Procedure in the United States*. New York: Quorum Books.

Lewis, H. Gregg. 1983. *Union Relative Wage Effects: A Survey*. Chicago: University of Chicago Press.

———. 1963. "Relative Employment Effects of Unionism." *Industrial Relations Research Association Proceedings* 16:104–115.

Li, Elizabeth H. 1986. "Compensating Differentials for Cyclical and Noncyclical Unemployment: The Interaction Between Investors' and Employees' Risk Aversion." *Journal of Labor Economics* 4 (April):277–300.

Lincoln, James, and Arne Kalleberg. 1985. "Work Organization and Workforce Commitment: A Study of Plants and Employees in the U.S. and Japan." *American Sociological Review* 50 (December):738–60.

Linneman, Peter D., and Michael L. Wachter. 1986. "Rising Union Premiums and the Declining Boundaries Among Noncompeting Groups." *American Economic Review* 76(2) (May):103–108.

Linneman, Peter D., Michael L. Wachter, and William H. Carter. 1990. "Evaluating the Evidence on Union Employment and Wages." *Industrial Labor Relations Review* 44(1) (October):34–53.

Machin, S. 1988. "Unions and the Capture of Economic Rents: An Investigation Using British Firm Level Data." Mimeographed paper. Department of Economics, University College, London.

Marshall, F. Ray. 1987. *Unheard Voices*. New York: Basic Books.

———. 1961. "Independent Unions in the Gulf Coast Petroleum Refining Industry." *Labor Law Journal* 12 (September):823–40.

Masters, Stanley H. 1969. "Wages and Plant Size: An Interindustry Analysis." *Review of Economics and Statistics* 51 (August):341–45.

McCormick, Janice. 1987. "Challenges in Industrial Relations." *Sloan Management Review* 28 (Winter):76–79.

McDonald, I. M., and R. M. Solow. 1981. "Wage Bargaining and Employment." *American Economic Review* 71(5) (December):896–908.

McKenzie, Richard B. 1989. "Labor Policy in a Competitive World." In *Advances in the Study of Entrepreneurship, Innovation, and Economic Growth*, edited by Gary D. Libecap, pp. 45–71. Vol. 3 of *Issues in American Competitiveness*. Greenwich, CT: JAI Press.

McKenzie, Richard B., and Bruce Yandle. 1982. "State Plant Closing Laws: Their Union Support." *Journal of Labor Research* 3 (Winter):101–110.

Metcalf, David. 1990. "Union Presence and Labour Productivity in British Manufacturing Industry: A Reply to Nolan and Marginson." *British Journal of Industrial Relations* 28(2):249–66.

———. 1989. "Water Notes Dry Up: The Impact of the Donovan Reform Proposals and Thatcherism at Work on Labour Productivity in British Manufacturing Industry." *British Journal of Industrial Relations* 27:1–32.

Michael, Robert T., and Heidi I. Hartmann. 1989. "Pay Equity: Assessing the Issues." In *Pay Equity: Empirical Inquiries*, edited by Robert T. Michael Heidi I. Hartmann, and Brigid O'Farrell, pp. 1–19. Washington, DC: National Academy Press.

Michael, Robert T., Heidi I. Hartmann, and Brigid O'Farrell, eds. 1989. *Pay Equity: Empirical Inquiries*. Washington, DC: National Academy Press.

Milkovich, George T., and Jerry M. Newman. 1984. *Compensation*. Plano, TX: Business Publications.

Millis, Harry A., and Emily C. Brown. 1950. *From the Wagner Act to Taft-Hartley*. Chicago: University of Chicago Press.

Millward, Neil, and M. Stevens. 1986. *British Workplace Industrial Relations, 1980–1984*. Aldershot, England: Gower.

Mitchell, Daniel J. B. 1972. "Union Wage Policies: The Ross-Dunlop Debate Reopened." *Industrial Relations* 11 (February):46–61.

Mitchell, Olivia S., and Gary Fields. 1985. "Rewards to Continued Work: The Economic Incentives for Postponing Retirement." In *Horizontal Equity, Uncertainty, and Economic Well-Being*, edited by Martin David and Timothy Smeeding. Chicago: University of Chicago Press for the National Bureau of Economic Research.

Montgomery, David. 1987. *The Fall of the House of Labor: The Workplace, the State, and American Labor Activism*. New York: Cambridge University Press.

Mulvey, C. 1986. "Wage Levels: Do Unions Make a Difference?" In *Wage Fixation in Australia*, edited by John Niland. Sydney: Allen & Unwin.

Munnell, Alicia H. 1990. "Why Has Productivity Growth Declined? Productivity and Public Investment." *New England Economic Review* (January-February):3–22.

Muramatsu, Kuramitsu. 1984. "The Effect of Trade Unions on Productivity in Japanese Manufacturing Industries." In *Economic Analysis of the Japanese Firm*, edited by Masahiko Aoki, pp. 103–23. Amsterdam: North-Holland.

Murphy, Kevin M., and Robert H. Topel. 1987. "Unemployment, Risk, and Earnings: Testing for Equalizing Wage Differences in the Labor Market." In *Unemployment and the Structure of Labor Markets*, edited by Kevin Lang and Jonathan Leonard, pp. 103–40. New York and Oxford: Basil Blackwell.

Nakamura, K., H. Sato, and T. Kamiya. 1988. *Do Labor Unions Really Have a Useful Role?* (in Japanese). Tokyo: Sogo Rodo Kenkyujo.

National Commission on the Public Service. 1989. *Leadership for America: Rebuilding the Public Service*. Paul A. Volcker, Chair. Washington, DC.

Nelson, Daniel. 1975. *Managers and Workers*. Madison: University of Wisconsin Press.

New York Stock Exchange. 1982. *People and Productivity: A Challenge to Corporate America.* New York.

Nolan, Peter, and Paul Marginson. 1990. "Skating on Thin Ice? David Metcalf on Trade Unions and Productivity." *British Journal of Industrial Relations* 28(2):227–48.

Oates, David. 1973. "Sensing Aids Candor in Aerospace Firm." *International Machinist* (April).

Orazem, Peter F., and J. Peter Mattila. 1990. "The Implementation Process of Comparable Worth: Winners and Losers." *Journal of Political Economy* 98 (February):134–52.

———. 1989. "Comparable Worth and the Structure of Earnings." In *Pay Equity: Empirical Inquiries*, edited by Robert T. Michael, Heidi I. Hartmann, and Brigid O'Farrell, pp. 179–99. Washington, DC: National Academy Press.

Osawa, M. 1989. "The Service Economy and Industrial Relations in Small and Medium-Size Firms in Japan." *Japan Labor Bulletin* (July 1).

Oswald, Andrew J. 1982. "The Microeconomic Theory of the Trade Union." *Economic Journal* (September):576–95.

Parker, Mike, and Jane Slaughter. 1989. *Choosing Sides: Unions and the Team Concept.* Boston: South End Press.

Parsley, C. J. 1980. "Labor Union Effects on Wage Gains: A Survey of Recent Literature." *Journal of Economic Literature* 18 (March):1–31.

Pencavel, John H. 1989. "Employment and Trade Unions." Mimeographed paper. Stanford University.

———. 1984. "The Tradeoff Between Wages and Employment in Trade Union Objectives." *Quarterly Journal of Economics* 99(2) (May):215–31.

Pencavel, John, and Catherine E. Hartsog. 1984. "A Reconsideration of the Effects of Unionism on Relative Wages and Employment in the United States, 1920–1980." *Journal of Labor Economics* 2(2) (April):193–232.

Personick, Martin E. 1974. "Union and Nonunion Pay Patterns in Construction." *Monthly Labor Review* 97 (August):431–52.

Personick, Martin E., and Carl B. Barsky. 1982. "White-Collar Pay Levels Linked to Corporate Workforce Size." *Monthly Labor Review* 105 (May):23–28.

Pesando, James E., and Morley Gunderson. 1988. "Retirement Incentives Contained in Occupational Pension Plans and Their Implications for the Mandatory Retirement Debate." *Canadian Journal of Economics* 21 (May):244–64.

Pesando, James E., Morley Gunderson, and John McLaren. 1990. "Pension Benefits and Male-Female Wage Differentials: A Canadian Perspective." Mimeographed paper. Institute for Policy Analysis, University of Toronto.

Piore, Michael J., and Charles F. Sabel. 1984. *The Second Industrial Divide: Possibilities for Prosperity.* New York: Basic Books.

Podgursky, Michael, and Paul Swaim. 1987. "Job Displacement and Earnings Loss: Evidence from the Displaced Worker Survey." *Industrial and Labor Relations Review* 41 (October):17–29.

Porter, Glenn. 1973. *The Rise of Big Business.* Arlington Heights, IL: Harlan Davidson.

Portugal, Pedro, and John T. Addison. 1989. "Accelerated Failure Time and Proportional Hazards Models of Unemployment Duration." Mimeographed paper. University of South Carolina.

Reder, Melvin W. 1952. "The Theory of Union Wage Policy." *Review of Economics and Statistics* 34 (February):34–35.

Reid, Joseph D., Jr. 1982a. "Labor Unions and Labor Management: 1900–1930." *Business and Economic History* 11 (Second Series) (December):150–58.

———. 1982b. "Labor Unions in the American Economy: An Analytical Survey." *Journal of Labor Research* 3 (Summer):277–94.

———. 1976. "Sharecropping and Agricultural Uncertainty." *Economic Development and Cultural Change* 24 (April):549–76.

Reid, Joseph D., Jr., and Roger L. Faith. 1987. "Right-to-Work and Union Compensation Structure." *Journal of Labor Research* 8 (Spring):111–30.

Reid, Joseph D., Jr., and Michael M. Kurth. 1990. "Union Militancy Among Public Employees: A Public Choice Hypothesis." *Journal of Labor Research* 11 (Winter):1–23.

———. 1988. "Public Employees in Political Firm: Part A. The Patronage Era." *Public Choice* 59 (December):253–62.

———. 1984a. "The Contribution of Exclusive Representation to Union Strength." *Journal of Labor Research* 5 (Fall):391–412.

———. 1984b. "The Organization of State and Local Government Employees: Comment." *Journal of Labor Research* 5 (Spring):191–200.

Reynolds, Lloyd G. 1978. *Labor Economics and Labor Relations*. 7th ed. Englewood Cliffs, NJ: Prentice Hall.

Rosenfarb, Joseph. 1940. *The National Labor Policy and How It Works*. New York: Harper.

Ross, Arthur M. 1948. *Trade Union Wage Policy*. Berkeley: University of California Press.

Salter, Malcolm S., and John T. Dunlop. 1989. *Industrial Governance and Corporate Performance: An Introductory Essay*. Cambridge, MA: Harvard Business School.

Saposs, David J. 1936. "Organizational and Procedural Changes in Employee Representation Plans." *Journal of Political Economy* 44 (December):803–11.

Schultz, Theodore. 1981. *Investing in People: The Economics of Population Quality*. Berkeley: University of California Press.

Schwab, Donald P. 1985. "Job Evaluation Research and Research Needs." In *Comparable Worth: New Directions for Research*, edited by Heidi I. Hartmann, pp. 37–52. Washington, DC: National Academy Press.

———. 1957. "Section 8(a)(2): Employer Assistance to Plant Unions and Committees." *Stanford Law Review* 9 (March):351–65.

Selekman, Benjamin M. 1947. *Labor Relations and Human Relations*. New York: McGraw-Hill.

Shore, Harvey. 1966. "A Historical Analysis of Thompson Products' Successful Program to Discourage Employee Acceptance of Outside Unions, 1934–1947." D.B.A. thesis. Harvard Business School.

Shostak, Arthur B. 1962. *America's Forgotten Labor Organization: A Survey of the Role of the Single-Firm Independent Union in American Industry*. Research Report No. 103. Industrial Relations Section, Princeton University.

Simpson, W. 1985. "The Impact of Unions on the Structure of Canadian Wages: An Empirical Analysis with Microdata." *Canadian Journal of Economics* 18:164–81.

Slichter, Sumner H., James J. Healy, and E. Robert Livernash. 1960. *The Impact of Collective Bargaining on Management*. Washington, DC: Brookings Institution.

Smith, Robert S. 1988. "Comparable Worth: Limited Coverage and the Exacerbation of Inequality." *Industrial and Labor Relations Review* 41(2) (January):227–39.

Soskice, David. 1990. "Reinterpreting Corporatism and Explaining Unemployment: Coordinated and Non-Coordinated Market Economies." In *Labour Relations and Economic Performance*, edited by Renato Brunetta and Carlo Dell'Aringa. Basingstoke: Macmillan.

Statistics Canada. 1986. *Pension Plans in Canada 1984*. Catalogue 74–401. Ottawa: Government of Canada.

Stock, James, and David Wise. 1988. "The Pension Inducement to Retire: An Option Value Analysis." Working Paper No. 2660. Cambridge, MA: National Bureau of Economic Research.

Swoboda, Frank. 1990a. "Cooperation: A Bone of Contention for Unions." *Washington Post*, May 20, pp. H1, 6, 7.

———. 1990b. "Unions Rethinking Role of the Strike." *Washington Post*, March 18, p. H3.

Taft, Philip. 1956. "Independent Unions and the Merger." *Industrial and Labor Relations Review* 9 (April):433–46.

Tauman, Y., and Y. Weiss. 1987. "Labor Unions and the Adoption of New Technology." *Journal of Labor Economics* 5 (October):477–501.

Terleckyj, Nestor E. 1990. *Changing Sources of U.S. Economic Growth, 1950–2010: A Chartbook of Trends and Projections*. Washington, DC: National Planning Association.

Thompson, Earl. 1980. "On Labor's Right to Strike." *Economic Inquiry* 18 (October):640–53.

Tiebout, Charles M. 1956. "A Pure Theory of Local Expenditures." *Journal of Political Economy* (October):416–24.

Tomlins, Christopher L. 1985. *The State and the Unions*. Cambridge: Cambridge University Press.

Topel, Robert H. 1984. "Equilibrium Earnings, Turnover, and Unemployment: New Evidence." *Journal of Labor Economics* 2 (October):500–522.

Treiman, Donald J., and Heidi I. Hartmann, eds. 1981. *Women, Work, and Wages: Equal Pay for Jobs of Equal Value*. Washington, DC: National Academy Press.

Troy, Leo. 1961. "Local Independent Unions and the American Labor Movement." *Industrial and Labor Relations Review* 14 (April):331–49.

———. 1960. "Local Independent and National Unions: Competitive Labor Organizations." *Journal of Political Economy* 68 (October):487–506.

Troy, Leo, and Neil Sheflin. 1985. *U.S. Union Sourcebook*. West Orange, NJ: IRDIS.

Tullock, Gordon. "1974. Dynamic Hypothesis on Bureaucracy." *Public Choice* 26 (Fall):127–31.

Ulman, Lloyd. 1955. *The Rise of the National Trade Union*. Cambridge, MA: Harvard University Press.

Ulph, Alastair, and David Ulph. 1989. "Labor Markets and Innovation." *Journal of the Japanese and International Economies* 3(4) (December).

U.S. Bureau of Labor Statistics. 1990. Unpublished data. Washington, DC. May.

———. 1988. "International Comparisons of Manufacturing Productivity and Labor Cost Trends, 1987." Washington, DC.

———. 1969. "Unaffiliated Intrastate and Single-Employer Unions, 1967." Bulletin No. 1640. Washington, DC.

———. 1962. "Unaffiliated Local and Single-Employer Unions, 1961." Bulletin No. 1348. Washington, DC.

U.S. Bureau of the Census. 1977. *U.S. Census of Manufacturers*. Vol. 3. Geographic Area Series: California. Part 1, Table 2b, pp. 5–8.

———. 1960. *Historical Statistics of the United States*. Series D-57, 60–62, p. 74. Washington, DC.

U.S. Department of Labor. 1981. *Employment and Training Report of the President, 1980*. Washington, DC: U.S. Government Printing Office.

———, Division of Foreign Labor Statistics. 1988. "Union Membership." Washington, DC.

U.S. Senate Committee on Labor and Public Welfare. 1947. "Statement of Paul Herzog." 80th Cong., 1st Sess., pt. 4, p. 1912.

van der Ploeg, F. 1987. "Trade Unions, Investment, and Employment: A Noncooperative Approach." *European Economic Review* 31 (October):1465–92.

Verma, Anil. "1985. Relative Flow of Capital to Union and Nonunion Plants Within a Firm." *Industrial Relations* 24 (Fall):395–405.

Vernon, Raymond. 1988. "On the Significance of the Privatization Movement." *French-American Commerce* (Winter).

Visser, J. 1989. *European Trade Unions in Figures*. Netherlands: Kluwer Deventer.

Voos, Paula B. 1984. "Trends in Union Organizing Expenditures, 1953–1977." *Industrial and Labor Relations Review* 38(1) (October):52–63.

Voos, Paula B., and Lawrence Mischel. 1986. "The Union Impact on Profits: Evidence from Industry Price-Cost Margin Data." *Journal of Labor Research* 4(1) (January):105–33.

Wadhwani, Sushil. 1989. "The Effect of Unions on Productivity Growth, Investment, and Employment: A Report on Some Recent Work." *British Journal of Industrial Relations* 27(2).

Wadhwani, Sushil, and M. Wall. 1989. "The Effects of Unions on Corporate Investment: Evidence from Accounts Data, 1972–86." Discussion Paper No. 354. London School of Economics, Centre for Labour Economics.

Walker, Kenneth F. 1970. *Australian Industrial Relations System*. Cambridge, MA: Harvard University Press.

Walsh, K. 1985. *Trade Union Membership: Methods and Measurement in the European Community*. Luxembourg: Eurostat.

Webb, Sidney, and Beatrice Webb. 1897. *Industrial Democracy*. London: Longman Green & Company.

Weiler, Paul C. 1990. *Governing the Workplace: The Future of Labor and Employment Law*. Cambridge, MA: Harvard University Press.

————. 1983. "Promises to Keep: Securing Workers' Right to Self-Organization Under the NLRA." *Harvard Law Review* 96:1769.

Weiss, Leonard W. 1966. "Concentration and Labor Earnings." *American Economic Review* 56 (March):96–117.

Weiss, Leonard W., and George A. Pascoe, Jr. 1986. "Adjusted Concentration Ratios in Manufacturing, 1972 and 1977." Statistical Report of the Bureau of Economics to the Federal Trade Commission.

Wever, Kirsten R. 1988. "Works Councils in the United States? Exploring a Public Policy Solution to Private-Sector Problems." Unpublished ms. Cambridge, MA: Harvard Law School.

White, Joseph B. 1990. "Car Makers Gear Up to Turn Good Marks in Quality Poll to Competitive Advantage." *Wall Street Journal*, July 3, p. B1.

Williamson, Oliver E. 1975. *Markets and Hierarchies: Analysis and Antitrust Implications*. New York: Free Press.

Williamson, Oliver E., Michael L. Wachter, and Jeffrey E. Harris. 1975. "Understanding the Employment Relation: The Analysis of Idiosyncratic Exchange." *Bell Journal of Economics* 6 (Spring): 250–78.

Wood, W. Donald, and Pradeep Kumar. 1980. *The Current Industrial Relations Scene in Canada*. Ontario: Industrial Relations Centre, Queen's University.

Zax, Jeffrey S. 1989. "Employment and Local Public-Sector Unions." *Industrial Relations* 28 (Winter):21–31.

Ziskin, Ian V. 1986. "Knowledge-Based Pay: A Strategic Analysis." *ILR Report* 24 (Fall):16–22.

Zuboff, Shoshona. 1988. *In the Age of the Smart Machines*. New York: Basic Books.